An Architecture of Education

Gender and Race in American History

Alison M. Parker, The College at Brockport, State University of New York
Carol Faulkner, Syracuse University

The Men and Women We Want
Jeanne D. Petit

Manhood Enslaved:
Bondmen in Eighteenth- and Early Nineteenth-Century New Jersey
Kenneth E. Marshall

Interconnections:
Gender and Race in American History
Edited by Carol Faulkner and Alison M. Parker

Susan B. Anthony and the Struggle for Equal Rights
Edited by Christine L. Ridarsky and Mary M. Huth

The Reverend Jennie Johnson
and African Canadian History, 1868–1967
Nina Reid-Maroney

Sex Ed, Segregated:
The Quest for Sexual Knowledge in Progressive-Era America
Courtney Q. Shah

An Architecture of Education:
African American Women Design the New South
Angel David Nieves

An Architecture of Education

African American Women Design the New South

Angel David Nieves

UNIVERSITY OF ROCHESTER PRESS

The University of Rochester Press gratefully acknowledges generous support from Hamilton College.

Copyright © 2018 by Angel David Nieves

All Rights Reserved. Except as permitted under current legislation, no part of this work may be photocopied, stored in a retrieval system, published, performed in public, adapted, broadcast, transmitted, recorded, or reproduced in any form or by any means, without the prior permission of the copyright owner.

First published 2018
Transferred to digital printing and reprinted in paperback 2020

University of Rochester Press
668 Mt. Hope Avenue, Rochester, NY 14620, USA
www.urpress.com
and Boydell & Brewer Limited
PO Box 9, Woodbridge, Suffolk IP12 3DF, UK
www.boydellandbrewer.com

hardcover ISBN-13: 978-1-58046-909-8
paperback ISBN-13: 978-1-58046-976-0
ISSN: 2152-6400

Library of Congress Cataloging-in-Publication Data

Names: Nieves, Angel David, author.
Title: An architecture of education : African American women design the new South / Angel David Nieves.
Other titles: Gender and race in American history.
Description: Rochester, NY : University of Rochester Press, 2018. | Series: Gender and race in American history, ISSN 2152-6400 ; v. 7 | Includes bibliographical references and index.
Identifiers: LCCN 2018014789 | ISBN 9781580469098 (hardcover : alk. paper)
Subjects: LCSH: African Americans—Education—Southern States—History. | Institution building—Southern States—History. | School facilities—Southern States—History. | African American educators—Southern States—History. | African American social reformers—Southern States—History. | African American women—Southern States—History.
Classification: LCC LC2802.S9 N55 2018 | DDC 371.829/96075—dc23 LC record available at https://lccn.loc.gov/2018014789

A catalogue record for this title is available from the British Library.

Cover image: Students at Tuskegee Normal and Industrial Institute, Tuskegee, Alabama, ca. 1902–6. Courtesy of the Prints and Photographs Division, Library of Congress, Washington, DC. Photographer: Frances Benjamin Johnston.

For Richard

Contents

	Acknowledgments	ix
	Introduction	1
1	Contested Monument-Making and the Crisis of the Lost Cause, 1865–1920	12
2	The Impact of Chicago's "White City" on African American Placemaking	30
3	Tuskegee Utopianism: Where American Campus Planning Meets Black Nationalism	46
4	The "Race Women" Establishment: Elizabeth Evelyn Wright, Jennie Dean, and Their All-Black Schools	65
5	Manassas and Voorhees: Models of Race Uplift	89
6	Historically Black Colleges and Universities: In Service to the Race	106
	Notes	113
	Bibliography	155
	Index	185

Illustrations follow p. 88.

Acknowledgments

This book has been a long time in the making and the thank-yous and acknowledgments now owed are legion. *An Architecture of Education* was first conceived during the relative optimism of the Clinton presidency and what I now recall as the last years of my youth. The twenty-plus years have been a journey indeed, and with the publication of this book, several chapters of my life and my research are now coming to a close. I want to thank the many stalwart contributors to my personal and professional journey, which has now spanned a number of locales—the American West, South Africa, the East Coast—reminding myself that it's been a privilege to befriend, study, teach, and work for two decades now with some of the finest in those environs. I have situated most people mentioned in these acknowledgments where I first met them, but many have moved on to other institutions, while a few others have passed from this world to be with our ancestors. For me, regardless of where they are physically or spiritually, they remain a part of my life.

Dear family and lifelong friends and colleagues who have helped me to realize this book in myriad ways, and whom I want to thank at this time, include my parents Angel and Ana Nieves, my sister Irma Nieves, my brother-in-law, my nephew, nieces, great-niece and nephew; Lois and Paul Foote and the extended Foote family clan; Isabel Martinez, Robb Hernandez, Janet T. Simons, Greg Lord, Marla Jaksch, Siobhan Senier, Dorothy Kim, Kim Gallon, Tara McPherson, Cecilia Hwangpo, M. G. Lord, David Dunlap, Scott Bane, Scot Coughlin, David Kesselman, Larry Sicular, Curt Sanburn, Ralph Teyssier; Chris, Lori, and Chelsea Lytle; Lisa Snyder, Elaine Sullivan, Ellen Hoobler, Yumi Pak, Courtney Thompson, Michele Simms-Burton, Kim Miller, Abdul Alkalimat, and Deborah A. Coquillon, and Katie Van Heest.

This book evolved from a seminar paper in a graduate-level African American women's history course at Cornell University in the late 1990s that was taught by the always inspiring Margaret Washington. Her seminal work on the Gullah and Geechee of Georgia's Sea Islands, and on Sojourner Truth helped to shape my future work. I had a wonderful interdisciplinary committee at Cornell—Maria Cristina Garcia, Mary Woods, and James Turner. Other Cornell teachers and friends have included: Lois Brown, Sherm Cochran, Marti Dense, Jacquelyn Goldsby, and Abdul Nanji.

The student cohort from my time at Cornell includes Leslie M. Alexander, Juan Barahona, Nicole Guidotti-Hernandez, Jean Ju Kim, Susie Lee, Liz Pryor, Gabriela Sandoval, Michelle Scott, and Jennifer Wilks. Remembering the wonderful times we shared back then, I salute and thank them all.

I left the Cornell nest on the eve of 9/11 in August 2001 and headed for the University of Colorado–Boulder for my first tenure-track teaching gig. Colorado is a stunning place and the personnel and students at CU–Boulder's Ethnic Studies Department were lively and intelligent. I want to give a shout-out in particular to: Kerry Callahan, Evelyn Hu DeHart, Erika Doss, Elisa Facio, Kenneth Foote, Lane Hirabayashi, Deborah Hollis, Alex Lubin, Jose Martinez, Karen Moreira, Tim Oakes, Lisa Park, David Pellow, and Darrin Pratt.

My partner, Richard Foote, who had elected to remain in upstate New York for the time being, found it difficult to travel west with any regularity in the aftermath of 9/11, so I would find myself back East in short order. It was my great privilege to teach at the School of Architecture, Planning and Preservation at the University of Maryland–College Park in their Preservation Program. Randall Mason, program chair, made me feel particularly welcome. One of this impressive cohort of faculty, Mary Corbin Sies, has remained the most steadfast of mentors and the dearest of my very close friends. I first met Mary on the professional conference circuit in Seattle in 1997. Her commitment and interest in cultural heritage and preservation across diverse communities was one of the things that first drew me to her, not to mention her passion for social justice. I can't thank Mary enough at this time and suspect I will always be in her debt and will forever remain in awe of her intellectual energies. Other Maryland acknowledgments include Renee Ater, Steve Boyle, Elsa Barkley Brown, Val Brown, John Caughey, Erve Chambers, Alex Chen, Kandice Chuh, Patricia Hill Collins, Ann Denkler, Stephanie Frank, Isabelle Gournay, Dawn Green, Patrick Grzanka, Wendy Hall, Christina Hanhardt, Marie Howland, Steve Hurtt, Katie King, Mary Konsoulis, Willow Leung, Marilee Lindemann, Don Linebaugh, Amy McLaughlin, Monica Mora-Herrera, Zita Nunes, Jo B. Paoletti, Phyllis Peres, Ann Petrone, Kelly Quinn, Connie Ramirez, Garth Rockcastle, Ana Patricia Rodriguez, Stephanie Ryberg, Paul Schackel, Martha Nell Smith, Nancy Struna, Erika Thompson, Wendy Thompson, Maria Velazquez, Daryle Williams, Psyche Williams-Forson, and Brooke Wortham.

It was my good fortune during my tenure at UMD–College Park to launch a relationship across the Atlantic with some remarkable people in South Africa. My faculty partnership with the Maryland Institute for Technology in the Humanities (MITH) enabled me to conduct research in South Africa for over ten years and from which emerged my earliest critical digital scholarship. Beloved lifelong South African friends, along with those who have proved critical to my research there, include Prinisha Badassy, Dinesh Balliah, Keith Breckenridge, Liz Delmont, Jo-Anne Duggan, Zac Gumbo, Sarah Haines, Ali

Hlongwane, Nicolene van Loggerenberg, Gabi Mohale, Michele Pickover, Brenda Schmahmann, and Jacques Stoltz.

In 2008 I was able to rejoin Richard in upstate New York, where I began what I regard as a period of remarkable personal and professional growth on the beautiful, sheltering campus of Hamilton College. First welcomed to Hamilton by Shelley Haley and her colleagues in the then-Africana Studies Program, I was able to help build (and found) the Digital Humanities Initiative (DHi) there—greatly assisted by generous funding from the Andrew W. Mellon Foundation and the support of Joe Urgo, dean of the faculty at the time—along with my amazing codirector, Janet T. Simons. I also want to thank the dean of faculty's office for their support of this manuscript by providing a generous subvention grant to assist with final publication. At Hamilton, many thanks are owed to, among others, Rich Alexander, Abhishek Amar, Erol Balkan, Lori Barone, Joyce Barry, William Billiter, Steve Humphries Brooks, J. Monique Collier, Crystal Endsley, Shay Foley, Lisa Forrest, Todd Franklin, Ella Gant, Margaret Gentry, Nathan Goodale, Amy Gowans, Martine Guyot-Bender, Tina Hall, Jan Howarth-Piayai, Carol Kentile, Gill King, Anne Lacsamana, Chaise LaDousa, Terri Lapinski, Doran Larson, Amy Lindner, Peter MacDonald, Lisa McFall, Linda Michaels, Kyoko Omori, Patricia O'Neill, Sam Pellman, Tammy Rotach, Patrick Reynolds, Nhora Serrano, Krista Siniscarco, Dave Smallen, Tami Stevens, Joan Hinde Stewart, Kristin Strohmeyer, Amit Taneja, Margie Thickstun, Kelly Walton, Nigel Westmaas, Thomas Wilson, David Wippman, Steve Yao, Penny Yee, and Steve Young. I have had the good fortune to teach a number of remarkable students at Hamilton during my tenure there. In particular, I remain indebted to, and in awe of, Samantha Donohue, Robyn Gibson, Robin Joseph, Stephanie Tafur, and Will Weston.

With my almost ten years at Hamilton College now drawing to a close, I want to thank new colleagues, mentors, and friends at Yale University: these include Weili Cheng, Cathy DeRose, Joe Fischel, Maureen Gardner, Inderpal Grewal, Linda Hase, Peter Leonard, Joey Plaster, Elihu Rubin, and jub sankofa. Laura Wexler of Yale has been a close friend, mentor, and intellectual powerhouse at a pivotal moment in my scholarly life. Her generosity and unwavering support have meant so much more than I can express in just a few words.

My intellectual journey carries me to San Diego, California, in the fall of 2018. I join a dynamic cohort of old and new colleagues, Bonnie Akashian, Norma Bouchard, Joanna Brooks, David P. Cline, Clarissa Clo, Sarah Elkind, Pam Lach, Angel Daniel Matos, William Nericcio, Walter Penrose, Beth Pollard, Jessica Pressman, Adriana Putko, Nathian Rodriquez, and Andrew Wiese. Andy, Jessica, Joanna, Pam, and Bill are welcoming me to San Diego State University (while also making it possible for me to spend an intervening year at Yale), making a new academic home for me, and permitting me to remain committed to research, teaching, and social justice.

I must also thank library personnel and libraries at the following: Hollis Burke Frissell Library, Tuskegee University; Harvey Library, Hampton University; Olin Library, Cornell University; McKeldin Library, University of Maryland; Norlin Library, University of Colorado; Burke Library, Hamilton College; and Sterling Memorial Library, Yale University. And a very personal shout-out and acknowledgment must be made to Barbara Opar, arts librarian, Syracuse University, for instilling in me during my undergraduate days at Syracuse University's School of Architecture the proper love and respect for her passionately held collection of fine arts volumes.

I also want to thank the many people with whom I've networked and befriended outside the walls of my respective institutions but who, in other respects, have been as important as those on the inside. First, I'd like to thank the program officers and administrators at the Andrew W. Mellon Foundation for their support and generosity. Hamilton's DHi was made possible, in large part, by two generous grants from Mellon and I will remain forever grateful for the early believers and risk takers there. Mellon Foundation people include Armando Bengochea, Patricia Hswe, Phil Lewis, Gene Tobin, and Don Waters. At the National Endowment for the Humanities Office of Digital Humanities, I would like to thank Brett Bobley, Perry Collins, Jason Rhody, and Jennifer Serventi. At the Society of American City and Regional Planning Historians (SACRPH) it was my great good fortune to meet the aforementioned Mary Corbin Sies. Other SACRPH scholar-activists include Robin Bachin, Gail Lee Dubrow, Howard Gillette, Walter Greason, Joseph Heathcott, Lynne Horiuchi, Marsha Ritzdorf, David Schuyler, Daphne Spain, June Manning Thomas, and the aforementioned Andy Weise.

Finally, my growing community of digital humanities coworkers and friends are stellar and humbling, and, with their boundless generosity, they never fail to teach and inspire me. They include Lissette Acosta-Corniel, Taylor Arnold, Keisha N. Blain, Susan Brown, Vincent Brown, Micha Cardenas, Bryan Carter, Marie Sachiko Cecire, Sonia Chaidez, Mark Christel, Alan Christy, John Clarke, Brittney Cooper, T. L. Cowan, Anne Cong-Huyen, Constance Crompton, Nathaniel Deutsch, Craig Dietrich, Amy Earhart, Mark Edington, Kristen Eschelman, Diane Favro, Nicole Ferraiolo, Dawn-Elissa Fischer, P. Gabrielle Foreman, Neil Fraistat, Alex Gill, Alyson Gill, Tula Goenka, Amanda Golden, Edward Gonzalez-Tennant, Dene Grigar, Roger Hallas, Jacob Heil, Chuck Henry, Sharon Irish, Bruce Janz, Jessica M. Johnson, Matt Kirschenbaum, Anne Kelly Knowles, Carly Kocurek, Adeline Koh, Liz Losh, Kim Martin, Anne McGrail, Jim McGrath, Tara McPherson, R. C. Miessler, Greg O'Malley, Scott Nesbit, Reynaldo Ortiz-Minaya, Costas Papadopoulos, Marisa Parham, Jessica Parr, Annemarie Perez, Eric Poehler, Irena Polic, Miriam Posner, Todd Presner, Andrea Rhen, Lisa Marie Rhody, Roopsi Risam, Gretta Roman, Shawna Ross, Jentery Sayers, Susan Schreibman, Carrie Schroeder, Donnie Sendelbach, Lynne Siemens, Ray Siemens, J. Mark Souther, Jesse Stommel, Friederike

Sundarm, Lauren Tilton, Fiona Vernal, Jacque Wernimont, Meg Worley, Marta C. Youngblood, Paul A. Youngman, and Vika Zafrin.

The series editors at the University of Rochester Press (URP), Alison Parker and Carol Faulkner, have been extremely patient, insightful, and incredibly supportive at every moment in the book-making process. Sonia Kane, editorial director at URP, has been supportive and admirably persistent throughout this process. I must also thank Julia Cook, Tracey Engel, and Valerie Ahwee for their invaluable assistance in the final stages of this book project.

And, in closing, I want to recognize two beings in particular: the two loves of my life, one human and the other canine—I'll let the reader determine which one is which—and to whom I dedicate this book: Paul Richard Foote III (Richard) and Mitzy. They both opened my heart and made me a better scholar and person. Although Mitzy passed in December 2016 (unbelievably, almost reaching the age of twenty!) her feisty spirit, humor, beauty, and loyal companionship are never far from my thoughts.

Thank you all.
New Haven, Connecticut
December 2017

Introduction

> "She made the vision true."
> —Coleman, *Tuskegee to Voorhees*

African American racial uplift—that is, a gendered racial mutual history of self-help—has existed as a tradition since the early part of the nineteenth century. Yet African American educational history and readings of the built environment have too often heralded the achievements of Black men such as Booker T. Washington or John Hope Franklin at the expense of Black women's involvement in racial uplift and, more specifically, in the creation of industrial and normal schools throughout the South in the nadir of Jim Crow.[1] Incorporating research into African American community and culture, *An Architecture of Education: Black Women Design the New South* essays the critical influence African American women of the late nineteenth century had on the built environment in the South (figure 1), and who, as such, inscribed a social and political ideology of race uplift onto the very bricks of the industrial and normal schools they worked to found in "the Age of Washington and Du Bois" some thirty years after the Civil War.[2] Two notable women, Elizabeth Evelyn Wright (figure 2) and Jennie Dean (figure 3) founded, respectively, Voorhees College in Denmark, South Carolina, established in 1897 (figure 4), and the Manassas Industrial School, Manassas, Virginia, established in 1893 (figure 5). Wright (born in 1872 and died in 1906) and Dean (born a slave in 1848 and died in 1913), whose biographies and actions illuminate and are central to *An Architecture of Education*, both regarded education not only as a remedy for the trauma of years of chattel slavery but also as a means to enlarge the limited role of women in the often male-dominated process of Black community building.[3]

Race Uplift and the Built Environment

An Architecture of Education expands our understanding of this period in African American women's history by arguing that the intellectual project of race uplift as a social movement included the built environment as a primary vehicle for race-based advancement.[4] As historians of the South—from post-Reconstruction through the beginning of the Progressive era—have yet to study the work of African American women and the built environment in an extended monograph, this book begins to fill this critical gap. This book also attempts to incorporate more recent thinking on intersectionality into its historical narrative. *Intersectionality* is a term that was coined by legal scholar and critical race theorist Kimberlé Crenshaw in the 1990s to describe the intersecting identities that factor into discrimination and systems of oppression.[5] These identities include categories such as race, gender, class, sexuality, age, disability, ethnicity, nation, and religion, among many others. While there is no single way to implement intersectionality into interdisciplinary scholarship, there are numerous research strategies and theoretical frameworks with which to highlight and interrogate categories of diversity and difference.

Intersectionality

As historians Carol Faulkner and Alison M. Parker have argued, gender and race must be seen as linked categories that shape, reflect, and situate how power, privilege, and oppression act as historical forces overwhelmingly impacting African American women.[6] A fuller, more in-depth theoretical framework examines how these systems, interwoven identities, and emerging feminist politics intersected and dynamically catalyzed nineteenth- and early twentieth-century women's social movements. The struggle to integrate the kinds of identities that defined both their gender and race as African American women reformers, along with their struggle to organize and build institutions of learning for poor and working-class students, are best understood through an intersectional feminist framework.[7] Intersectionality allows us to interrogate the ways in which racism and sexism evolved in the late nineteenth century at this critical juncture of "freedom," segregation, and the continued exploitation of labor (especially of women) under capitalism during the Second Industrial Revolution in the latter part of the nineteenth and the first part of the twentieth centuries.[8]

As such, these intersectional identities and their histories are crucial subject matter for interdisciplinary research and activism as they tend to overlap or cut across traditional and often siloed disciplinary areas of study.[9] More particularly, the gendered, racialized agents of *An Architecture of Education*, Jennie Dean and Elizabeth Wright, operating in the face of daunting oppression during the nadir of the Jim Crow South, seized agency and, acting at the highest levels as the clients of both Black and white establishment architects, worked to upend the dominant culture's monopoly on monumental material culture.[10]

The Civil War inspired women, both Black and white, to work to educate African Americans across the South. Many of these women were abolitionists or missionaries who felt that their efforts to educate Blacks were a logical extension of their antislavery work. Northern religious and philanthropic organizations initiated efforts to educate slaves living in areas occupied by the Union Army. Of the more than nine hundred Northern teachers sent to freedom schools in the South, 75 percent were women.[11] The federal government's Freedmen's Bureau (the Bureau of Abandoned Lands, Refugees, and Freedmen) became involved in educating Blacks while providing federally mandated social welfare programs.[12] During Reconstruction more than three thousand Southern whites taught in new Black schools with men outnumbering women by a very small margin.[13] Later, women from across the North and South during the Progressive era would embrace schoolteaching as one of the few public occupations available to them. Teaching, understood as an extension of child care and the domestic sphere, would soon be dominated by women.

Contested Black Educational Historiography

The canonical (and siloed) historical narrative of the African American experience of the end of the nineteenth century has regarded vocational education for African Americans as the only feasible alternative to classical higher education then available.[14] This historiography of Black education has perpetuated a master narrative, since the 1970s and 1980s, that industrial and vocational training was little more than a program for social engineering and racial control to make better laborers and workers to advance white capitalist goals. Wright's and Dean's efforts fell strongly on the side of the industrial education advocates of the Black South. As women, they both understood that to advance the political project of race-based industrial and normal school education, they would ally themselves publicly with accommodationist Black male proponents—that is, consciously adopting or adapting to white political strategies and ideals.[15] Wright, founder of Voorhees College, herself was a follower of Booker T. Washington. Wright had attended the Tuskegee Institute and had befriended both Booker T. and his second and third wives, Olivia Davidson and Margaret Murray (his second wife had died during Wright's tenure at Tuskegee, and Booker T. remarried several years later). Her fondest wish, she claimed, would be "to try and be the same type of woman as Mr. Washington was of a man."[16] Jennie Dean modeled her institution on the industrial school, placing herself squarely on Booker T.'s side.[17] Yet if the accommodationist strategies employed at Tuskegee and Voorhees were seemingly designed to be inoffensive to the white elite, the built environments—that is, the evidence inherent in the material culture there—were fully competitive and monumental, organizing as they did at once the plan of whole communities. *An Architecture of Education* maintains that Manassas and Voorhees were intended to assist their race toward political self-determination and, from a scholarly perspective in the first years of the twenty-first century, acted as critical agents of a de facto strategy of nation building under the American segregationist policy of Jim Crow.

There were other Tuskegee disciple schools such as the Utica Institute, the Piney Woods School, the Palmer Memorial Institute, and the Calhoun Colored School, to name a few, that were founded by women.[18] For example, the Calhoun Colored School was founded in 1892 by Charlotte Thorn and Mabel Dillingham in Lowndes County, Alabama. Both white women and former Hampton Institute teachers, they worked in partnership with Booker T. Washington to start a school focused on industrial and vocational training. Charlotte Thorn, born in New Haven, Connecticut, was committed to training rural Blacks because of her support of Gen. Samuel Armstrong's Hampton model. Although Calhoun offered students an industrial education, it promoted land ownership for future economic stability.[19] In 1902 Charlotte Hawkins Brown founded the Palmer Memorial Institute in Sedalia, North Carolina, after raising funds across New England. The school emphasized manual and industrial training for rural African Americans. Palmer does not, however, reflect Tuskegee's influence on the built environment or that of other working-class school founders such as Wright or Dean. Palmer was a preparatory high school and not a fully designed industrial school campus as those built at Voorhees or Manassas.

Black Nationalism and Women Reformers

Black nationalism is a constructed world view characterized as a "quest for autonomy" on the part of all peoples of African descent throughout the African diaspora who are interlinked by the common history of enslavement. Black nationalism in the United States is best understood when linked to both pan-Africanism because of the international system of enslavement and an imagined community notion of nationalism.[20] Through an intersectional analysis we can more fully understand that Black nationalist reform efforts and protest in America, linked by race and gender oppression, have a long history in the United States. In the mid-nineteenth century women such as Maria Stewart and Mary Ann Shadd argued for a Black nationalism that supported economic independence and a sustained political activism.[21] Scholars have often viewed Black nationalism as inherently patriarchal and linked to the construction of separate spheres for women and men, with women being left outside most mainstream theorizations of nationalism until recently.[22] Scholars such as August Meier, Wilson J. Moses, and Tunde Adeleke have provided siloed academic discourses on Black nationalism that ignored the important contributions by feminist nationalists, especially those who used the built environment as significant parts of their race uplift and nation-making efforts.[23]

Today, it is understood that Black nationalism is the belief in distinct African group traits: the consciousness of shared oppression, the awareness of duties and responsibilities of African-descended peoples to assist one another, and the need for Black self-determination and solidarity.[24] Black nationalism reflects not only a sense of tradition and history, but an African value system predicated on collective advancement. Despite forced cultural deracination, virulent biologically determined racism (also understood as scientific racism), and the ravages of slavery, Black nationalism maintained its roots in an African core culture that espoused Black pride and identity through cultural and heritage preservation.[25] In the context of this book, Black nationalism centers on a conscious ideology of racial solidarity and self-help among African Americans, specifically as seen through these two women, who were committed to the vindication of the race by building bricks-and-mortar institutions. The collective self-determination and identity formation of African Americans in the late nineteenth century is clearly expressed through their attempts to build a nation within the American cultural landscape composed entirely of all-Black institutions such as the church, school, and home. Although separatism and emigration were once considered preferred solutions to the "race problem" of the eighteenth and early nineteenth centuries among many African American leaders, Black women nationalists of a different era sought to empower and liberate African Americans in other ways. For African American women, nation building was but a single aspect of the much larger Black nationalist agenda: a series of complex racial projects for social, economic, and political betterment expressed through the built environment.

An examination of African American industrial education, school building, and social welfare activism demonstrates that African American women were purposefully invested in the physical design of their many community-based institutions for race uplift. African American women were uniquely aware of the spatial power (and, in turn, a kind of spatial activism) that their social welfare institutions had in the making of what were radical agendas for social change and race-based advancement. These African American women were not simply the clients of architects (who, contemporaneously, were being rigorously trained and regulated as professionals in the latter part of the nineteenth century as industry, science, and mass education took hold in the United States) but as female clients, they were allying themselves with designers, although they themselves may have lacked training in architecture or its allied arts.[26] New scholarship is needed that cuts across traditional constructs of historical periodization for our broader understanding of race uplift institutions founded by those women, who were undeterred by boundaries of gender, class, and color—including gendered and racialized respectability—at the height of the Victorian era. As such, *An Architecture of Education* will employ an intersectional investigation into this particular arena of uplift.

This book is not intended to be a comprehensive history of Black women in education; instead, it documents and situates the architectural and social history of two particular instances of nation building, and, nodding to the *spatial turn* that animates so much scholarly conversation today, demonstrates linkages between the construction of autonomous spaces, resistance against racism, and promotion of collective identity and community in an historical epoch of American oppression—the late nineteenth-century U.S. South.[27] In spotlighting the work of Wright and Dean, this book acts as historical recovery, while also situating these women's efforts in the inter- and multidisciplinary field of African American studies, demonstrating linkages to women's spatial reform work while also employing architectural history, historic preservation, women's studies, and cultural studies.[28] This interdisciplinary and intersectional approach is intended to help the reader better understand the complex social and spatial dynamics of race, class, gender, and nation that were in play and that have shaped many of these cultural landscapes of educational reform. Rejecting subordinated assimilation, the institutions these women founded in the post–Civil War South may be understood as experiments in Black cultural and economic nationalism.[29]

Narrative Chapters

Chapter 1 examines the history of the postbellum Lost Cause and its contemporary relevance. Chapters 2 and 3 provide a historical framework with which to understand the architectural and social history of the period. Chapters 4 and 5 examine the histories of Wright and Dean, their respective schools, and how they claimed agency. The book does not frontload the careers of Wright and Dean; instead, it provides readers who might be unfamiliar with the period a critical spatial history of the late nineteenth century. Recent concerns in architectural history now consider historic preservation, historical recovery, and the social production of memory around the built environment in the African American community.[30] Narratives written by architectural historians today must begin to critically engage with the social, political, and economic world "in which such works [in the built environment] serve as cultural and historical agents."[31] The built environments of African Americans as proposed were sometimes not realized, in addition to those that were built; both, however, must be seen as important historical agents in the movement for race uplift.

In chapter 1, *An Architecture of Education* recounts how, in the decades after the Civil War, as white southerners maintained their own "official" culture through acts of racial violence, African Americans responded by continuing to develop a nationalist culture informed by the built environment and their heroic acts of agency. Despite white supremacists' assaults on Black homes, churches, schools, and even towns, the South remained home to fully 90 percent of the almost ten million (9,733,313) African Americans living in the United States in 1910. Over 60 percent alone were living in the states of Alabama, Georgia, Louisiana, Mississippi, North Carolina, and South Carolina. Education afforded hope, and eventually African Americans were to claim progress, with metrics such as illiteracy rates plummeting from 79.9 percent in 1870 to 44.5 percent by 1900.[32]

As a milestone in American political will, material culture, and the built environment, the 1893 World's Columbian Exposition still looms large in the historical imagination. Chapter 2 examines the significance of the 1893 World's Columbian Exposition on placemaking among African American women reformers and architects. Located on 690 acres on the South Side of Chicago, the Columbian Exposition opened its doors from May to October 1893 to great popular acclaim, with attendance reaching twenty-seven million (figure 6). At an event celebrating culture, commerce, and national ideology and narrative of the industrial age of the late nineteenth century, the so-called "White City's" Court of Honor and its neoclassical style "great buildings" contrasted with the chaos of the "savage" ethnological exhibitions of the nonwhite "other" in the Midway elsewhere on the fairgrounds.[33] The message to visitors was clear—there would be no doubt that the architectural spectacle of the Exposition had sublimely linked notions of Anglo-Saxon supremacy and Western expansion to the imperial Roman past.

By 1893 African Americans had enjoyed thirty years of widespread emancipation (although complicated by the wholesale collapse of Radical Reconstruction).[34] However, segregation or Jim Crow was now the law in much of the United States, and early twentieth-century eugenics brought added vehemence and violence to Jim Crow: African Americans were decried as an underdeveloped race and it was the right and obligation of white men—either the "Southern Best Man" or the "New Southern Man" of the Progressive era—to rule.[35] In the face of Southern segregation and terror, Ida B. Wells and many other Black female social reformers were laying out the political agenda of a gendered Black nationalism to counter American white hegemony.[36] African American architects and social reformers challenged claims concerning separatism and strategies for subordinated assimilation at the Columbian Exhibition, and reappropriated its divisive imagery. In doing so, they co-opted the hegemonic material culture of the Exposition (and other architectural production of the Beaux Arts era) and transformed it into a working model for race betterment in the built environment—transforming it from the imperial to the progressive—as they were forced to create their separate Black-based institutions.[37]

An act of Congress had authorized the creation of the Exposition, calling for "an exhibition of the progress of civilization in the New World"—with little acknowledgment that any such advances were achieved, in no small part, on the backs of the enslaved and indentured.[38] The Midway, depicting the supposed backwardness of peasant peoples from Africa, Asia, the Pacific, and the Middle East, essentially representing them as the "savage races"—Africans and American Indians, for example—were sequestered the farthest from the White City. Soon, however, by reappropriating the style of the "master class," African Americans "attempted to employ the racialization of the Southern landscape to their advantage."[39] African Americans promoted a narrative of a new Black nation with its own identity and citizenship, and actively constructed Black self-help institutions that could provide safe space and refuge for Black citizens from racist hostility.

Chapter 3 frames the influence of dominant architectural practice on American campus design during the growth of normal and industrial schools in the South in the latter part of the nineteenth century. The American college campus had by then reimagined itself as a kind of utopia and a city of learning.[40] The exurban settings of the prototypical American college—often far from settlements of any kind—required that "the college become even more fully a kind of miniature city."[41] Once imagined by Thomas Jefferson as a kind of "academical village," the design of the American campus also "became an experiment in urbanism" (figure 7).[42]

Perhaps no African American institution of higher learning more fully realized these aspirations than the Tuskegee State Normal School, founded in 1881 by African American reformer Booker T. Washington. The craft traditions—woodcarving, building, and ironsmithing—that built the antebellum South on the backs of the enslaved can be difficult to reconstruct because so much of the work went unrecorded. With African American higher education seemingly contested between classical versus industrial traditions, Washington and his "machine" were powerful advocates for industrial training, and so he required that his students participate in the construction of Tuskegee's campus as a key component of their educational and moral training. As such, Black students constructed seemingly autonomous Black spaces (figure 8) despite the compromises that were implicit in Booker T. Washington's larger compact with Northern capital and the dominant White Southern establishment. Washington wrote that although he "knew that our first buildings would [not] be comfortable or complete in their finish as buildings erected by the experienced hands of outside workmen . . . but that in the teaching of civilization, self-help, and self-reliance, the erection of the buildings by the students themselves would more than compensate for any lack of comfort or finish."[43]

"Jim Crow" laws—the name was derived originally from the minstrel song "Jump Jim Crow," written in 1828—were enacted primarily in Southern states in the latter half of the nineteenth century, restricting many of the rights granted to African Americans after the Civil War. Culminating in the U.S. Supreme Court's doctrine of "separate but equal" in the case of *Plessy v. Ferguson* of 1896, Jim Crow laws required that African Americans decamp to their own space—in the largest sense, that they make an exodus to their own lands or their own nation. As if to rally this nation, writer and social reformer Anna Julia Cooper employs the biblical Exodus tale, making an explicit comparison with this, the African American nation, and the nation of Israel in her work, *A Voice from the South* (1892): "We look within that we may gather together once more practical methods, address ourselves to the tasks before us. We look forward with hope and trust that the same God whose guiding hand led our fathers through and out of the gall and bitterness of oppression."[44] Sensing an opportunity in the face of what might otherwise be calamity, Cooper writes, "to be a woman of the Negro race in America, and to be able to grasp the deep significance of the possibilities of the crisis, is to *have a heritage*. . . . No plan for renovating society, no scheme for purifying politics, no reform in church or in state, no moral, social, or economic question, no movement upward or downward in the human plane is lost on her."[45]

In chapter 4, *An Architecture of Education* pivots to the personal biographies and microhistories of two African American women reformers of the Progressive era. One, Elizabeth Wright, had been forever altered by her experience at Booker T. Washington's Tuskegee Institute, an experience that led her to claim agency and seize the singular opportunity lying ahead for African American women who wished to better the race. Additionally, the relationships with key race women during her tenure as a student at the Tuskegee Institute had solidified her resolve to contribute to an expansive social movement, while at the same time it encouraged her further education. Much as Booker T. Washington had appealed to Northern capital and its agents—the Rockefellers, and Andrew Carnegie et al.—to bankroll the Institute, so would Wright appeal in the 1890s to another cohort of Northern philanthropists—Ralph Voorhees of New Jersey, in particular—to eventually establish Voorhees College in rural Denmark, South Carolina. Wright's initial vision of an all-Black *race-based* institution and model educational community was unique in the state of South Carolina, and was significant as a site spearheaded entirely by the efforts of an African American woman. Wright supported industrial education and believed that the school should follow Tuskegee's example in all its endeavors. Unfortunately, Voorhees's typically straitened finances were such that it was difficult to implement development for all its programs. Trades taught at Voorhees included farming, bricklaying, plumbing, carpentry, wheelwrighting, blacksmithing, painting, printing, cooking, laundering, sewing, millinery, housekeeping, nursing, and mattress making. Other curricula offered at Voorhees included reading, writing, and arithmetic.[46] Today, Voorhees College continues with its mission on the same campus that Elizabeth Wright founded in 1893.

During its tenure, Jennie Dean's Manassas Industrial School grew from a bare one hundred–acre site to a two hundred–acre campus. The school held classes in sewing, carpentry, laundry, blacksmithing, wheelwrighting, cooking, dairying, and poultry husbandry; its eight instructors also assumed the teaching of strictly academic subjects. Despite the abuse that slavery had inflicted upon her, Dean summoned the strength to promote training classes for African Americans in the face of national and, in particular, local white hostility as whites regarded the education of Blacks as a means of openly subverting the legitimacy of white supremacy.

Chapter 5 looks critically at these all-Black schools as early efforts to construct the physical sites of race betterment. Architectural training was considered one of the "most important divisions of Tuskegee's work," providing the basis for the erection of some twenty-three buildings at the school site by 1901. Booker T. Washington's experiment in campus planning in particular had provided young architects with the opportunity to design their own monumental Black City in microcosm and experiment with issues of urbanism. As at the Columbian Exposition, Beaux Arts monumentality would inform the plan "parti" for the Manassas Industrial School, where ten pavilion-like structures were to be interspersed along a series of one-story dormitories arranged around a terraced "great lawn," somewhat reminiscent of Thomas Jefferson's seminal arrangement of buildings around the open lawn at the University of Virginia's "academical village."[47] Manassas's placement of administration buildings and residences for various school officials and the incorporation of a secondary axis suggests the dual role of the industrial school to help educate its students in both the manual trades and provide them with elements of a liberal arts education. Meanwhile at Voorhees, the striking scale and grandeur of its overall design is a testament to the educational authority and permanence that was intended for this institution founded by African Americans. Moreover, it was believed that community building would be an essential part of African American architectural practice—in the words of Booker T. Washington, it would connect "the school with life, thus making it a center and a source of interest that might gradually transform the communities about them"—and, as such, architects initially trained at places like Tuskegee would approach the study and practice of architecture very differently from those trained only at elite Northern white schools.[48]

As African Americans painfully built upon their heritages under enslavement in the nadir of Jim Crow, Southern whites invented and promoted the Lost Cause, a white antebellum Southern cultural narrative of valor, chivalry, and martyrdom. The Lost Cause was recognized in particular as a literary phenomenon, shaped largely by journalists and fiction writers, who gave their audience a sense of belonging to an "imagined community" of the "Old South." With elite white Southern women assigned the mantle of "guardians of the past," they expanded the boundaries of propriety and voluntarism, allowing elite white women to influence the making of a Southern tradition in "public history." Thus, throughout the last decades of the nineteenth century, advocates of the Lost Cause (figure 9) would found a number of colleges and institutions throughout the South as memorials to their fallen Confederate heroes, seemingly in tandem with Black attempts to recover and commemorate their own heritage. Opposed to the narrative of the Lost Cause were those African American writers and reformers of the late nineteenth century involved in the production of race literature, who believed that such a literature would provide a "pattern-book" to promote race uplift strategies. Race literature would ensure the careful promotion and preservation of important events, "saving from obstruction and obliteration what is good, helpful, and stimulating."[49]

If white women believed that it was their primary goal to preserve Southern culture through a carefully scripted interpretation of the past, Black women, on the other hand, such as Jennie Dean and Elizabeth Evelyn Wright had determined that radical social reform would be made possible only through mass education for African Americans. Black women's efforts to exploit the junctures of public and private space in political culture had a lasting impact, despite whites' continued attempts to hinder African American institutions from maturing into viable centers of race education and community advancement. At school sites such as Voorhees and Manassas, African Americans were surrounded by the physical artifacts, stories, and traditions that testified to their enslavement and liberation. On these campuses, African Americans were no longer simply replicating traditional architectural forms: they would instead transform the symbolic meaning of white dominance and social control long embedded in the classical architectural orders as a means of expressing their own power over cultural production. By reconfiguring the American ideal of an all-white nationalist and exclusive spatial culture, African American women seized a place for themselves and their communities.

An Architecture of Education examines how African American women, as educators and reformers, built their educational institutions in racist and hostile environments throughout the New South in the last decades of the nineteenth century. The *spatial turn* of the academy over the past twenty years—popularized by the work of white male social theorists such as Henri Lefebvre, Michel Foucault, Manuel Castells, and Anthony Giddens—has failed to adequately theorize the lived experiences of African Americans and their complex relationship with the American cultural landscape.[50] Countless scholars have argued that spaces and places can be constituted as subjects and analyzed as material evidence, seemingly bearing witness to varying forms of violence and cultural trauma brought on by state-sponsored injustice. Few scholars have, however, made the linkage between Black women and their social reform work as it impacted the American built environment beginning in the late nineteenth century.[51] By addressing the absence of African American women in the spatial narrative of American public and civic culture, *An Architecture of Education* attempts to reinstate their presence.

Chapter One

Contested Monument-Making and the Crisis of the Lost Cause, 1865–1920

> If there were a school of this kind in every county or in every congressional district of the south the negro problem would soon be solved.
>
> —Jennie Dean

The spring of 1876 would find twenty-eight-year-old Jennie Dean in service in the ubiquitous domestic economy of urban Washington, DC, and, more particularly, the morning of April 15—Jennie Dean's birthday—would find her, in all likelihood, consumed by her morning chores: preparing the family breakfast and washing and ironing clothes from the previous day. Living as a domestic and working in the home of a prominent Washington, DC, family, Dean may have been awarded a little birthday holiday if her employer had made a rare exception and consented to it. However, festivities greater than her birthday were taking place nearby—a dedication ceremony at Lincoln Square (now Lincoln Park), one mile directly east of the U.S. Capitol building in the easternmost part of the city, was being held—and conceivably Dean could have used the pretext of her birthday to join the crowds there.[1]

It was little more than a decade ago when Jennie Dean and countless other formerly enslaved African Americans heard the news that an assassin's bullet had killed President Lincoln at Ford's Theatre in the District.[2] Although African Americans in Washington, for all intents and purposes a Southern city, had been freed by the Compensated Emancipation Act of 1862, many feared that with Lincoln's death, some measure of their equality might soon be taken away. At the time, their growing fears and a continued sense of insecurity were only further heightened by the swearing in of Andrew Johnson as president—a man whose political leanings were as uncertain as was his commitment to Black progress. Congress had a sizable bloc of Radical Republicans who supported

Black enfranchisement, but many felt that their future was still largely uncertain as congressional leaders continued to usurp control of the limited self-government and Black agency the District had once enjoyed.[3] Many African Americans who had lived in Washington had witnessed firsthand the collapse of the Freedmen's Bureau—another in a series of failed efforts by Northern whites to assist the race since the close of the Civil War. More and more it was clear that if African Americans were to make significant strides for race-based advancement, they would have to embrace a form of self-reliance and "uplift" and found their own institutions.

Born a slave herself and already a teenager at the time of the Emancipation Proclamation in 1863, Dean would have remembered hearing as a young girl—an oral tradition was very much alive back then—that much of the area surrounding what had become Lincoln Square had been a temporary home to slaves rescued by the Union Army where they were protected from bounty hunters in search of fugitives.[4] The area had changed little since then, with nothing more than a few dozen or so scattered houses and a large plot of land designated for a future park in honor of President Lincoln.[5] Much of Black Washington was expected to turn out for the day's festivities in commemoration of the fourteenth anniversary of Emancipation in the District (the crowds were celebrating in actuality Abraham Lincoln's signing of the Compensated Emancipation Act of April 16, 1862, not the date of the general Emancipation Proclamation itself of 1863). A statue of a standing Lincoln liberating a crouching African American male slave dressed only in a loincloth, the *Freedman's Memorial to Abraham Lincoln* (now known as the *Emancipation Monument*), funded solely by African American contributions collected since Lincoln's death, would soon be unveiled to help mark one of the first public celebrations openly acknowledging the ravages of American slavery in the Black community (figure 10).[6] Today, Emancipation Day continues to be celebrated as a public holiday in the District of Columbia.

Commemorating the Civil War

If she arrived at the gathering, Dean would have seen that the square was already filled with hundreds of people from various parts of the city. Although she might not have recognized the many banners and flags that filled the square with color, she might have remembered similar sights from the end of the war, when she had lived as a slave in Virginia,[7] where in towns of the old Confederacy soldiers had dressed in their uniforms and gathered in public squares to commemorate those who had fought against Lincoln's Union Army.[8] In Lincoln Square the festivities would include a procession of civil society "colored" troops: the Knights Templar, Knights of St. Augustine, the Sons of Purity, the Sons of Levi, Good Samaritans, the Labor League, Sons of

Zion, the Young Men's Island Benevolent Association, the Pioneer Corps, and many other uniformed benevolent associations.[9] That so many African American societies and their supporters gathered in one place—in this instance, to commemorate their involvement in the war and to honor the work of the slain President Lincoln—was unprecedented.

On a dais covered with banners, brightly colored flags, and spring flowers were seated guests, including members of the president's cabinet, justices of the Supreme Court, foreign ministers, senators, and some local representatives. The form of the celebration here in Washington would not be so different from ritual unveilings that were taking place throughout the white South—a parade through the city streets to a monument site, several welcoming addresses, musical selections, and a closing oration by a prominent Southern war hero.[10] However, this unveiling in Washington, on the border of what had been the old South, was, in fact, very different, something attested to by the presence of one figure seated at the dais. There, the celebrated African American Frederick Douglass was seated among the white dignitaries—something that would still be unheard of in the South a long decade after Emancipation.

The revered orator and former slave Frederick Douglass spoke formally to a mixed crowd of Blacks and whites at this, the border of the North and old South (mixed-race gatherings of this scale south of the border might be more typically concerned with lynchings or hangings). After a round of applause and cheers, Douglass greeted the large crowd:

> I warmly congratulate you upon the highly interesting object which has caused you to assemble in such numbers and spirit as you have today. This occasion is in some respects remarkable. Wise and thoughtful men of our race, who shall come after us, and study the lesson of our history in the United States; who shall survey the long and dreary spaces over which we have traveled; who shall count the links in the great chain of events by which we have reached our present position, will make a note of this occasion. . . . We stand today at the national center to perform something like a national act—an act which is to go into history; and we are here where every pulsation of the national heart can be heard, felt, and reciprocated.[11]

As his many other public speeches and writings had already made clear, Douglass made it his own personal quest to preserve the memory of the Civil War, which he believed should be remembered by both Blacks and the nation as a whole.[12] Emancipation, Douglass believed, was the event in Black history that had most redefined American nationalism.[13] Throughout the 1870s, he felt that the country was suffering from some form of collective amnesia, or that many Americans were simply "destitute of [any] political memory."[14] Believing that the postwar era would ultimately be controlled by those who could best shape and control the interpretation of the war and promote its significance to the teaching of American history, Douglass's speech at the commemoration of the Emancipation Monument would act as a corrective and help to preserve the memory of the struggle over slavery.

Douglass openly criticized Lincoln being cast as a war hero, taking exception to the Lincoln hagiography emerging even then: "It must be admitted, truth compels me to admit, even here in the presence of the monument we have erected to his memory, Abraham Lincoln was not, in the fullest sense of the word, either our man or our model. In his interests, in his associations, in his habits of thought, and in his prejudices, he was a white man."[15] He argued that Lincoln "was preeminently the white man's President, entirely devoted to the welfare of white men" and that slaves were never truly "the special objects of his consideration."[16] For Douglass, only African Americans themselves would best handle the challenges of their past and those that lay ahead in the era of rebuilding a so-called New South.[17] In concluding his speech, Douglass suggested that

> We have done a good work for our race today. In doing honor to the memory of our friend and liberator, we have been doing highest honors to ourselves and those who come after us; we have been fastening ourselves to a name and fame imperishable and immortal; we have also been defending ourselves from a blighting scandal. When now it shall be said that the colored man is soulless, that he has no appreciation of benefits or benefactors; when the foul reproach of ingratitude is hurled at us, and it is attempted to scourge us beyond the range of human brotherhood, we may calmly point to the monument we have this day erected to the memory of Abraham Lincoln.[18]

In his closing remarks at the Lincoln Square ceremonies, Douglass made certain that whites understood the significance of the monument to African Americans as a shared national memory and a way of reframing the history of the Civil War. Douglass understood that people and nations were shaped and redefined by their own history. More specifically, African American history and representation were being contested at that very moment. In the South at this time, effigies of Lincoln were being burned by whites nostalgic for a fictional, aggrandized Southern past.[19] Douglass hoped that the memorializing events of this day would somehow successfully resist ongoing efforts by Confederate sympathizers to impose on the public the South's history of the Lost Cause. In the Progressive era, when violence and terror enforced acquiescence along what Du Bois called the color line, new stakeholders in the South refashioned it into a feudal society of racial peonage. The question remained who would claim the material culture of the South, as evidence attesting to both was springing up in the postbellum South. In any event, African American women reformers such as Jennie Dean and Elizabeth Evelyn Wright asserted themselves, claimed agency, and pursued their reform strategies in the face of the Southern Lost Cause.

The Lost Cause and Its Effects

In the years after the war, white southerners sanctified their past with tales of valor, chivalry, and martyrdom.[20] These formed the myth of the "Sacred South," which was "made inviolable by those who loved it, baptized in the blood of those who died for it, and ordained to permanent changelessness by the God who guided it."[21] For many, Confederate life and culture consisted primarily of those ideals, symbols, or material artifacts that were believed best representative of a now-lost patrician way of life. The Civil War had brought about the formal end of chattel slavery, the end of the Confederacy as a political power in the South, a tremendous loss of life, and the physical destruction of the agrarian landscape. Escalating Klan violence, carpetbaggers, and scalawags forced federal troops to mobilize in an attempt to restore civil order to the South. Unfortunately, many of the Southern states' militias were also mobilized. Conservative attempts to oppose Reconstruction in several Southern states gained popular support as Republicans argued over the direction of the newly formed government. White southerners desperately wanted to champion their view of the Civil War and its impact on self-determination for Southern states, and unreconstructed Southern nationalists made attempts to launch vigorous social campaigns to uphold states' rights vis-à-vis secession as a just response to what they perceived as an ever-growing, oppressive federal government.[22]

Some historians see the Lost Cause as the struggle over collective public memory, which was shaped most often by a series of organizations and institutions and their formalized rituals. The abstract collective memory of the Lost Cause is objectified or physically realized in the South's many public monuments. Others consider the Lost Cause as a kind of Southern and American civil religion rooted in the rhetoric of the sacred past before the war, as well as in the rhetoric of many varying secular institutions. Proponents of the Lost Cause felt that patriotism to the South would honor their dead: "Let them live and shine in your hearts forever; not prompting you to empty boasting, but quickening every generous impulse, and stirring in you the purest ambition."[23] However, honoring the Confederacy signaled a refusal on the part of southerners both to comprehend the damaging effects slavery had on the abusive economy of the South or to reorder postbellum social relations there.

Southern myth-making became a way of blending basic historical truths with nostalgic emotions of the past that would promote a glorious Confederate history and restore the past dominant social order on the backs of newly freed African Americans.[24] The Lost Cause also served to reestablish and memorialize fading Confederate honor as an evolving myth of Southern virtue and victimization became a political device and a dominant force in postbellum literary production. Related institutions included memorial associations, the Southern Historical Society, the United Confederate Veterans, the United

Daughters of the Confederacy, and many other institutions devoted to the recovery of a mythical past.[25] Many of these institutions believed that the South had engaged in a "just cause" to protect states' rights—an appeal successful to many since it helped comfort white southerners during a period of massive social change. Not only did the Lost Cause narratives suppress the African American experience, they also attempted to erase the history of white Southern repression.

A series of well-organized memorial activities swept the entire South in an effort to vindicate a collective sense of the past and address Northern "misinterpretations" of American history. The growth of various forms of white cultural production—such as nationalistic writings, songs, illustrations, memorial statuary and other forms of "textual narratives"—soon became the material artifacts of Lost Cause ideology.[26] The immediate growth of journals and magazines such as *The Land We Love* (1866), which had begun publishing in North Carolina, were primarily "devoted to literature, military history, and agriculture" as a means of improving conditions exacerbated by the war. In an address to its patrons, the editors of *The Land We Love* argued that "we believed then and believe now that the land of our birth,—the land for which we had battled four long years—deserved the enthusiastic attachment for her children and the admiration of the world. We have acted upon this sentiment, and have ever maintained and avowed our fealty to our beautiful South."[27] Other journals, such as the *Banner of the South* (1868), *Our Living and Our Dead* (1874), and the *Confederate Veteran* (1890), soon became the primary documents that recorded the "history" of the war.[28] All of these journals concentrated their efforts on developing the theme of Confederate military power by arguing that Southern forces, although ultimately fewer in number, were superior to those of the Union.[29]

By the nineteenth century, Americans had become voracious consumers of the news who often borrowed newspapers or publications from one another. Even the poor and illiterate had access to newspapers and asked friends to read to them.[30] Confederate proponents used print culture and the media to propel their nation-building process, and after the Civil War, white southerners mythically rebuilt their vanquished nation through a culture of "history and hope."[31] The Lost Cause, seen as a literary phenomenon, was shaped largely by journalists and fiction writers, among them Confederate apologists, "local color" writers of the 1880s, and the many white novelists of the 1890s who argued for national reconciliation.[32] By disseminating a uniform version of their collective memory, these literary texts gave their audience a sense of belonging to an "imagined community" of the "Old South." As a reactionary movement emerging from an agrarian tradition, the Lost Cause only complicated efforts to rebuild the former slave states into a New South.[33] Many proponents, both male and female, of the Lost Cause actually disavowed any references to the New South—some even considered the "New South" a kind of expletive.[34] In sharp contrast to an emerging New South ideology, these men and women believed in upholding the values of the Old South, and were determined to vindicate their fallen heroes and heroines by preserving the common values of states' rights and white supremacy.

By the late 1870s and 1880s, Southerners were fully invested in writing and revising the history of the Civil War South.[35] Especially for white women, the Lost Cause was seen as a campaign to honor and vindicate the Confederacy through diverse social programs. Many of these programs included building monuments, caring for indigent Confederate soldiers and their wives, sponsoring historical publications of the war, and teaching subsequent generations to revere the South's former way of life.[36] Along with the promotion of narratives that espoused a national mythology of the Old South, white women also perpetuated the stereotype of the Black Mammy figure beginning in the last decades of the nineteenth century and extending well into the twentieth.[37] By drawing bold lines between white and Black womanhood, white women found themselves at the center of Anglo-Saxon supremacist campaigns for public memory.

The United Daughters of the Confederacy imagined itself as a cultural authority guarding representations of the past.[38] In an advertisement for the United Daughters of the Confederacy in later years, Thomas Nelson Page wrote that "she [the antebellum white Southern woman] was not versed in the ways of the world, but she had no need to be. She was better than that; she was well bred. She had not to learn to be a lady, because she was born one. Generations had given her that by heredity."[39] As Page describes, elite white women were best suited to carry the mantle of "guardians of the past." Expanding the boundaries of propriety and voluntarism allowed elite white women to influence the making of a Southern tradition in "public history." As historian W. Fitzhugh Brundage has suggested, "these women architects of whites' historical memory, by both explaining and mystifying the historical roots of white supremacy and elite power in the South, performed a conspicuous civic function at a time of heightened concern about the perpetuation of social and political hierarchies."[40] Brundage maintains that these elite women understood how power could make certain historical narratives possible while silencing many others. In doing so, they turned to the print media as a way of recasting antebellum class and racial privileges.[41] Historian Drew Gilpin Faust has even argued that women were not only faced with the "failures and incompetence of their traditional protectors," but also had to deal with an injured and broken sense of white manhood.[42] Their rehabilitation became a central postwar responsibility for Confederate women, who now had to defend their honor and that of the entire defeated South. The Confederated Southern Memorial Association suggested that:

> In the struggle for a noble and just Cause, for which the men of the South sacrificed their all, the women with a faith and confidence, sublime almost in

its intensity, cheered and encouraged Fathers, Sons and Husbands in their gallant defense of their rights, weaved, spun, nursed the sick, and wherever a woman's hand could tend or soothe, there her mission. With a courage undaunted by the perils that beset her path of duty and love, from 1861 to 1865, she hoped, endured and prayed for her struggling land and her heroes, and when defeat came passed through the fiery ordeal of ruined hopes, to accept with a brave and dignified resignation, a fate so adverse, its memory can never be effaced.[43]

The Civil War literary genre, whose beginnings are often attributed to Stephen Crane's *The Red Badge of Courage* (1895), depicted the war as the domain of chivalrous male fighters and the war novel as a uniquely male form of cultural production. But women, both Black and white, were actively engaged in the war as civilians and in combat. Beyond organizing at home, many women worked in the army as cooks, laundresses, nurses, spies, scouts, and even as soldiers. The Civil War succeeded in opening venues for women in the public sphere and blurring the boundaries between the male-dominated "battlefront" and the female-identified "home front." Although these boundaries did not typically exist among African Americans under enslavement, much of their war effort was simply an extension of their fight for freedom and self-determination. White women were, in effect, responsible for the maintenance of an ideology of a Southern past through the development of new political and social organizations.[44] Literature became the immediate arena where white women could maintain a sense of their collective past to help shape the South's recovery. Women responded to the call for a uniquely Southern literature that had begun during the war and continued well into the post-Reconstruction era.

At the same time, African American women writers of the 1890s were grappling with a new sense of identity and understanding of the Civil War in the service of race consciousness, while also promoting a Black nationalist agenda through race history. It becomes important to see how the Lost Cause genre emerged with the full participation of Southern white women, and to understand its impact on African American women writers of the same period. African American women had to rewrite dominant culture history, not only as a rebuttal to the Lost Cause, but as a way to secure a stronger voice in social welfare issues. Many literary critics have argued that the Civil War genre was primarily a social project to reinforce the links between Southern nationalism and masculinity among whites. However, there is little evidence to suggest that a male-only canon by male-only writers ever truly flourished, and often it was women such as Harriet Beecher Stowe, Julia Ward Howe, Mary Chesnut, and others who proposed an alternative Civil War history through literature and memoirs.[45]

African Americans were invested in promoting community news and events through print culture, although their resources were often limited. African American reformers of the late nineteenth century who were involved in the production of race literature felt that it would provide a "pattern-book" to promote race-uplift strategies. Conventional historical texts might have appeared too controversial, so a literary genre was used—one perhaps more accessible to the broad readership found among Black women—that addressed issues including slavery, American imperialism, the Civil War, and Reconstruction. As such, it becomes necessary to reconsider the novels of women such as Frances Ellen Watkins Harper and Pauline Hopkins, two of the most influential Black writers at the turn of the century, as a part of their politically motivated community-based feminist pragmatism.

Race literature would ensure the careful promotion and preservation of important events, "saving from obstruction and obliteration what is good, helpful, and stimulating."[46] Following the collapse of Radical Northern Republicanism in the years after Reconstruction, these fictional works served as a remedy for the persistent disenfranchisement of Blacks. Among African American women, efforts to build institutions were also promoted in the various literary works of the period, particularly in many newspapers, magazines, and literary journals of the Black press, such as the *Colored American*.[47] These texts form "living monuments" or informal archival records of the past. They show how nationalism took another critical turn for the expression of civic ideals.

For whites, the myth of the Lost Cause became intimately interconnected to the economic and political recovery of the embattled Southern landscape and its many institutions. For many African American reformers, it was tacitly understood that their attempts to purchase property for Black institutions might only further heighten the growing frustrations of Confederate supporters. Even the titles of journals, such as *The Land We Love* or *The Sunny South* (1875), demonstrated the significance of the Southern landscape in an idealized and imagined past under the dominance of a model white planter class. In describing the Southern homestead of the Upshur family, one white writer tells how the family "had lived upon the eastern shore two hundred year, cultivating the soil and adorning society." The property "is situated upon Hungar's creek, about three miles from its mouth, and was in the years not so very long gone, the loveliest spot in all that beautiful wave-girdled garden—the eastern shore of Virginia."[48] The author does make a distinction between the home's atmosphere and its "architectural effect." He writes, "there was genial home-beauty, in every line and angle of its capacious and hospitable proportions, besides that un-transplantable je ne sais quoi, which marked it as the residence of the Old Virginia gentry."[49] Filled with descriptions of a mythical Southern past, these journals provided an escape from the turbulent memories in those initial postwar decades.

Throughout the last decades of the nineteenth century, advocates of the Lost Cause worked as if in parallel with Black attempts to commemorate their own history, founding a number of colleges and institutions throughout the South as memorials to their fallen heroes. A series of campaigns to build colleges and universities were seen as a way of providing for a "greater concentration of instructed opinion."[50] The Lost Cause provided an immediate avenue for establishing a series of "authoritative cultural institutions,"[51] including these colleges throughout the South. At the end of the war, these schools were established to teach a "proper" understanding of the Old South and the many reasons for the Confederacy's justifiable secession.[52] As early as October 1865, William Gordon McCabe, a former soldier, had opened the University School for Boys in Petersburg, Virginia.[53] Attempts to instruct young southerners in the Lost Cause were further reinforced by the large number of Confederate officers who entered the teaching profession after the war. Gen. Robert E. Lee accepted the presidency of Washington College in Lexington, Virginia, in October 1865.[54] The most striking holdovers of the Confederacy were seen at the University of the South in Sewanee Tennessee, and at Carr-Burdette College for Women in Sherman, Texas. Both institutions required all students to wear Confederate gray uniforms—at Carr-Burdette women also carried rifles while in uniform as late as 1904.[55] A later example, the Stonewall Jackson Institute in Abingdon, Virginia, was dedicated as a "Memorial to Stonewall Jackson's Army . . . when completed [it] is to be a shrine for all those who admired and loved this great Confederate chieftain . . . the opportunity and invitation is extended to those who desire to contribute and share in the honor of erecting and perpetuating this shrine."[56] At Jackson's death, a local clergy member, Rev. C. D. Waller, suggested that a fitting tribute would be the erection of a "living monument" or institution for the training of Southern youth. The students themselves would act as memorials "of his [Jackson's] unselfish devotion to duty and to God."[57] Women who attended the Stonewall Jackson Institute or even the Confederate Home and School in Charleston, South Carolina, were taught to be "true daughters of the Confederacy."[58]

White southerners clearly understood that it was not enough to erect traditional memorials to their Confederate dead; they were compelled to rebuild their war-ravaged landscapes with institutions that would perpetuate the mythology of an ideal Southern past filled with subservient "Uncle Toms" and the ever-obedient "Black Mammy." As seen in their deliberate choice of architectural styles, most often employing classical iconography, these schools and public monuments sought ways to materially represent ideas of Southern mythology based on a sacred and imagined mystical past. Historian Eugene D. Genovese terms the system of ideas and beliefs based on the "Legend of the South" as the era of "Moonlight and Magnolias."[59] By the 1870s, some white southerners went so far as to suggest that they should erect monuments to their former slaves, particularly to the "Black Mammy" figure, for her bravery in helping to fend off advancing Union soldiers (figure 11).[60]

Efforts to build monuments throughout the South continued to grow in number in the closing decades of the nineteenth century, and as one writer suggested, "this abounding of monumental plans and work is one of the greatest tributes that can ever come to magnify the splendor of Southern character and glorify Southern manhood and womanhood . . . and with one voice the South bids this splendid work go until no battle and no hero shall be without some testimonial of the South's courage and patriotic sacrifice."[61] As late as the 1920s, white clubwomen of the South were so invested in preserving the myth of the Old South that they remained advocates for a memorial to the "Black Mammy" on the National Mall in Washington, DC, but by then African American women had institutionalized resistance to the Lost Cause movement through their own efforts to recast the history of the war and the post-Reconstruction years (figure 12).

"A Monument Not of Marble or of Brass, but a Monument of Education"

At the time of the Emancipation Monument's dedication in 1876, Black Washingtonians were already engaging in memorial activities of their own.[62] As early as 1865, the Colored People's Educational Monument Association was working to erect a national school for freedmen to honor Lincoln's memory.[63] The school/monument was "to be a seat of learning, dedicated to God, to Literature, and to the Arts and Sciences, and shall be held and appropriated for the education of the children of freemen and freedmen, and their descendants forever."[64] Education would remain a lasting tribute to Lincoln, but would also provide a way of responding to the immediate needs of the Black community. The written appeal for the school reflects the need for a kind of "living monument"—"a monument not of marble or of brass, but a monument of Education. Marble may crumble, brass may tarnish, but the light of learning is as enduring as time."[65]

Higher education assumed a new role in American society by the 1860s, with intellectual historian Thomas Bender arguing that the college or university was emerging as a fundamental institution of modern social and intellectual life.[66] If the emerging white professional and educated classes were assuming critical leadership, Black reformers believed that a college or university run entirely by African Americans would similarly propel their self-help efforts. Frederick Douglass, for one, was in support of African Americans taking the lead in building institution for themselves. He had indeed spoken at the unveiling of the statue in Lincoln Square in Washington—and he had made clear his ambivalence about the memorial to Lincoln—but the financial impetus for that monument came first from a former slave: Charlotte Scott of Marietta, Ohio.[67] Even on that occasion, however, it was clear to many of the District's Black leaders and other onlookers that Douglass would not be publicly in favor of the proposed school in the president's honor, which the Colored People's Educational Monument Association was to build with shared support from white philanthropists.

In a series of letters exchanged over several months with the association's leader, Rev. Henry Highland Garnet, the tangled politics of Black education and monument-making are revealed with Douglass challenging the premise of the memorial in the pages of New York's *Anglo African*. Careful to make clear that he was not opposed to memorials or to schools in general, Douglass nevertheless thought that the two types of projects should be distinct:

> a college is a college, and has its own peculiar claims and ought to stand upon its own merits. A monument is a monument, and has its own peculiar claims and merits ... for a college-monument, or for a monument-college I do not say good; for the things however good separately, are incongruous and offensive when connected as now proposed ... it carries on its front a distasteful implication. It looks to me like an attempt to wash the black man's face in the nation's tears for Abraham Lincoln.[68]

Despite the generalized grief over Lincoln's martyrdom, Frederick Douglass was, no doubt, once again recalling Lincoln's complicated history vis-à-vis slavery: in the 1850s Lincoln had expressed his opposition to expanding slavery into the western American territories, but he also insisted he would not oppose it in the South, despite finding it personally repugnant. The Civil War, of course, finally forced Lincoln's hand with respect to emancipation. Given the choice, Douglass opted not to promote African American education while capitalizing it in Lincoln's memory. In closing his letter to Garnet, Douglass writes, "when they [colored people] want to raise a college for themselves out of the general affection of the American people for the dead, I am not with them."[69]

Arguing that any institution founded by Blacks should be solely funded on their own terms, Douglass supported the creation of a monument under the condition that Blacks use the opportunity to influence public opinion as to their worthiness of equal rights as full citizens:

> A monument of this kind, erected by the colored people—that is by the voluntary offerings of the colored people—is a very different thing from a monument built by money contributed by white men to enable colored people to build a monument. We should bury our own dead and build our own monuments, and all monuments which we would build to the memory of our friends, if we would not invite the continued contempt of the white race upon our heads.[70]

Garnet responded to Douglass's letters by pointing out the many contradictions in his objections to the "monument school," especially in his insistence that the school would be supported only by African Americans. Garnet writes, "You object to our movement because white people are invited to contribute to it; but would have no objection if it should be built by colored people alone. Can you fail to see your inconsistency? Such a monument, according to your views, would be exclusive and separate." Garnet's letter does reveal something far more significant than debates over assimilation or possible difficulties in establishing racial alliances: Black leaders at the close of the Civil War fully recognized the significance of monumental building sites to foster a nationalist political agenda for Black education. In questioning Douglass's motives, Garnet writes, "Has it escaped your notice that in Richmond, New York, and in other places in this country, we have 'monumental churches?' . . . [people] have built monumental schools to the memory of their great and glorious dead? Can it be possible that you do not know that a fine monument school has lately been built in the native town of the late Samuel Gurney as a monument to his memory?"[71]

Garnet not only understood the importance of building monuments to the "great and glorious dead" but also their potential impact for documenting significant events in Black history. Members of the Colored People's National Lincoln Monument Association also proposed to build another monument school to the memory of John Brown and his nineteen Black compatriots who were killed at Harpers Ferry and "who set the great ball in motion that crushed out the devilish life of slavery."[72] The 1865 feud between Douglass and Garnet persisted over several months and only highlighted the debates surrounding Black educational reform and the divide between many male and female reformers. In seeking to combine a memorial site with an industrial institute, these reformers felt that the significance of events surrounding the Civil War could not be so easily forgotten or ignored, especially in the nation's capital. Although Douglass and Garnet disagreed on the tactics by which they could raise the level of historical consciousness in the Black community and foster a more authentic interpretation of the past, they did agree that they could no longer allow whites the sole control over shaping national memory. This foreshadowed W. E. B. Du Bois's essay of 1903 entitled *The Talented Tenth* in which Du Bois wrote that "education and work are the levers to uplift a people. Work alone will not do it unless inspired by the right ideals and guided by intelligence. Education must not simply teach work—it must teach Life. The Talented Tenth of the Negro race must be made leaders of thought and missionaries of culture among their people."[73] For Du Bois and many others, the elite so-called Talented Tenth, whom he considered to be exclusively male, were those solely responsible for the preservation of the race and the advancement of their many causes for social betterment.

Neither Douglass nor Garnet could have imagined the obstacles African Americans would continue to face as they attempted to transform the built environment and build their own monuments in the postbellum South. Whites during Reconstruction immediately feared Black educational advances and saw the Freedmen's Bureau as an instrument of radical social and economic reform. However, many Americans, since the beginning of the nineteenth century, felt strongly that the school model was the most proper institutional instrument of social and moral regeneration. Some northerners felt that a sufficient number of teachers from New England existed to "make a New England out of the whole South, and God helping, we will not pause in our work until the free school system . . . has been established from Maryland to Florida and all along the shores of the Gulf."[74] The Freedmen's Bureau accounts suggested that "the school room must supplant the fort, the primer and the Bible, the rifle and the sword. . . . schools and the Gospel were to be the new munitions of war, munitions more effective than Congressmen, President, Supreme Court, or U.S. Army."[75] The immediate threat to whites was that these Black school sites would impede their continued hegemony over the social order of the South. White southerners even argued that the North hoped to "redeem and regenerate the South" through the schools as a way of accepting the "moral code of the North." Yet concurrently, with the Tuskegee machine firmly in control of educational orthodoxy by the 1890s, Black Victorians had formalized strategies for race uplift through institution building.

Another dedication ceremony outside the South—this commemoration was in 1897—bookends the dedication at Lincoln Park some twenty years earlier and highlights the ongoing African American struggle for freedom and equal rights. There, at Boston's old Music Hall, speaker Booker T. Washington addressed a crowd awaiting the unveiling of sculptor August St. Gaudens's classicizing monumental relief in Boston Common (public park), in honor of Col. Robert Gould Shaw and members of the all-African American 54th Regiment of the Massachusetts Infantry. Washington addressed his speech in part to those who had served the Confederacy:

> there can [now] be no prouder reward for defeat than by a supreme effort to place the negro on that footing where he will add material, intellectual, and civil strength to every department of state. This work must be completed in public school, industrial school, and college. The most of it must be completed in the effort of the negro himself . . . after all the real monument, the greater monument, is being slowly but safely built among the lowly in the South, in the struggles and sacrifices of a race to justify all that has been done and suffered for it.[76]

The debates between Douglass and Garnet some thirty years previously in 1865 demonstrated that African American men would lay claim to the public arena in support of their causes while Black women would seek reform in the South through institution building. There, women's monuments to Black nation building not only included schools along the lines of Booker T. Washington's, but also other civic and cultural institutions such as churches, missions, lyceums, settlement houses, day care centers, and societies. As such, these women were creating alternative, spatially constituted race narratives through their built environment.

Women Building the African American Experience

By Reconstruction, the ruling classes of white America had already been using the built environment to assert a national narrative. Through their use of architectural language, typology, and precedent, nineteenth-century cultural institutions—including the museum, school, library, and university—used America's colonial past as an instrument in their struggle to assimilate thousands of European immigrants, and also as a means to address the growing "Negro problem." White social reformers attempted to incorporate within these institutions an architectural fabric and iconography that memorialized a mythical community that its users maintained to have existed in America's past. As historian Mark Girouard has put it, many "recreated the past as an ideal world of pre-industrial simplicity" shortly after reunification, and as a reminder of the Christian Anglo-Saxon roots of the country.[77]

In Mrs. T. P. O'Connor's text, *My Beloved South* (1914), she addresses a letter to Thomas Nelson Page, a novelist, essayist, and lawyer, who was at the time one of the more prominent apologists for the white Southern point of view on race relations.[78] O'Connor writes:

> To Thomas Nelson Page—Each day the memory of the old South becomes more and more a cherished dream. Its bounteous hospitality, its quixotic chivalry, its daring courage, its spotless honour, its poetic understanding, are receding into the heroic past. Therefore, we of the Old Guard must stand together, and do what we can to keep the younger and more practical generation Unforgetting. My pen is freighted with appreciation, but is, alas, inadequate, while already your genius has made "The tender grace of a day that is dead" immortal; and so. After many years of affectionate friendship, I dedicate this book to you.[79]

If white women believed that their primary goal was to preserve Southern culture through a carefully circumscribed interpretation of the past, Black women such as Jennie Dean and Elizabeth Evelyn Wright, on the other hand, knew that radical social reform would be made possible only through education for African Americans. Wright's and Dean's efforts to test the junctures of public and private space in political culture had a lasting impact, despite whites' continued attempts to prevent these institutions from maturing into viable centers of race education and community advancement.[80] Anna Julia Cooper believed that she could now:

> honor my name and vindicate my race! Something like this, it strikes me, is the enthusiasm which stirs the genius of young Africa in America; and the memory of the past oppression and the fact of present attempted repression only serve to gather momentum for its irrepressible powers. Then again, a race in such a stage of growth is peculiarly sensitive to impressions. . . . What

a responsibility then to have the sole management of the primal lights and shadows! Such is the colored woman's office.[81]

During Reconstruction, the concept of race woman had emerged from the abolitionist movement, drawing lessons from the antebellum self-help tradition as a way of combating white oppression and a failing Southern economy.[82] African American women helped form some of the earliest neighborhood schools, missions, and churches shortly after the war. In her early work on Georgia's African Americans during Reconstruction, *Soldiers of Light and Love* (1992), historian Jacqueline Jones reflects on how "demonstrating an 'ethos of mutuality' had permeated African American culture for some time, and how communities formed Black churches; Republican party clubs and Union Leagues; fire companies; mutual aid, protective, and fraternal associations; and schools."[83] Jones points directly to the legacy of mutuality and self-help that persisted despite the supposed full-scale degradation of the Black race and its inability to build communities under enslavement. Although Jones acknowledges that education was deemed an expensive proposition and luxury for people of all ages and for all sexes, it provided an impulse for applying all-Black strategies for social reform.[84]

The making of school buildings—an exercise in monument-making to which Black communities bore witness—became the actual narratives and physical reminders of the trauma that began with enslavement. The concept of "family" that emerged under enslavement had reflected the larger slave-quarter society. Frequently, entire families were separated by the trade in slaves, forcing the creation of familial groups and extended families that would share common experience under enslavement.[85] These familial groups persisted well into the post-Emancipation era, as in the case of Dean's own local community. By forming alternative family structures, the enslaved were able to repropose kinship relations critical to social identity formation.

A strong sense of family and local community also mitigated the pernicious effects of dominant institutional infrastructures in the civic and public realms, such as the judicial system, which provided Black women with next to no support. Left with little recourse, they understood the significance placed on land ownership and development as access to agency through identity formation and collective self-determination. In the founding of their own all-Black educational institutions, African American women could respond to their needs, and those of the community, in their own ways. Despite the threat of legally sanctioned lynchings and rape, these women recognized the importance of institution building as a way of garnering the necessary elements for a Black nation. African American women such as Wright and Dean responded to white supremacy and mob violence by developing their own educational institutions on the now "sacred grounds" of the old plantation system. It was only in the 1890s that Black male leaders such as Washington, Douglass, and Garnet began to realize how the many educational institutions founded by women reformers might memorialize their Exodus from slavery and transform their limited civil rights into self-empowerment, even at the height of repressive Jim Crow legislation.

African American Space to Place

Representation in architectural design and placemaking provide a school's users—students, faculty, and administration—with experiences that situate themselves in the larger society. Buildings and boundaries make a campus unique and contribute to the user's memories and to collective memory in general. The use of scale, form, light, and texture are all important elements that impact the user's perceptions of place and provide meaning to the individual parts of a larger campus plan. The symbolic environment of Manassas is marked not only by the edge of its physical boundaries, but also by its meaning to the race as an experimental site in Black institution making.[86] As such, Dean not only designed a model school for her race, but also, by situating her school on a former Civil War battlefield, helped redefine the meaning of this formerly contested site for its African American users. The buildings at Manassas, along with those at Voorhees, physically marked resistance against the existing racial order, as disguised as that purpose may be.

For Black women, the American ideal of an all-white nationalist and exclusive spatial culture meant reconfiguring a "place" for themselves and their communities. If we begin to examine these sites and their many layers of meaning, it might be possible to identify the tangible elements or symbols of space making as it relates to Black nationalism. "A landscape," historian Hilary Winchester says, "may be read in the same way as a text may be read; the layers of meaning within it may be dissected and analysed."[87] For Blacks, monument-making suggested an unofficial narrative or "hidden transcript" that operated outside the popularly accepted version of history, one perceived in the public sphere by everyday passersby. This subordinate architectural discourse of difference in the presence of the dominant is a *public transcript*, while the term *hidden transcript* can be used to characterize a discourse that takes place beyond the perception of those who hold power—much like the meanings embedded at these school sites. The hidden transcript is produced for a different audience and under very different circumstances than a public transcript.[88] Three characteristics of the hidden transcript are significant if we apply this approach to our understanding of those industrial schools founded and built by women such as Wright and Dean: (1) the hidden transcript is specific to a given social site and to a particular group of people, typically those who share common experiences of repression; (2) the hidden transcript contains a wide range of representational possibilities; and (3) the frontier between the public and the hidden transcript is always in a state of constant struggle. The dominant group, in this case white southerners, would not always prevail. The sites of the hidden transcript are those places that speak only to its intended audience and away from the gaze of the dominant order.[89] Played to best use were the "cards" dealt to Booker T. Washington—the Jim Crow South demanded that he build in the margins and he did so successfully. For example, many whites believed that Booker T. Washington was a strong proponent of segregation because of the school's distance from town: "this segregation of the negro families is the best for the school, and best for the white community of Tuskegee."[90] Along with his many disciple students who founded industrial and normal schools throughout the South, Washington in some ways allowed white fears to play out in his favor as the work of building the physical artifacts of Black nationalism continued.

After Reconstruction, African Americans were not simply invested in replicating traditional architectural forms; they were instead committed to transforming the long established symbolic meaning of white dominance and social control—embodied in the columnar portico, as it were—as a way of expressing their own power over cultural production. At industrial school sites such as Voorhees or Manassas, Blacks were surrounded by the physical artifacts, stories, and traditions of their enslavement and deliverance. The architectonic qualities of the various buildings provided "an experience of past and present, of primary and secondary and emergent qualities, of the present space itself as a physical stimulus coupled with associations, recollections, recallings, and memories of the past which arise by means of significant activities that take place in that space or by means of signs that are in some way attached to it."[91] White constituencies' repression of Black history and culture—despite their futile attempts to assert superiority in service to the Lost Cause—was now in question. If these industrial school sites are perceived as "living or working monuments," it becomes clear how critical they were to African American nation making.[92]

Chapter Two

The Impact of Chicago's "White City" on African American Placemaking

> There can be no doubt that this fourth centenary of America's discovery which we celebrate at Chicago, strikes the keynote of another important transition in the history of this nation; and the prominence of woman in the management of its celebration is a fitting tribute to the part she is destined to play among the forces of the future.
>
> —Anna Julia Cooper, *A Voice from the South*

> Why are not the colored people, who constitute so large an element of the American population, and who have contributed so large a share to American greatness, more visibly present and better represented in this World's Exposition?
>
> —Ida B. Wells, *The Reason Why the Colored American Is Not in the World's Columbian Exposition*

Since its publication in 1892, *The Reason Why the Colored American Is Not in the World's Columbian Exposition*, a pamphlet written by journalist and activist Ida B. Wells, has remained an important contribution to our understanding of race relations at the close of the nineteenth century (figure 13). Wells, already well known among African Americans because of her tireless efforts to expose the injustices of lynching and its stain on American civilization,[1] had included in her pamphlet a self-authored article as well as articles by Frederick Douglass, Irvine Garland Penn, and Ferdinand Lee Barnett, and made public comment on the exclusion of African Americans from the Columbian Exposition.[2] In 1892 the Council of Administration refused to allow African Americans to take part in Exposition preparations. Although several projects were proposed free of charge by the Colored Men's Association, Exposition organizers would still not allow their equal participation.³ African Americans were originally not welcome to attend the event at all until the idea of a "Negro Day" or "Colored American Day" at the Exposition was approved. Wells adamantly opposed this solution because it could be seen as an excuse for continued disenfranchisement. Others, such as Douglass, saw Colored American Day as an opportunity to highlight African American achievement since emancipation.⁴

Expositions prior to the Columbian Exposition of 1893 had excluded the participation of all women. For that year's event, however, Congress had specifically allowed for the national commission to name a white Board of Lady Managers at the Exposition. Many female participants were members of Chicago's elite class of clubwomen who shared a concern over the "woman's question." At their first board meeting, Rebecca Felton acknowledged the significance of allowing women to participate: "Let us remember we are on trial before a great nation. There is a large class in this country who are inimical to us ... who suppose that we are a superfluous appendage to the ... Commission."⁵ The Exposition also provided women with a forum for advancing several key issues, particularly suffrage. With the appointment of Bertha Palmer as president of the board came a sizable donation of $200,000 for the construction of a separate Woman's Building (figure 14). After a lengthy national competition, Sophia Hayden was chosen, the first female graduate of the Massachusetts Institute of Technology (MIT). As some of the first professionally trained African Americans architects were also MIT graduates, some of them were no doubt aware of Hayden's participation at the Exposition.⁶ At the opening of the Woman's Building, Palmer insisted that the course of women's progress would "meet whatever fate life may bring, not only to prepare her for the factory and workshop, for the professions and arts, but, more important than all else, to prepare her for presiding over the house." Palmer dedicated the building to "an elevated womanhood, knowing that by so doing we shall best serve the cause of humanity."⁷

Regrettably, the cause for humanity did not include the equal participation or inclusion of African American women on the Board of Lady Managers. Before the World's Congress of Representative Women, Wells spoke of progress and achievement despite scientific findings in the age of Darwinism: "There is no wish to overstate the obstacles to colored women or to picture their status as hopeless. There is no disposition to take our place in this Congress as faultfinders or supplicants for mercy. As women of common country, with common interests, and a destiny that will certainly bring us closer to each other, we come to this altar with our contribution of hopefulness as well as with our complaints."⁸

Essentially, Wells and many other Black female social reformers were laying out the political agenda of a gendered Black nationalism, claiming leadership roles despite the fact that African American men were at this point effectively denied representation under Jim Crow. Definitions of nationalism among these women reformers no longer relied on the paternalistic rhetoric of Black figures such as Alexander Crummell or Martin Delany—they understood that women's leadership was vital to race progress. Nineteenth-century writer Frances Ellen Watkins Harper also addressed the World's Congress of Representative Women and suggested that they were "on the threshold of [a] woman's era" and that they must be prepared for the "responsibility of political power."[9]

After much debate, Black women were appointed to serve in various capacities on several boards. Joan Imogene Howard, a member of the Committee on Education, was influential in collecting several important works by prominent African American women reformers and writers. African American women from New York State and three Black educational institutions—Atlanta University (now Clark Atlanta University) in Georgia, Hampton Institute in Virginia, and Wilberforce University in Ohio—also exhibited some important works.[10] Atlanta University alone occupied some three hundred square feet of floor space and four hundred of wall space. Photographs of the faculty, student body, and physical plant were on display; examples of students' work in academics, home economics, nursing, and crafts were also shown. Hampton Institute showed off woodwork and student-produced clothing. Wilberforce University's academic contribution to the Exposition included two large books filled with student work in rhetoric, grammar, logic, and mathematics. Wilberforce also submitted work in taxidermy, needlework, and woodcraft.[11] The promotion of works produced at these schools revealed the importance of African American education at a venue celebrating nationalist progress and achievement. Thomas J. Bell of Atlanta University wrote that "the friends of colored people and those interested in Southern education often remark, 'This exhibit and that of Hampton are enough to convince the most skeptical, that the colored people of the South are people capable of learning just as other people are.'"[12] The Exposition helped Black women gain the space in which to articulate their political presence and call into question notions of republican motherhood, despite the opposition of white women reformers.

Ida B. Wells and Women at the Exposition

The near but not total exclusion of African Americans from the Exposition paradoxically presented women with an opportunity to openly address race-based issues in the public sphere before a mixed audience.[13] Wells and other African American activists saw the World's Columbian Exposition in Chicago as a national venue where notions of Black nationhood and political autonomy could be reinforced. Wells made it clear that "the absence of colored citizens from participating therein will be construed to their disadvantage by the representatives of the civilized world there assembled."[14] The leading African American newspaper of the day, the *New York Age*, openly protested the exclusion of a Black woman from the Board of Lady Managers: "We object. We carry our objection so far that if the matter was left to our determination we would advise the race to have nothing whatever to do with the Columbian Exposition or the management of it."[15] The editorial continued by suggesting that "the glory and the profit of the whole thing, is in the hands of white 'gentlemen' and 'ladies' and in all charity they should be allowed to share all the glory or failure of the undertaking."[16] African American women felt strongly that if they were to have a say in the Exposition, they would have to hire someone to insure that Black exhibits would receive equal attention. In Wells's opinion, the accomplishments Africans Americans had made in just thirty years of emancipation would have best provided examples of American's moral stature and civilization. Wells even went so far as to suggest that African Americans had indeed "contributed a large share to American prosperity and civilization."[17] Wells was keenly aware that she needed to underline the contributions of Black women to American progress while also making certain to expose their continued sexual exploitation. Wells was already well versed in the ways that race and gender intersected in American life, and how social issues particular to African American women demanded greater attention from both Blacks and whites. Lynching, for Wells, was also a virulent assault on Black womanhood—something deemed unworthy of any true concern or social response in the dominant culture because Black women were still considered inferior to white women and even Black men.[18]

Black female reformers, such as Wells, were agitating for a broader social order that would empower women to further shape the civic realm and expand Victorian gender and spatial boundaries outside the home or parlor. Although Exposition officials were unwilling to allow African Americans equal involvement, Blacks saw the fair as a way to promote social change with national implications. Some fairgoers commented that Black exhibits had been "buried so deep that Gabriel's trump [*sic*] could not waken them."[19] One visitor complained that "there is a lump which comes up in my throat as I pass around through all of this . . . and see but little to represent us here."[20] As Wells firmly suggests, African Americans "were given to understand that they were persona non grata."[21] Wells's pamphlet underlined the divisions that existed within the African American community. Many Blacks were ashamed that their lack of participation in the Exposition had been brought to the attention of an international audience. Others feared that future African American progress would be thwarted because of whites' adverse reaction to the pamphlet. Some questioned Wells's motives in preparing the pamphlet as merely an attempt to become a national spokesperson for African Americans.

World's Columbian Exposition of 1893

At the dawn of the Progressive era, marking the four-hundredth anniversary of Columbus's arrival in the New World, the World's Columbian Exposition of

1893 in Chicago was a "neoclassical wonderland" that exposed late nineteenth-century Americans to an ideal, classicizing blueprint for a future urban imaginary.[22] Set in the marshlands of Lake Michigan's waterfront only some seven miles south of downtown Chicago's Loop, the Columbian Exposition was "a little ideal world, a realization of Utopia"(figure 15).[23]

Much like U.S. society at the time, the Columbian Exposition was divided into two distinct worlds: the first, or "civilized," section was known as the *White City*, a half-mile-long basin surrounded by massive buildings in the classical tradition with a "Court of Honor" as a focal point (figure 16).[24] There, six buildings framed the reflecting pool and represented the highest achievements of Western technology and civilization: machinery, manufactures, mines, agriculture, art, and electricity. The White City was in essence a celebration of Victorian manhood, power, capitalism, and masculinist perfection, "A Vision of Strong Manhood and Perfection of Society."[25] The second section of the Exposition, the Midway, depicted the supposed backwardness of peasant peoples from Africa, Asia, the Pacific, and the Middle East, essentially representing them as savages and barbarians who had yet to secure any form of civilization (figure 17).

The Midway was organized under the auspices of the Exposition's Department of Ethnology. It provided a closely scripted, pseudoscientific view of the nonwhite world as "barbaric and childlike" and gave an American blueprint for building an ideal industrialized nation-state.[26] Driven by the new disciplinary conventions of American anthropology, the Exposition's exhibits and its displays of "other" cultures spatially reinforced white ideologies of superiority and domination.[27] All ethnic displays were placed along the periphery of the fairgrounds, far removed from the Exposition's celebration of Western European and American achievements. These abject displays along the Midway were arranged according to their supposed or imagined proximity to Anglo-Saxon culture: the Teutonic and Celtic races—represented by the German and Irish exhibits, respectively—occupied the space closest to the White City at the center of the Exposition (figure 18). The implied, racialized spatial logic of the Midway was clear and reinforced the current white Anglo-Saxon social order (figure 19). One white female journalist noted, "these people are they who, in the mad race of nations for power and self, seem to have been left far behind, and, compared with the nations of today, are like untutored children."[28] For such a journalist it might have been important to maintain solidarity with her white male colleagues and reinforce Victorian fears and racialized stereotypes, and to infantilize the "other" for as wide an audience as possible given the Exposition's broad consumer popularity. The chaos of the Midway was cast in direct opposition to the buildings in the Exposition center, replete as they were with Western industrial, social, and artistic achievements.[29]

The model city of the Exposition was admired for the innovations it promoted in American city planning and was controversial because of its overt display of colonial histories, imperialism, and power.[30] Expansion was a popular national theme by the 1890s as the ability to meet and control new territorial frontiers was understood to be an indicator of the American destiny.[31] The American cultural narrative of the day, with strong religious undertones, was replete with words such as "pride," "duty," and "destiny" with the city of Chicago and the Exposition becoming models for the transformation of America from a largely premodern agricultural society into a modern landscape of interstate and international commerce and industry.

American Architects and Education

The overwhelmingly male and white American architectural students who were trained at the Ecole des Beaux-Arts in Paris—the very practitioners who would dominate American architectural discourse—were searching for an architectural style that would express a strong American national identity. In their search, many of the Beaux-Arts architects applied their French educational models to restore order to what was perceived as the chaos of revival styles.[32] American practitioners trained at the Beaux-Arts bluntly disavowed architectural production of the recent past; some even argued that, regarding history, a national style should take strictly architectural, not archaeological, considerations into account. A national style should use "all the resources which modern science has placed at the disposal of the architect, which, if used logically that is, with the aid of reason, will call for new, fresh forms."[33]

It has been suggested that the Columbian Exposition's Auditorium Building, designed by architect Louis Sullivan, raised the neo-Romanesque style of Henry Hobson Richardson to its greatest level of monumentality, but by the 1890s a fixation with the alternative "Capital" style of Greece and Rome was undeniable. Some leading architects, such as Sullivan, criticized the Exposition for its deviation from an American style of protomodernism in favor of the Beaux Arts.[34] Instead, Sullivan lauded Richardson's work at the Marshall Field Wholesale Store for inspiring the unadorned skyscraper style: "four-square and brown, it stands, in physical fact, a monument to trade, to the organized commercial spirit, to the power and progress of the age, to the strength and resource of individuality and force of character."[35]

Montgomery Schuyler, a widely quoted and respected architecture critic of the period, often remarked that the bourgeois mansions of the 1850s had mushroomed by the 1890s into palaces with symbolic connections to European aristocracy. The commercial power of the American robber barons and their houses signified a revolution in American life and culture.[36] Industrialism had triumphed as did the social revolution it helped create. Membership in elite society had now changed: "all of the old fortunes were being dwarfed, in fact and in publicity, by the riches which accrued between the Civil War and the

Great War—the longest crescendo in the history of American wealth."[37] Middle-class culture emulated bourgeois life, albeit bourgeois life circumscribed by limited resources and, as some critics have argued, by limited taste. The middle class conceived of domestic architecture as simply a modest version of the rich man's mansion.[38]

In its design, the Columbian Exposition promoted an international classicizing iconography, upholding in this instance the triumph of Anglo-Saxon nationalism, whose proponents harbored pretensions to an ancient Greek and Roman architectural inheritance. The Columbian Exposition was also, as was the earlier Centennial Exposition of 1876 in Philadelphia, a major venue for the promotion of the Colonial Revival style through its architecture, interior decoration, historical exhibitions, and commemorative activities.[39] The Colonial Revival style reflected the growing nostalgia for America's colonial history and a desire to strengthen connections to an idealized past. The architectural language adopted and put on display at the Exposition by men such as Daniel Burnham or Frederick Law Olmsted fashioned an imagined and idealized conception of Western whiteness in the Court of Honor. The structural spectacle linked notions of Anglo-Saxon supremacy with Western expansion and an imperial Roman past. The message to visitors was clear—Americans of the 1890s had inherited the glory of ancient Rome and reflected the renaissances of Italy, Spain, France, and England.[40] Much as Western Europeans had done before, these nationalist American architectural planners were grafting their country onto the lineage of the great ancient Mediterranean civilizations, intending to grant cultural continuity to a still-young United States, simmering with racial and class tensions.

Classicism and Urbanism

Efforts to revive classicism in urban architecture became a consequence of the Exposition's stylistic victory over an emerging American commercial modernism. The return to classicism seems inevitable in retrospect: the style offered Chicago as a city, and the nation as a whole, cultural and aesthetic validation. As some have argued, "for a nation searching for roots, the belief in its own progress as the natural extension of European history was reassuring."[41] Montgomery Schuyler considered the White City one of "the most admired group of buildings ever erected in this country."[42] But the Exposition alone did not foster the national interest in classicism. The architects of the Court of Honor—George B. Post, Charles B. Atwood, Charles F. McKim, Richard Morris Hunt, Robert S. Peabody and Stearns, Henry Van Brunt,[43] and Frank Maynard Howe—had all embraced Beaux-Arts classicism well before the Chicago World's Fair. The Exposition further popularized classicism for both the larger public and a new class of eager patrons. Much like Thomas Jefferson, who had turned to the classical styles and historical references of Rome for inspiration—making reference to an ennobled and republican past in the first part of the nineteenth century—Exposition organizers had done likewise decades later in an effort to inculcate the growing number of urban immigrants with the values of an American democracy. In practice, architecture would be an instrument to expose the otherwise unschooled in the political constructions of whiteness and remind African Americans of their place in the social hierarchies of the reunited nation and in the New South itself.

Many reformers saw Chicago as an all too earthly metropolis to be contrasted to the celestial White City. As historian Alex Krieger has suggested, "the raw, often disorderly pattern of postbellum urban life" made classical structures like those emulated at the Court of Honor "very seductive"[44] to the late Victorians on the other side of the Atlantic. American cities lacked such clear divisions and clean facades, leading one journal writer to conclude, "life in our cities would be vastly easier if only they had been planned with some reasonable foresight as to results and some common sense provision in behalf of the people who were coming to live in them."[45] Those provisions could include the white Anglo-Saxon Protestant ruling class's complete social control of the "other." It was also the "responsibility of wealth" to exhibit its civilizing influence in the public realm, and it has been argued that as a result of the Exposition, the physical footprints of many of the country's leading cultural institutions were expanded. By providing avenues for civic improvement, these cultural institutions influenced the design of cities as a way of further displaying elite modes of philanthropy. The combination of architecture and civic design secured the maintenance of a proper civic order and a way to provide solutions for the "Negro and immigrant problems." Victorian-era magazines such as *Collier's*, *Harper's Bazaar*, and *The Country Gentlemen* often depicted the differences between the refined Victorian white man and nonwhite ethnic groups. On the cover of *Harper's Weekly* appeared depictions of a Black man and a Chinese man with the captions "The Chinese Must Go" and "The Nigger Must Go."[46] During the Exposition, *Harper's Weekly* published a fifteen-part Saturday cartoon series about the fictional Black Johnson family. The cartoon made clear that African Americans were not welcome at an Exposition that served to codify America's national identity.[47]

"Civilization" and Nation

Mainstream discussions of civilization in the 1890s were often predicated on Darwin's theories of evolution. For white Victorians, "civilization" meant the precise moment or stage in human evolution following the primitive stages of "savagery" and "barbarism."[48] Scientists and ethnologists argued that human races progressed in historical steps from the earliest stages of savagery to the more advanced stages of civilization. Ruling classes argued that they had evolved to an advanced level of civilization and attributed its many qualities to an inherent racial trait. In upholding the doctrine of "separate but equal" in *Plessy v. Ferguson* (1896)—a doctrine that would stand until repudiated by the court's ruling in *Brown v. Board of Education* (1954)—the United States Supreme Court established the constitutionality of statutory segregation and the maintenance of the South's social order through stringent Jim Crow legislation. The court's decision would legitimize a construct of race based on biological determinism and the tenets of social Darwinism.[49] The Columbian Exposition would only help to further reinforce the power of middle-class manliness and its associated discourses of civilization as reflected in the built environment through official "classicizing" architecture.

The Columbian Exposition's central mission was not only a symbolic national reunification between Northern industrialists and their Southern agrarian counterparts, it was also a collective response to an unresolved social crisis in race relations. The potential economic gains made possible by technological advances on an international level were largely restricted to whites under the umbrella of white nationhood. American nationalism meant purity, piety, and, most importantly, whiteness as the critical means of advancement politically, socially, and economically. Americans were not simply inventing traditions constructed around whiteness, but were also inventing definitions of Blackness that had brought a divided nation to war and questioned civil liberties.[50] The White City lived in the American imaginary—and in its memory—because so few Americans of Anglo-Saxon heritage would comprehend or validate the radical impact of race (and African Americans in particular) on the transformation of republican nationalism and civic form. To white Americans, the Exposition's layout was an affirmation of the country's reunification after the Civil War; its very legible design bolstered self-confidence and progress despite the turmoil of urban industrialization and the further racial and ethnic violence that loomed ahead. Just how reunified the nation could ultimately be when African Americans were not welcome to participate at the Chicago World's Fair, however, was left unsolved.

Spectacles, Space, and Lynching

The White City was certainly a spatially manifested culmination of American civic and national ideologies at the close of the nineteenth century that further reinforced racial inequality, social segregation, and white supremacist campaigns of superiority. African Americans were perceived as direct counterparts to the "noble savages and barbarians" exhibited at the Exposition—and were assumed bereft of any civilizing tendencies.[51] For many social Darwinists at the time, the Midway Plaisance—with its voyeuristic display of the West African Fon people in their "authentic" Dahomey village—was a public spectacle of modern scientific eugenic thought (figure 20). To many African Americans, the spectacle of the Fon's physical bodies recalled the public display of lynched Black bodies throughout the South (figure 21). The display of Black bodies at either the Chicago Columbian Exposition or from the branches of a "dogwood tree" exposed America's racial hatred for the "other" and its white Anglo-Saxon nationalism physically constructed of bricks and mortar.[52] As historian Robert Rydell has argued, "As the racist underpinnings of the utopia projected became clear, many African Americans concluded that the World's Columbian Exposition, with its radiant 'White City,' had become nothing less than a Frankenstein, the cultural counterpart to the lynchings that claimed 161 African-American lives in 1892 alone."[53]

With the lynching deaths of three close friends in March 1892, Wells clearly supported a national campaign against white supremacy and racial bigotry.[54] In one of the many newspaper editorials she authored against lynching, she strongly argued, "nobody in this section of the country believes the old threadbare lies that Negro men rape white women. If Southern white men are not careful they will over-reach themselves and public sentiment will have a reaction, or a conclusion will be reached which will be very damaging to the moral reputation of their women."[55] Wells knew that her earlier condemnation of white womanhood in the Memphis papers made her a popular target for ridicule and personal attacks. Some white papers even called Wells a "slanderous and nasty-minded mulatress."[56]

Wells's persistent questioning of white womanhood and failed white moral values only further escalated the uneasiness many white male southerners faced about their own manliness. In the pages of her newspaper, the *Memphis Free Speech*, she portrayed rape and lynching as key expressions of white manliness. White southerners' loss during the Civil War had brought into focus their inability to regain control over the Southern values and traditions they desperately sought to maintain. With their men on the battlefields, white Southern women were forced to assume the duties of both husbands and fathers, effectively displacing men from their traditional role as heads of households. Southern men were not alone in their struggle to maintain social order. Wells knew that in launching her campaign against lynching, she would also be able to manipulate the general fears of the middle class and its own waning male hegemony. By exposing the inherent gender tensions in the late-Victorian era, Wells problematized the dual constructions of American manhood and civilization and questioned the democratic ideals of the nation.[57]

The spectacle of lynching made certain that southerners, Black and white, male and female, understood their place in a long established social hierarchy that had changed little since enslavement (figure 22).[58] Lynchings reminded Black men and women of their vulnerability to mob violence in the racial and sexual order of the South.[59] Lynching was more than a form of physical violence; it signaled the many failures of democracy in the post-Reconstruction South. Historian Leon Litwack maintains that throughout the Southern landscape the ordinary modes of execution no longer satisfied the crowd of spectators witnessing acts of mob violence. Litwack contends that "to kill the victim was not enough; the execution needed to be turned into a public ritual, a collective experience . . . not only a public spectacle but also public theater, often a festive affair, a participatory ritual of torture and death that many whites preferred to witness."[60] Much as the American ruling classes were indifferent to the assaults on African Americans; the Columbian Exposition's serene Court of Honor and its associated buildings along the Basin were at far remove from the public spaces of the teeming, contested, and potentially violent spaces of the Midway.

Although it can certainly be seen as evidence of white hegemony and colonial social control, the Columbian Exposition of 1893 also testifies to an attempt on the part of African Americans—fully cognizant of their enslaved past—to employ the racialization of the Southern landscape to their advantage. At the Exposition, African Americans who reinserted the memory of enslavement into American history publicly contested the collective amnesia of Southern whites vis-à-vis slavery. The year 1893 would also mark a significant turning point in African American social welfare politics and in the growing field of American city planning. Scholar Hazel Carby asserts that the "Columbian Exposition . . . inaugurated an age that was to be dominated by 'the problem of the color-line.'"[61] The "color line" clearly demarcated the failures of Reconstruction and the impending success of a white supremacist ideology to shape the future of the architectural profession. African Americans in the South at that time struggled against the memorialization of the Civil War at the hands of Confederate sympathizers. Monuments to the Confederacy had dotted the Southern landscape as the physical landmarks of whiteness and had made African Americans conscious of the potential power of the built environment to recast Southern history and civic identity. Nineteenth-century Americans considered public monuments as civic markers and as vessels for the transmission of patriotism. African Americans soon realized that the establishment of their own physical landmarks of race pride and history were necessary for communal self-empowerment.

That most democratic ideal in American placemaking—the public square or outdoor space of assembly—had spurred disenfranchised African Americans to reappropriate it and reclaim its symbolic significance. In the postbellum era, African Americans were attempting to construct autonomous public "Black space," or what geographer David Harvey might call "spaces of hope," in response to the racial violence and political exclusion they continued to face.[62] Blacks knew that acquiring land was not simply symbolic of freedom and citizenship, but the only assured way of garnering independence and social mobility despite restrictive Jim Crow covenants of sale. In acquiring land, African

Americans understood that by establishing their own public sphere they could foster new forms of self-respect, group identity, and Black civic pride, and promote their own vision of a more inclusive nationalist struggle.

African Americans' struggle for public space, or "the parallel polis," involved major acts of resistance among the disenfranchised. Enslaved Blacks, of course, had left behind a legacy of African American underground activism. The fight over public space extended beyond the streetscape of the Southern landscape and became for Blacks a way of testing the boundaries of their rights under Emancipation. The 1883 struggle over civil rights in Danville, South Carolina, resulted in the deaths of countless African American men, women, and children. The "appropriation of public space" was a strategy used "to assert their humanity, demonstrate their political rights, and stake their claim to equal citizenship."[63] By the 1890s African Americans believed they could control public space only if they constructed a new civic order through their own all-Black-based institutions. Building separate African American organizations and structures was a viable strategy for security and advancement, a response to the white ruling classes' continued control over the national space. Anthropologist Ghassan Hage contends that, in their ceaseless attempts to construe whiteness (or even race) as a natural category, white nationalists do symbolic damage to the real, diverse populace by laying claim to shared spaces such as the Columbian Exposition, ostensibly an event held not only for the nation but for the world.[64] The Exposition established order in the chaos of the immigrant city and allowed for the emergence of other institutions such as schools, universities, and museums to promote social control through design in architecture. Controlling such spaces, and constructing them as somehow "white," legislates how the "other" is defined in the public sphere and emphasizes the racialized rituals of spatial organization. "Spatial purification" in the closing decades of the nineteenth century maintained the social control of deviant populations and those unproductive groups who threatened white capitalism.[65]

Americanization and the Public Sphere

Efforts to Americanize a growing foreign-born population reached their peak between 1880 and 1930 as industrial centers began expanding.[66] Many whites felt that immigration would destroy the American way of life that promulgated distinctly Anglo-Saxon, Protestant forms of "American" ideals. A growing immigrant population throughout the New South was also seen as endangering the stability of order in the region. English-language classes and instruction in American government and history were to instill a set of core values that could then be portrayed in the architectural styles presumed appropriate to a shared sense of whiteness.[67] Since the late eighteenth century, Americanism was a concern of many men, including President Thomas Jefferson (an amateur architect himself), who felt that buildings related to key events, such as the signing of the Declaration of Independence, should be preserved. This thinking was summarized some thirty years ago by architectural historian William B. Rhoads along these lines: "so long . . . as we can preserve the material objects . . . which these great men saw, used, or even touched, the thrill of vitality may still be transmitted as unbroken."[68]

The White City made certain that by manipulating the physical appearance of the built domain, the public sphere acted as a voice of precedented authority, surrounding the individual with new and imagined definitions of American citizenship. Historians such as Alan Trachtenberg have long maintained that creating a unified, nationalized, and ordered constituency was necessary for industrial progress after the Civil War, but that those most marginalized might have adopted a very different social agenda.[69] The legacy of the Ecole des Beaux-Arts—the French institution that informed many of the designs on display at the Exposition—had a profound effect on future attempts to create a formal program of nation making among African Americans. With its depictions of the United States as the most advanced nation in all of history, the Exposition compounded already prevalent ideas of racial and cultural superiority. By separating the Court of Honor from the Midway, the accomplishments in art, architecture, and technology were compared and contrasted by visitors with the many living "exotic" ethnological exhibits of the dark uncivilized ghetto.

In clear response, African Americans took the opportunity to present "a small nation of people, picturing their life and development without apology or gloss"[70] through their own display of advances initiated by industrial and normal education. African Americans understood that normal and industrial schools were an important part of the larger Black civic discourse to assert power and control over the production of cultural capital[71]—quite literally through the founding, establishment, and building of these racialized landscapes in the "New South."[72] These educational landscapes legitimated African American attempts at redefining a new public order in the American landscape. The buildings themselves act as sites of "racially inflected national identities" and memory.[73] The confluence of Southern history and identity with the lessons of the White City required African American women reformers and architects to build institutions ready to challenge the order of the "New South."

The White City and African American Social Movements

The narrative of the new Black "nation" had been formulated by the time of the Exposition, articulated by self-help institutions that were often the target of white racist attacks. African American women reformers especially understood the significance of the domestic sciences in creating public institutions and political forums for advancing the causes of racial betterment. Through the very public founding and leading of normal and industrial schools, African American women created educational institutions that reconceived the city and shaped a new nationalist civic realm.[74] African American women participating at the Exposition had also developed a model for future reform of the built environment, and a political model for a gendered Black nationalist campaign. Black women understood that they could act as nationalist agents for the race despite the constraints of the era, and they were unwilling to suppress the role of gender in the formation of a nation-building campaign. Many African American women reformers understood how a powerful agent shapes the landscape by employing particular techniques to promote order and organization; the techniques include the process of domination and legitimation. Domination may involve the taking of prime space, the control of space, or the creation of space in such a way as to effect control. Legitimation may involve the use of other power or authority to validate this control.[75]

For African American women in particular, the White City became a site of political contest over the right to speak out against lynching, mob violence, and civil disorder throughout the South.[76] Reformers such as Ida B. Wells publicly challenged white women at the Columbian Exposition, clearly establishing new, more radical venues for political autonomy and self-empowerment.[77] Wells and many other Black women reformers looked upon their own exhibits at the Exposition, which displayed their educational efforts at normal and industrial schools, as an open critique of Western ideals on race and culture.

Even if constructed only of sparkling white painted plaster and lath, the buildings at the Exposition did offer some kind of new utopian view for the future of American nationalism.[78] African Americans could relate to the invocation of a "promised land" if that built environment could be modified to reflect their pursuits of self-empowerment and self-definition instead of commenting on their spatial exclusion from the public sphere. And so through the creation of Black-based institutions, those African American architects and social reformers exposed to or made aware of the Exposition reappropriated its divisive imagery into a working model for race betterment in the built environment.

The classical City Beautiful or Urban Art movement plans—acting as a sort of visual text for civic improvement—were seen as "models of excellence for America, teaching both citizens and new immigrants aesthetic standards and moral values."[79] Municipal art, civic improvement, and outdoor art were at the root of the movement. Public sculpture was seen as a way to familiarize people with the fundamental values of past and present cultures and to ultimately eliminate congestion, poverty, prostitution, and corruption in city government.[80] A *Harper's New Monthly Magazine* article entitled "A Dream City" compared the Exposition's founders to builders of biblical utopia: "perhaps some freed spiritual intelligence who had had experience in the building of the New

Jerusalem became conscious of a possible improvement, and longing to verify it, came down for a brief period to join the band of builders and distinguish his share of work in the Dream City."[81]

African Americans, only three decades removed from enslavement, did not share whites' agendas for effecting change through the domestic sphere of the built environment. But by appropriating elements of the Colonial Revival and the Anglo-Saxon "origin myth,"[82] African American designers and reformers were actively engaged in rewriting the nation's narrative to include their many contributions in shaping the Southern landscape. African American experimentation with forms of higher education and the massive building campaigns that accompanied them not only provided their people with the power of literacy, but also provided them with the physical signs of an emerging Black nation. By reappropriating the style of the "master class," African Americans were again pressing their rights to their own national identity and citizenship.

Since Emancipation, Black women social reformers and architects had adapted the City Beautiful model as a means of contesting spatial formations of whiteness, and had asserted their own claims to American space making.[83] African American women clearly understood the power of a monumental architecture to act as a stage for their political and social enfranchisement in the face of the racist imagery of the White City and the ethnic savagery and carnival atmosphere of the Midway.

The Reason Why . . . and Public Discourses of Reform

Spread along Chicago's Lake Michigan, the 1893 World's Columbian Exposition provided African American women reformers with the opportunity to propel their social and political causes onto an international stage. Some contemporary historians have questioned the role of Wells's pamphlet: perhaps it constructs a false sense of the reality of African American involvement at the Exposition. However, the pamphlet is a profound cultural artifact not only because it contests the strength of white supremacy in the 1890s but also because it effectively disrupts our fascination with the Exposition and questions the reliability of the American imaginary. The Exposition clearly embodied the rhetoric of white superiority and white nationhood in its exhibits, in its architecture, and in its publicity. For Black southerners such as Ida B. Wells, the Exposition was a direct statement about the failures of Emancipation and the social engineering that remained intact in the post-Reconstruction decades.

Indeed, many Americans saw the Chicago Exposition as a blueprint for a future course of American "civilization" that excluded the contributions of African Americans entirely. Wells's pamphlet, however, refuted any claims made by fair leaders of a manly, all-white civilization in opposition to supposed "Negro savagery." Wells understood that the social production of race histories, such as her own publication in response to the Columbian Exposition, could play a significant part in reconstructing a collective self-identity and promoting race-uplift projects on the part of the formerly enslaved.

The Exposition's monolithic architectural campaign also demonstrated to African American reformers the importance of performative institution building, such as that on display at the White City, in promoting radical social change and new nation-making strategies.[84] A new public discourse among Black leaders and reformers would soon emerge, based largely on the well-established intellectual tradition of the nineteenth century, that upheld values of race heritage and cultural preservation. Du Bois best described it as a "nation stored with wonderful possibilities of culture [the destiny of which] was not a servile imitation of Anglo-Saxon culture, but a stalwart originality which shall unswervingly follow Negro ideals."[85] Reformers such as Wells helped to redefine notions of civilization and progress among African Americans throughout the decade of the 1890s with the construction of community-based social welfare institutions. Du Bois himself would advocate for the erection of "a Negro School of literature and art" to establish an autonomous aesthetic in education and civic values that would uplift the race.[86] Wells herself was active in the social settlement movement that helped build community-based outreach centers and venues for women's political engagement in the civic arena.[87]

And yet many educated women reformers, such as Wells and Elizabeth Evelyn Wright, were still seen as unfit for public life, even by their fellow African Americans. Jennie Dean, a former slave (with its implications of chattel "savagery") who overcame enslavement to found a Black industrial school, would not have even been judged a woman suitable for *race work* by the growing elite Black middle class, as if this would reflect negatively on them as a group. Elizabeth Evelyn Wright and Jennie Dean both assumed the dual role of social welfare reformers and catalysts for a space-making, gendered Black nationalism.[88] Dean's work to establish the Manassas Industrial School on the site of a former Civil War battlefield, for example, reflects the complexity of her lived experience and her commitment to social reform despite her lack of formal education and a working-class background.[89]

While a legacy of social welfare reform among African American women had existed since the late eighteenth century and had blossomed in the post-Emancipation era, the history of Black educational advancement, especially those efforts by African American women educators, is still being written. The work of these race women, especially the work of Black clubwomen, is an object of historical recovery, but it is a legacy that is often difficult to record in light of few extant primary documents. The built environment that they shaped is our best source of critical evidence about these African American women reformers.

Chapter Three

Tuskegee Utopianism

Where American Campus Planning Meets Black Nationalism

> Before going to Tuskegee I had expected to find there a building and all the necessary apparatus ready for me to begin teaching. To my disappointment, I found nothing of the kind. I did find, though, that which no costly building and apparatus can supply,—hundreds of hungry, earnest souls who wanted to secure knowledge.
>
> —Booker T. Washington, *Up from Slavery*

> A work that requires no sacrifice does not count much in fulfilling God's plans. . . . He who makes no such sacrifice is most to be pitied. He is a heathen, because he knows nothing of God.
>
> —Samuel C. Armstrong

As they contested the legitimacy of a white American nation-state, African Americans were already proposing an alternative identity for themselves and the institutions they were creating for their new nation. The church alone could not build a national community for African Americans: other institutions were needed. Black women reformers established a series of institutions, including industrial schools and other spaces of education, that were predicated on African Americans instructing their community by invoking race pride and representations of an authentic historical past, as they also worked to counteract white attempts to rewrite the South's defeat in the Civil War. For example, reformers—including Anna Julia Cooper and Pauline E. Hopkins and their circle of nationalistic intellectuals, some of them former slaves—worked under the banner of the Negro Society for Historical Research (founded in 1911) and published papers, books, and essays on topics related to "race-history."[1] Cooper and Hopkins sought to depict an "authentic folk memory before the hegemonizing power of the state ... [could] ... do its work."[2] Cooper described the role of women in developing new institutional models for the race. She writes,

> As far as my experience goes the average man of our race is less frequently ready to admit the actual need among the sturdier forces of the world for woman's help or influence. That great social and economic questions await her interference, that she could throw any light on problems of national import, that her intermeddling could improve the management of schools systems, or elevate the tone of public institutions ... that she has a word worth hearing on mooted questions in political economy, that she could contribute a suggestion on the relations of labor and capital...[3]

For Cooper, Black nationalism meant that women must help to redefine their role in the public and civic realms for race betterment. Cooper's *A Voice from the South* of 1892 acted as a clarion call for Black women to represent the race through racial betterment and social advancement during the decade of the "Woman's era." For Cooper, the Black woman was solely responsible for the care and maintenance of the family and its only member capable of representing the entire race in the quest for new freedoms and self-determination. She writes, "Only the BLACK WOMAN can say 'when and where I enter, in the quiet, undisputed dignity of my womanhood, without violence and without suing or special patronage, then and there the whole Negro race enters with me."[4] Cooper felt strongly that it was the Black woman who could be the only agent for drastic social change. Cooper frequently argued that Black autonomy and the right of self-determination were the only formulas for racial self-improvement.[5] In that very same year, in what some have considered a response to Cooper, Frances Ellen Watkins Harper would write that "the greatest need of the race is noble, earnest men, and true women."[6] Harper, a long-time abolitionist, lecturer, and social welfare crusader, understood the importance of breaking down the boundaries of silence on matters pertaining to institutionalized racism and sexism. Her novel, *Iola Leroy or Shadows Uplifted* (1892), would soon come to signify the dissatisfaction of many African Americans with the failures of Reconstruction while proposing new solutions to improve conditions throughout the South.

Black women such as herself, argues Cooper, are uniquely suited to redefining American civilization in part because of their former enslavement. She writes, "to be a woman of the Negro race in America, and to be able to grasp the deep significance of the possibilities of the crisis, is to have a heritage."[7] She also contends that

> No plan for renovating society, no scheme for purifying politics, no reform in church or in state, no moral, social, or economic question, no movement

upward or downward in the human plane is lost on her. . . . All departments in the new era are to be hers, in the sense that her interests are in all and through all; and it is incumbent on her to keep intelligently and sympathetically en rapport with all the great movements of her time, that she may know on which side to throw the weight of her influence. She stands now at the gateway of this new era of American civilization. In her hands must be moulded the strength, the wit, the statesmanship, the morality, all the psychic force, the social and economic intercourse of that era. To be alive at such an epoch is a privilege, to be a woman then is sublime.[8]

African Americans as Planners and Builders

African American involvement in the planning and building of the antebellum South is difficult to reconstruct because so much of the work went unrecorded. Enslaved Africans arrived in America skilled in traditional crafts such as woodcarving, building, and ironsmithing.[9] Their skills were utilized on Southern plantations in the construction of the manor or big house and their many associated outbuildings, and, as master carpenters, enslaved and free Blacks also constructed the furniture found in many of these houses. Historians James E. Newton and Ronald L. Lewis have argued that "if slave occupational categories were given modern terminology, many bondsmen would have such titles as architect, industrial engineer, graphic artist, landscaper, and other titles representing highly skilled fields associated with the visual arts."[10] Slaves also constructed their own dwellings, typically one-room cabins made of clay, thatched roofs, dirt floors, and fireplaces, many with clear evidence of West African building traditions. On many plantations "a considerable number of Negroes uniting the function of both the architect and the builder led almost free and independent careers although nominally held as slaves."[11] For example, when John Sims's house at Gippy Plantation in South Carolina was destroyed by a massive fire, it was later rebuilt by slave artisans. In accounts of his thirty years spent under enslavement, Louis Hughes tells of how a group of slaves was sent ahead to make bricks for their master's new mansion, which they later erected. A school of the manual arts for skilled slaves was even established in Alabama.[12] Referring to his early years in Florida after the Civil War, author and poet James Weldon Johnson, a leading figure in the Harlem Renaissance, writes, "All the most interesting things that came under my observation, were being done by colored men . . . they built houses, they laid the brick, they painted the buildings. . . . When I was a child, I did not even know that there existed such a thing as a white carpenter or bricklayer."[13]

Unforeseen was the rapid decline in the number of Black craftsmen employed in nineteenth-century Southern cities. The legacy of Denmark Vesey's failed 1822 insurrection in Charleston had helped to stigmatize the Black artisan class as untrustworthy and politically volatile for many fearful whites across the South. Vesey, a free Black carpenter, attempted to launch a slave rebellion and sail to freedom in Haiti with his followers, leaving much of white Charleston in constant fear of any possible involvement of skilled Black craftsmen in insurrection. Other reasons for the decline in available Black artisans included the steady stream of immigrant craftsmen arriving from Europe working for less than normal wages, and stringent regulations that restricted the spaces where African Americans could work.[14]

Religion, Democratic Space Making, and Nation Building

Immediately after Emancipation, African Americans began to erect bush arbors and log houses where they could hold community meetings and voice their opposition to their former masters. Indeed, the only Black cultural institution that remained largely intact after the Civil War was the Black church. As the Bible's Exodus story had recounted the tale of the Israelites in search of a land where they could rebuild their nation, so African Americans felt that they, too, would find a similarly reconstructed homeland under the leadership of the God who had already taken them out of enslavement. By the latter part of the nineteenth century, the civic realm among African Americans was not only made up of churches and religious organizations, but various other social welfare institutions, including schools, as well. For example, in 1893 social reformer Frances Ellen Watkins Harper used nation language to invoke some of the emerging civic realm's material culture. Harper writes, "not simply a nation building up a great material prosperity, founding magnificent cities, grasping the commerce of the world, or excelling in literature, art, and science, but a nation wearing sobriety as a crown and righteousness as the girdle of her loins."[15] The formation of a new civic order was predicated on a belief that freedom was not guaranteed unless African Americans worked collectively to construct the racialized landscape for their collective self-benefit. Also critical to the success of any model community and industrial school for African Americans was the role of the church and its place in promoting advancement through liberation theology and biblical scriptures.[16] The construction of this physical, social, and morally just national identity was based, in part, on the biblical Exodus tale as a way of imagining a Black New South.

African Americans continued to envision their liberation struggle, even into the 1880s and 1890s, as a reenactment of the Bible's Exodus story. Under enslavement Blacks believed they were the children of God and, like the Israelites, would leave Egypt behind and escape to freedom.[17] Race women often invoked the Exodus tale in their literary works (including novels and newspapers) to contest the prevailing narrative of white supremacy and the racial purity of the American nation. Their stories often provided a countermemory or even a countermonument to the master narrative of the white nation.[18]

Commemorative activity, such as freedom celebrations, as one form of public display openly challenged white collective memory of the Civil War and its significance for a reunified American nation. Marches, parades, and the use of public ceremonial places in cities across the country, such as New York, Atlanta, Chicago, and Richmond, also helped African Americans reclaim and honor their role in American civic life.[19]

Despite past attempts by historians such as Eugene Genovese, who argued in the 1970s that paternalism only weakened Blacks' attempts at self-determination, some assert that out of Black religious life came a distinctive Black national identity. Genovese himself posits that religion "made possible a universal statement because it made possible a national statement. [This] national statement expressed a duality as something both black and American, not in the mechanical sense of being an ethnic component in a pluralistic society, but in that dialectical sense of simultaneously being itself and the other, both separately and together, and of developing as a religion within a religion in a nation within a nation."[20] Historically, the Black church provided African Americans a mediated space where they could come together and construct a collective identity. As they sought to better address their common woes, African Americans beheld the church as a safe space for public discourse where white supremacy and racial violence could be openly questioned.

African American women could also publicly deliberate contemporary social concerns within the church walls—the home and hearth were not the only spaces reserved for the conversations of African American women. Anna Julia Cooper maintained that "Religion, science, art, economic, have all needed the feminine flavor; and literature, the expression of what is permanent and best in all of these, may be guaged [sic] at any time to measure the strength of the feminine ingredient."[21] African American women credited their reform commitments, in part, to their strong devotion to the church and its teachings: "the duty of enlightened Christians to send out their light and emulate their Master's aggressive labors of love."[22] Black women reformers organized around two basic tenets, theology and community, which allowed local churches to erect religious buildings and schools, provide food and clothing for the poor, and help "spread a gospel of self-help, self-discipline and self-determination."[23]

Black Nationalism and Nation Making

Undertaking the challenges of a Black nationalist agenda meant that African American women would respond to "their second enslavement" in the post-Reconstruction South in ways that might have included the implementation of multiple racial projects at any one given time. This first in a long series of racialized projects helped Africans Americans bear witness to their collective past under enslavement and testify to a now growing political consciousness, despite enraged white supremacists' attempts to thwart their progress. Benedict Anderson's definition of nationalism as an "imagined community" (one that is both limited and sovereign) is insufficient for understanding how national belonging is imagined, remembered, and recorded among these impassioned African American women reformers.[24]

Some historians maintain that the idea of a Black nation was not conceived specific to any geographical territory or even as an independent nation-state, but rather articulated within the confines of a "race language" reacting to white patriarchal oppression. For other scholars, Black nationalism is the expression of racial solidarity on issues impacting the larger African community. Some have even suggested that Black nationalism "generally has no ideological or programmatic implications beyond the desire that black people organize themselves on the basis of their common color and oppressed condition."[25] Black nationalism, therefore, demanded that African Americans take full responsibility for their own liberation and the maintenance of their own culturally specific institutions. In addition, Black nationalism, according to some scholars, often falls short of advocating for the absolute and total control of a geographic or spatial territory.[26] Certain ideals, presumably utopian, are upheld, however, that will one day advance the collective cause of self-determination. Black nationalism does occupy a geographic territory or space—a physical ideal—that moves us well beyond the limited conceptualization of a "race language" used only in literary forms of cultural production. That spatialized or geographic territory appears prominently in the founding of institutions designed by Black architects and building craftsmen and founded by African American women, many of whom were graduates of Tuskegee and its peer institutions.[27]

Many of Booker T. Washington's students, women in particular, understood that a more radical social agenda could be achieved by establishing schools similar to Tuskegee. The campus was a site where women could address changing gender roles and begin to assume responsibility for shaping Black civic life. Women reformers understood the importance of commemorative narratives that provided African Americans with a story of their community's origin, and the built environment could do its part toward institutionalizing that new ideal Black nationhood.[28] Women believed strongly that by the 1890s, "the fundamental agency under God in the regeneration, the retraining of the race, as well as the ground work and starting point of its progress upward, must be the black woman."[29] Especially in the late nineteenth century, national self-determination among African Americans was evident in the spaces fashioned by female reformers, trained at schools such as Tuskegee, who went on to found normal and industrial schools of their own.[30]

"Campus Beautiful" Planning

An Architecture of Education situates itself in the crisis that is Jim Crow where acculturation and the hard work of African American community building continued under the most contested of circumstances. As the architecture at the Columbian Exposition's White City projected elite ideals and embodied the mission of elite institutions, so African Americans seized upon the validating iconography on display there. Much as the Beaux Arts had applied its problem- and program-solving design formulas onto the template of the emerging industrial city—reviving and codifying European architectural and urban planning principles—by the end of the nineteenth century, the City Beautiful movement turned its attentions to the face of the American university campus.[31] Thus, to the City Beautiful argument is coupled the American "campus beautiful," which addressed imperatives such as changing ideas about curriculum, specialized study, and the institution's relationship to the larger society.[32] Many leading critics of the early Progressive era had noted that the traditional American campus was seemingly not designed at all, composed as it was of often barren, isolated, and unrelated buildings.[33] Since the time of the Puritans, the dormitory, the classroom building, and the administration building had been identified as independent units—no more, no less—and not parts of any kind of materially unified whole or identity. An architecture critic of the day, Ashton Willard, had even dismissed the design of Harvard's venerable Massachusetts Hall, dating from the eighteenth century, as nothing more than an aggrandized, existing colonial building type.[34] Mid-nineteenth-century campus designs might feature a collection of separate and distinct buildings grouped around a central grassy area, a green or quad, often situated in rural and semirural regions, with a campus's architectural style and form—as dictated by a particular institution's president, trustees, or donors—often influenced by the design already in evidence in its extant buildings.[35]

Nationwide, university education was seen as a means of civilizing American society amid perceived urban chaos while assigning social roles—gendered and racialized—to its graduates. Beginning in the mid-nineteenth century, the land-grant institutions were adding colleges and programs of engineering, agriculture, and science as a way of combining the education of "head-workers and hand-workers."[36] With the nation rapidly transforming in the face of massive industrialization and urbanization, new educational mechanisms were required to educate and assimilate immigrants and others without means during the post–Civil War era.[37]

By the first decade of the twentieth century in the Progressive era, architectural critics such as A. D. F. Hamlin and Claude Bragdon were arguing for a more unified plan for American campus planning. A European country such as England might have had a well-established tradition based on the inward-looking academic cloister.[38] However, increasingly concerned with the quality of American scholarship after the Civil War, educators modeled their efforts after the outward-looking empiricism of the German university system.[39] The German university model had an enormous impact in the United States, ultimately merging with the American undergraduate teaching-focused tradition as a "marriage between collegiate and university ideals."[40] Eventually promoting the opportunity for an education to the public, the university now had to create a series of academic programs, departments, and facilities to meet the growing demands of its evolving student body. The American university required "a fine architectural effect which [would] represent to its students the ideals and purposes of a university and command the attention and admiration of the public."[41] The linkages between collegiate architecture and the Columbian Exposition were pithily acclaimed by Henry Van Brunt in a series of articles written about the fair[42] (figure 23) as a kind of university "open to all . . . and so ordered that to see is to learn."[43] A Columbia University trustee noted that the Columbian Exposition's most significant contribution was its overall plan for "an extensive group of buildings as one consistent whole, symmetrical in arrangement and harmonious in design."[44]

As consensus shifted toward advocacy for comprehensive university and college plans, the Beaux Arts tradition was made manifest in American campus planning with a coherent legacy in evidence even today. By 1900, journal writers were interested in how the unified design of the Beaux Arts ideal could be used in a university master plan, subsuming to it the design of individual buildings while employing stylistic references to the glory of past republics. According to architectural historian Mary N. Woods, the arrangement of the buildings at the Chicago Exposition's Court of Honor suggests a strong correlation with Jefferson's "Lawn" at the University of Virginia.[45] A uniquely American character was said to be inherent in the design of educational institutions, such as Jefferson's own University of Virginia, as "the tendency of academic architecture is conservative . . . in America . . . the university atmosphere tends to place exaggerated value on the historic traditions which it possesses, and this is a marked feature in university life . . . we shall find only rare instances of radicalism in collegiate architecture."[46] The architectural firm of McKim, Mead, and White (later responsible for the initial design of a relocated Columbia University in Manhattan's Morningside Heights) was considered at the forefront of promoting a unique American template (despite adapting Beaux Arts models and precedents) in architecture through their civic designs.[47] The firm was recognized abroad as one of America's leading architectural firms—the Royal Institute of British Architects had even awarded its gold medal for achievement to principal Charles McKim in 1903. Among the firm's landmark commissions were not only Columbia's Morningside Heights campus, but also the Pennsylvania Railroad Station, the Rhode Island State Capitol, and renovations of the White House interiors.[48]

Decades before the Exposition, Frederick Law Olmsted's campus plans for the University of California at Berkeley, the University of Maine, Amherst College, and Gallaudet College reflected his belief in the school as a total community comprised of much more than just a group of buildings and the landscape. These schools, along with homes, churches, stores, and museums, grew to comprise a uniquely American environment.[49] Olmsted, who designed at least nine colleges and universities in the decades following the Civil War, felt strongly that the American campus could extend the civilizing mission of higher education throughout the United States.[50] In his treatise, *A Few Things to Be Thought of before Proceeding to Plan Buildings for the National Agricultural College* (1866), Olmsted made clear his belief that the material culture of a well-designed campus provides uplift for the behavior of its students as much as subjects such philosophy, mathematics, and language do—something that places him squarely in the Jeffersonian camp of collegiate design advocacy.[51]

In 1906 an idea known as the "group plan" was featured in the pages of *The Brickbuilder*. In a five-part series, Alfred Morton Githens discussed how the arrangement of different buildings could be made according to their functions and need. He analyzed and compared a series of group plans, acknowledging the lack of an existing American model for these institutions.[52] Githens was concerned that no distinct typological plan existed in the United States and was particularly critical that Americans "have attempted far more pretentious and monumental architecture. . . . We Americans are architectural libertines and have no restraining traditions. . . ."[53] With the broad acceptance of the City Beautiful or Urban Art Movement, and the subsequent publication of Githens's group plan models, many American universities were fully prepared to think of themselves as cities of learning. Architectural historian Paul Venable Turner has even argued of American campus design that because of its frequent isolation in nature—for instance, in the rural American countryside—"the college had to become even more fully a kind of miniature city. And its design became an experiment in urbanism."[54]

The Project of the Tuskegee Institute

In the final decades of the nineteenth century, African American architects and reformers helped transform the traditional campus model into an institution of social welfare reform and political advocacy. Perhaps no institution of higher learning more poignantly realized these aspirations than the Tuskegee Normal School, founded in 1881 by African American reformer Booker T. Washington (figure 24). Washington, having left his teaching post at the Hampton Normal and Agricultural Institute in Virginia, was approached by veteran African American politicians from Tuskegee, Alabama, who were eager to have him establish a school there.[55] Lewis Adams, a former slave and mechanic by trade, had asked Washington to help him preserve the trades that Blacks had long dominated for generations throughout the South. Adams's downtown Tuskegee tinsmith and blacksmith shop had become an informal trade school for poor Blacks after the Civil War. Unfortunately, many Black artisans had already left the county and had dispersed throughout the state in an effort to find better employment and higher wages. Washington understood the significance of teaching these important vocational skills to a younger generation of men, especially after his own experiences while enrolled at Hampton.[56] Washington himself described the Tuskegee campus as "a city in itself built by young colored men, most of whom were totally ignorant of systematic mental or menial training when they asked to be admitted to Tuskegee."[57] The *Chicago Record Herald* would eventually describe Tuskegee as "the most astonishing educational center on the continent. Despite the volumes written upon Booker T. Washington and his school, the visitor is never prepared for the marvels he finds. A school? Tuskegee is not a school in the ordinary sense of the word. It's a city in itself, a community that dominates a whole county."[58]

Architectural education became an important part of the industrial school movement among African Americans, famously emphasizing the dual "training of the head and hand" in the service of the race.[59] Architectural and mechanical drawing were in particular a critical component in the industrial training program at Tuskegee—a program of study that many of the other schools founded by Tuskegee graduates soon adopted.[60] Providing the curricular foundation for the construction of some twenty-three buildings at the school site by 1901, architectural training was considered one of the "most important divisions of Tuskegee's work."[61]

Responding to the needs of African Americans, Tuskegee's architecture curriculum would more or less combine William Robert Ware's curriculum at the Massachusetts Institute of Technology (MIT) and Nathan Ricker's curriculum at the University of Illinois, along with the Ecole des Beaux-Art's emphasis on architecture as a fine art. These early program models, coupled with Booker T. Washington's self-help tenets, made Tuskegee's approach to architectural education unique in many respects. Tuskegee's architects also differed greatly from other late nineteenth-century practitioners who would consistently denounce all earlier, nonacademic architectural production, a luxury unthinkable to the many African Americans who were less than one generation removed from enslavement.

Both Ware and Ricker believed that students could complete their design education by working in offices over school holidays and vacations. Tuskegee students, however, did not have to leave campus as faculty and students used the school as a laboratory for design and construction. Washington had adopted the Sloyd system of manual training, working closely with mechanical drafting and scaled models throughout the design process (figure 25).[62] The school catalog described the four-year course and emphasized the training of students in the workshop system: "in addition to time spent in the drawing room, students must spend some time in the work shops, to give them a more intimate knowledge of the materials with which they will deal, and to supervise work intelligently. The amount of time required depends on the knowledge the student already has of materials and construction."[63]

Nathan Ricker's Illinois curriculum would influence training at Columbia University and would soon have an enormous influence at Tuskegee, as Columbia University President Seth Low also served on the Tuskegee Institute's Board of Directors. While traveling abroad, Low had purchased a multivolume set of texts on German university architecture.[64] The German university system already had an enormous impact on the curriculum at most institutions of higher learning by the mid-nineteenth century. Architectural historian Mary Woods also maintains that "the Tuskegee synthesis of craft training, architectural education, and building experience was unique in American architectural education.... Few American architects were as thoroughly trained and experienced in both architecture and building before they left school as Tuskegee graduates."[65]

Photographer Frances Benjamin Johnston (1864–1952) famously documented the classrooms and workshops of the Tuskegee Institute, following her *Hampton (Institute) Album*, which had been exhibited at the Exhibit of American Negroes at the Paris Exposition of 1900. Johnston was well connected, and her work over the decades was wide-ranging with subjects drawn from white society—including President Theodore Roosevelt's daughter's wedding portrait—to celebrities, including Booker T. Washington, to series featuring American Indigenous peoples and African Americans. George Eastman himself had once provided her with one of his new compact Kodak cameras, but Johnston's use of oversize glass plate negatives at Hampton and Tuskegee (requiring several seconds of exposure) lent her compositions a classicizing affect. The subject matter of the classrooms and workshops is gendered: some monolithically so while other subjects are provocatively mixed. However, I believe Johnston would not have taken it upon herself to "gender" the space of classrooms and workshops outside existing practice at these institutions.

Macon County, Alabama's Black Belt

Home to the Tuskegee Institute, Macon County was one of the more prosperous regions in Alabama prior to the Civil War, with a large population of enslaved African Americans working on local plantations. After the war, the county quickly adapted to the raising of cotton, corn, peas, beans, oat, sweet potatoes, peanuts, watermelon, and various other kinds of fruits and vegetables. Africans transplanted to the area had brought with them new harvesting and agricultural practices that soon helped to transform the region. Before the

Civil War, Macon County was considered one of the chief centers of culture and learning in the state, with the earliest academy founded exclusively for elite white women. By 1860, the town of Tuskegee included some twenty-five Black carpenters, one blacksmith, three painters, two wheelwrights, three tinsmiths, two tanners, five masons, and fourteen shoemakers.[66]

After the close of the Civil War, a large portion of the population, especially newly freed Blacks and poor whites, immediately left the county. The primary reason for this rapid decrease in population was the soil, depleted after consecutive decades of monolithic cotton production. The thick, dark, and naturally rich soil of Alabama's Black Belt had been left impoverished. By 1881, the county was in the midst of an economic crisis with cotton prices at all-time lows. Although Blacks had been emancipated only a little over a decade and a half prior, many former slaves and their children were newly threatened with a second form of enslavement through debt peonage or the sharecropping system. Many were living only somewhat better than chattel, while many others were even worse off, trying to eke out a modest existence through subsistence farming. Poor farm families lived in crowded, one-room cabins, often working in the fields with only a meager diet of pork fat and cornbread. Unfortunately for sharecropping Black families, the soil was too often poorly prepared and rarely tilled more than three or four inches deep. Subsoiling, fall plowing, fallowing, and crop rotation were seldom practiced by the local farmers, who knew little of the many recent innovations in agricultural technology.[67]

Many African American families felt that as soon as children were able to carry a hoe, they should be sent to the fields to assist with menial agricultural tasks. This attitude, combined with pervasive and open white hostility, makes it unsurprising that most public schools in the region were open to Black children only three to five months during the entire year and were closed during the farming season. Macon's public schools were a major concern to Washington and his Tuskegee faculty because so few facilities were made available to Black children. School sessions were often held in church buildings or wherever space might be made available. Many teachers across the county were ill-trained, and used the time left to them in the classroom inefficiently.[68] Washington held "little respect for the farmer who is satisfied with merely 'making a living.' It is hardly possible that agricultural life will become attractive and satisfactory to ambitious young men or women in the South until farming can be made as lucrative there as in other parts of the country."[69]

Booker T. Washington believed that the post-Reconstruction government had not adequately prepared African Americans for total emancipation. Moreover, in efforts to reassert control over their former slaves in the nadir of Jim Crow, Democrats had initiated a series of legislative maneuvers to disenfranchise African Americans: a series of poll taxes set too high for poor Black farmers to pay, a campaign of literacy testing designed to disqualify undereducated Blacks, "grandfather clauses" requiring the voter to produce evidence that his grandfather had voted in previous elections, and a procedure called the "understanding test."[70] The above tested Washington's resolve to counteract discriminatory laws that disenfranchised African Americans. Black southerners had already been freed by this time and enjoyed limited privileges as free laborers, citizens, and voters. The failure of Reconstruction to secure their rights left them once again disenfranchised and politically segregated by virtue of the law.[71] The challenges of this de facto captivity at the hands of former masters were settled on educational institutions that, many have argued, were ill-equipped for the task of nation building that lay ahead. However, these former slaves turned educators effectively brought national attention to their causes, and succeeded in providing the Black community with an institutional base for massive social reform. Booker T. Washington describes firsthand the struggle that freed men and women experienced: "Few people who were not right in the midst of the scenes can form any exact idea of the intense desire which the people of my race showed for education. It was a whole race trying to go to school. Few were too young, and none too old, to make the attempt to learn. As fast as any kind of teachers could be secured, not only were day-schools filled, but night-schools as well."[72]

Disrupting the Accommodationist Master Narrative

Booker T. Washington's biography and legacy remain fiercely contested today. For some, he is the power at the center of the "Tuskegee Machine," the strongman who tolerated no challenge to his uplift orthodoxy or his unparalleled access to white capital and political influence, as Washington, charismatic and ruthless, intimidated or even promised bodily harm to such a rival.[73] However, if Washington was the boss, he also made efforts to empower certain of his supporters and, although Washington is widely regarded as accommodationist, his "Tuskegee Machine's" seeming acquiescence to white society and societal norms was complicated: witness how behind the scenes at Tuskegee, Washington was effectively funding Black radical reformers such as T. Thomas Fortune and Victoria Earle Matthews. He was also especially interested in funding efforts on the part of African American women journalists and educators who could make an immediate impact on the lives of the formerly enslaved and their children.[74]

For many whites, Booker T. Washington was considered a moderate because he publicly advocated vocational training over a more classically based education for African Americans. Historian Louis R. Harlan, author of Washington's early 1980s biography, critically questions Tuskegee's educational approach and its effectiveness in promoting self-help strategies. Harlan writes, "Was it [Tuskegee] the instrument for achieving a black man's dream of self-sufficiency through a marketable skill, or was it a white man's dream of preparing black people to fill the subordinate places, the only ones available to them in the new order of white supremacy?"⁷⁵ In addressing criticisms that industrial education restricted the opportunities of African Americans, Washington said that he saw a "danger . . . that most seriously threatens the success of industrial training, [it] is the ill-advised insistence in certain quarters that this form of education should be offered to the exclusion of all other branches of knowledge. . . . It is evident that a race so largely segregated as the Negro is, must have an increasing number of its own professional men and women."⁷⁶ Vocational training would be one critical path toward racial uplift.

Black schooling, as historian James D. Anderson has argued, emerged at a time when American popular education was being transformed across all intersectional boundaries into a critical and highly formalized endeavor. In the face of a changing educational landscape, Washington expended his initial efforts to grow his first generation of graduates into race educators. Those enrolled in the normal school classes were the first line of defense in the battle against illiteracy, poverty, and discrimination. Washington urged his teachers to return to their plantation districts and show people new ideas in farming as well as help them develop their intellectual, moral, and religious training. One of his primary objectives was to provide rural communities with an extension program that allowed farmers, who could not attend the school, to access progressive ideas for raising crops and training for race betterment. Washington also wanted to equip his students with the occupational skills necessary for the growing number of jobs available in the building trades and agriculture.⁷⁷

Industrial Schools as Community Laboratories

Because of the culture of racial segregation, campus designs of the time could not reflect a truly inclusive, reformist vision—one of a new social order that would have included African Americans.⁷⁸ But, as if taking into account an African American nation in exodus, Booker T. Washington considered his experimental campus and industrial school a model *Black City*, one might say, in microcosm,⁷⁹ with African American educators on the whole envisioning their model industrial schools as physical laboratories for community development. As such, the schools founded by African Americans would be havens set far away and aside from the attentions of white society. Some scholars have maintained that Washington went so far as to internalize the white Southern view of African Americans as unable to acquire basic life skills. Mindful of the intimidation and terror that Jim Crow could impose on African Americans, Washington stressed the importance of manual labor while maintaining good working relationships with whites as a form of political pragmatism. Washington affirmed that to physically rebuild the race, it was first necessary to undertake industrial and manual training programs in an emerging industrial economy.

Tuskegee reinforced the link between the physical design of its overall campus and the kinds of programs administered for race-based advancement. In the early 1890s, just before Chicago's Columbian Exhibition, the Tuskegee Institute underwent a period of massive expansion that would bring its total number of buildings to well over a dozen (figure 26). Numerous building projects were made possible by the income from the Institute's brick manufacturing, established by Washington. Porter Hall (1882), Alabama Hall (1886), Armstrong Hall (1886), and the Pavilion (1886) had already been erected when Wright arrived in the fall of 1888.[80] Washington recalls, "The school was constantly growing in numbers, so much that, after we got the [early] farm [site] paid for, the cultivation of the land begun, and the old cabins which we had found on the place somewhat repaired, we turned our attention towards providing a large, substantial building."[81] Porter Hall contained the administrative offices, library, reading room, chapel, six recitation rooms, girls' dormitories, dining room, kitchen, and laundry. Although unfinished at the time of its inauguration on Thanksgiving Day in 1882, it was a physical statement of the power of Black institution building in the state of Alabama.[82] As architectural historian Barbara Mooney has noted, that with Washington distributing architect-drawn plans and specifications to farmers attending regional conferences, home and school typologies became "agents for further advancement as well as celebrations of what had already been accomplished [as a race]."[83]

For Washington, "the school is a community unto itself, in which buildings can be erected, finished, and furnished, the table supplied the year round, and economic independence achieved in a large measure."[84] On Sundays, Tuskegee faculty and students visited surrounding communities and assisted with local church outreach to the poor. These efforts provided the Tuskegee faculty and its students with the opportunity to discuss important issues with community members, such as home improvement, home ownership, the latest advances in farming techniques, and partnerships that might lead to the establishment of better public schools. Through his own innovative planning, Washington soon provided the first teacher's institute to be held on campus for all nearby rural and surrounding counties. The teacher's institute had an enormous impact at both the local and regional levels, particularly in promoting self-help education.[85]

The Campus Quadrangle, Community Building, and African American Architects

With the study of architectural and mechanical drawing for male students becoming an important part of the all-Black racial project of uplift and nation making—tracing its earliest beginnings to a course of study at the Negro State Normal School in Montgomery, Alabama, and Claflin University in Orangeburg, South Carolina[86]—these experiments in campus planning provided young African American architects with the opportunity to design their own monumental Black City in microcosm and experiment with issues of urbanism. In the late nineteenth century, there may have been a general absence of accepted, canonical forms of collegiate planning, but civic design and campus design had similar objectives: to generate a sense of place that served and symbolized institutional values and purposes.[87] For African American architects and reformers, the campus quadrangle in particular provided a physical, social, and metaphorical space for exploring issues of self-governance, identity, and citizenship. The quadrangle or square—a constructed physical center for communal self-expression—persisted as the critical public space and a source of symbolic civic power. Washington believed that requiring his students to participate in the construction of Tuskegee's campus, while setting aside these critical communal spaces, was key to their educational and moral training (figure 27). With the benefit of hindsight, he wrote, "I knew that our first buildings would [not] be comfortable or complete in their finish as buildings erected by the experienced hands of outside workmen . . . but that in the teaching of civilization, self-help, and self-reliance, the erection of the buildings by the students themselves would more than compensate for any lack of comfort or finish."[88]

Black Towns as Utopia

As early as 1865, African Americans were beginning to act, building themselves de facto utopias in the "Black or Negro towns" that spread throughout the South. Some of the most significant settlements included Cedarlake, Greenwood Village, Plateau, and Shepherdsville in Alabama; Biscoe, Edmonson, and Thomasville in Arkansas; Eatonville and New Monrovia in Florida; Archery, Burroughs, Cannonville, Grenough, and Leroy in Georgia; and Expose, Renova, and Mound Bayou in Mississippi. The state of Oklahoma had the largest number of Black towns, including Boley, Bookertee, Clearview, Porter, Grayson, Lima, Mantu, Redbird, Rentiesville, Taft, Tatums, Tullahassee, and Vernon.[89] Black towns in the South were more substantial than those established in Northern or western states, and, although smaller in size, Southern settlements developed their own resources for self-improvement and support. Residential school settlements, founded by African Americans, such as Wilberforce in Ohio, the Institute in West Virginia, and Langston in Oklahoma, developed alongside the establishment of large institutions for race betterment.[90] Sites such as Mound Bayou, Mississippi, began as one way of refuting claims that without whites' civilizing influence, Blacks would revert to savagery. This sort of argument—ultimately refuted—is synopsized in a 1909 history of Mound Bayou: "Removed from under the immediate restraint of the white governing hand we start on the path of retrogression and revert back to the original condition from whence we have come only by difficult slow steps. Any considerable number of Negroes left entirely to themselves, it was said, would inevitably drift in the direction of their own mutual debasement and destruction."[91] Official or political landscapes foster order, security, and continuity of society by reminding people of their rights, their obligations, and the history of the nation or state.[92] Efforts to memorialize the Confederate past, for example, can be seen as the expressions of an official culture since they sought to maintain social order and reinforce existing institutions by discouraging disorder and radical change. These displays of official white culture stress the duties of citizens to the state or nation above their individual rights. Vernacular landscapes, in contrast, reinforce individual decisions, traditions, customs, personal relationships, and utility by illustrating "how individuals or groups within a society organize local spaces."[93] A vernacular culture is a local grassroots expression of diverse interests based on individuals whose reality reflects their personal experience within the local community.[94] Since white southerners maintained their own officializing culture through acts of racial violence, African Americans responded by continuing to develop a nationalist culture with strong ties to the built environment.

Greenwood Village, Washington's own planned community, is adjacent to the Tuskegee Institute and is an example of Washington's race-uplift project expressed through the built environment. Planning for Greenwood began with the school's founding in 1881, and reflected Booker T. Washington's belief that every teacher and worker should own a home (figure 28). Washington had the Institute purchase as much of its adjacent property as possible and then allow easy terms for teachers and workers to obtain homes. At its height, the community boasted some 175 homes with 1,500 residents living and working in close proximity.[95] Greenwood became a prime example of Washington's self-help communal model and a readily adapted prototype for progressive living throughout the South. By 1901, some 200 acres at Greenwood were purchased and subdivided into 40 wide streets and 45 wide avenues.[96] Washington used all the available resources of the architecture department to help design affordable model cottages for it. The town was described as "A Progressive Village Adjoining the Tuskegee Normal and Industrial Center for Colored People in the South." The model school building originally located on campus, as well as the Mount Olive Baptist Church, was moved to Greenwood. Washington's village was self-supporting with its own industry, retail stores, and local shops.[97] Washington biographer Louis Harlan suggests that Greenwood, like Tuskegee, "was a preparation for life, and for assimilation into the mainstream of American life, as Washington strongly believed, then Greenwood was that life in miniature."[98] While some architectural historians applaud the overall classicizing proportions governing these simpler structures, including those found at Greenwood, Emmett Scott, Booker T. Washington's closest adviser and Tuskegee's first publicist, maintained that these structures were only "good enough for a Negro school."[99] Other historians have argued that these buildings were "not so challenging of the social order."[100] I instead argue that in their domestic order, they presented a formal challenge to the accepted social norms of segregation, racism, and mass public lynchings.

Greenwood Village as a cultural landscape reflects the struggle of African Americans to survive on their own economically and participate in community life. Constructing their own houses of brick and mortar, a mere thirty years after enslavement, hinted at a form of radicalism that would soon be spread throughout the South by Tuskegee graduates—by men and women very much like Wright—committed to social, economic, political, and spatial self-empowerment. Landscape historian J. B. Jackson contends that these vernacular landscapes are "the image of our common humanity—hard work, stubborn hope, and mutual forbearance."[101] The Black nation would not only be made up of institutions such as the industrial school, but would also transform the domestic and communal realms. Were Washington and his Tuskegee architects truly advocating eventual assimilation into dominant culture by promoting Greenwood as a model community for African Americans? White responses to Tuskegee initiatives suggest the delicate balance that Washington was able to achieve between campus and town. School administrators often cautioned their students to avoid the hostility of local white townspeople, even urging them not to carry too many books while walking around town.[102]

The space-making agenda of Black nationalism attempted to effectively counteract white social dominance. As one southerner explained, "The end of the war brought new ideas; the individual demanded a place and a reward no matter what was his family backing. . . . Energy, business ability and general efficiency were the watchwords that opened the door to success now. We were living in a new world."[103] Many Blacks hoped that they had witnessed the birth of a "new civilization."[104]

Urban historian M. Christine Boyer, in *The City of Collective Memory* (1994), argues that

> the physical form and shape of a city, its official plan and ceremonial places are articulated by political and social configurations that a nation or municipality wants to instill within its public. Monuments and civic spaces of the city designed as emblematic scenes are the sites of rhetorical meaning. As staged events they are a studied representation of civic authority, becoming the official memory book of significant events or the metaphors of national life.[105]

These sites can be seen as a kind of *memory theater*, which implies a reordering of civic discourse that now conceptualizes an idealized space of nationhood. Perhaps it is a community in which African Americans could physically reclaim their lost heritage and redefine a civic discourse within the confines of these engendered educational spaces by somehow demarcating a new order on the larger Southern landscape (figure 29). For African American educators, architectural education in particular became an expression of utopianism because it allowed practitioners and clients to transform structures of oppression in place since the earliest days of enslavement.[106] Pragmatic progressive political and educational work would begin at the margins or intersections of institutional sites such as these industrial schools, where people not only lived their daily lives but were active members in a participatory democracy. Ultimately, these democratic spaces provided educators, particularly women, with the kinds of public forums or civic spaces normally denied them as African American women, thus allowing them to participate more actively in decision-making processes for their community.

Chapter Four

The "Race Women" Establishment

Elizabeth Evelyn Wright, Jennie Dean, and Their All-Black Schools

The race women of *An Architecture of Education*—the founders of two industrial and normal schools in particular—were working-class African Americans who developed strategic and pragmatic race-uplift programs in the service of their communities' built environments. Elizabeth Evelyn Wright and Jennie Dean were both committed to building schools and campus sites that provided comprehensive normal and manual school training to young African American men and women for race betterment. By schooling an "intelligent citizenship" through an "academic education," these educators commanded resources, political opportunities, and organizational strength.[1]

During Reconstruction, the concept of race woman emerged from the abolitionist movement and developed in opposition to a growing white supremacist ideology. Race women drew their lessons from the antebellum self-help tradition as a way of combating white oppression and the stagnation of the Southern economy, which fueled further hostility.[2] African American women helped form some of the earliest neighborhood schools, missions, and churches shortly after the war. In historian Jacqueline Jones's early work on Georgia Blacks during Reconstruction, *Soldiers of Light and Love* (1992), she reflects on how "demonstrating an 'ethos of mutuality' that had permeated Afro-American culture for some time, communities formed black churches; Republican party clubs and Union Leagues; fire companies; mutual aid, protective, and fraternal associations; and schools."[3] Jones points directly to the legacy of mutuality and self-help that persisted despite the perceived degraded condition of the Black race and its inability to build communities under enslavement. Although Jones acknowledges that education was an expensive proposition and luxury for people of all ages and sexes, it provided an impulse for applying all-Black strategies for social reform.[4]

Historian and media studies scholar Brittney C. Cooper asks, "What does it mean to be a race woman?" In *Beyond Respectability* Cooper answers her own question thusly: "Race women were the first Black women intellectuals. As they entered into public racial leadership roles beyond the church in the decades after Reconstruction, they explicitly fashioned for themselves a public duty to serve their people."[5] The concept of "race woman" describes how Black women across the country formed a movement dedicated to combating racism and sexism, serving the needs of Black women, and uplifting the race through their efforts to transform the built environment. Not all race women considered themselves equal to those they perceived as less fortunate—working-class, poor, or formerly enslaved women generally approached uplift differently from elite women. Race uplift was at the core of their social agenda, enacted in various forms through architecture, literature, etc., and backed by an overarching Black nationalist political ideology.[6] Booker T. Washington often acknowledged the unique efforts of race women in his many public speeches. In 1912, he wrote, "Perhaps the most remarkable example of what these women have accomplished is the work of Elizabeth Evelyn Wright, the founder of Voorhees [Industrial School]. She came to us at Tuskegee, a frail young woman without means, and as it often seemed, without the physical strength to complete her course . . . Voorhees stands today as a monument to this young woman's faith and persistence."[7]

Although the term *feminism* did not exist in nineteenth-century America, debates over the "Woman Movement" among white women developed as they sought to improve their status and expand their roles beyond the parlors of domestic life. Images of idealized women—including those of true womanhood, real womanhood, public womanhood, and new womanhood—overlapped as attitudes toward gender shifted and power receded from long-held patriarchal strongholds.[8] Public womanhood provided women with a rationale to move from the private domestic sphere into the public in the "legal, political, *spatial*, and cultural sense."[9]

Exemplifying this shift in dominant culture, 1890s Southern white women were drawn into the newly emerging national and local club movements. Between 1894 and 1907 federations of cultural and self-help groups formed in every Southern state. By 1890, these groups had consolidated into the General Federation of Women's Clubs (GFWC). Their goals included statewide library and adult education programs, sanitary milk supplies, guardianship laws for divorced women, child labor laws, protective legislation for women, and a host of other reforms. As suggested by some historians, these clubs served as "alternative universities" that mobilized public opinion, promoted the suffrage movement, and kept white clubwomen informed of current events. Black women, however, were excluded from the GFWC, so after Margaret

Murray Washington began the Tuskegee Woman's Club in 1895, they formed, in response, their own Southern Association of Colored Women's Clubs. Black clubwomen were especially concerned with issues impacting poor women, working mothers, and tenant wives. Mutual aid societies to provide medical care and burial assistance also formed in response to concerns of Black Southern women.[10]

In 1896 the National Association of Colored Women's Clubs (NACW) came into being after the merger of the National League of Colored Women and the National Federation of Afro-American Women. The NACW became the largest network of African American women dedicated to improving the lives of others, and many members worked to bridge the gap between the educated and elite middle class and poor women. Although they were advocates of broad institution building "regardless of ethnic or racial group," the deeply embedded class divisions and Victorian gender ideals espoused by the "cult of true womanhood" made some of this work problematic for Black women.[11] Like dominant society, Black communities, too, were divided by binaries of rural and urban, educated and laboring, and established and poor. Despite these obstacles, a New South Progressivism promoting an emerging and now growing educated Black middle class was taking shape in the midst of the larger Progressive era. Ending patriarchal Southern principles of propriety that strictly defined family, work, and home meant that elite Black women reformers resolved to include poor and working-class women to make significant race progress possible.[12]

Historian Ula Taylor's research on Marcus Garvey's second wife, Amy Jacques Garvey, and her work following the Progressive era and throughout the 1920s on behalf of the Pan-African Movement, suggests an important maneuvering between the domestic sphere of family and the public world that even at this later date required a "strategic performance of private and public."[13] Taylor provides a useful framework for understanding Garvey's reform and activist strategies using the term *community feminism*.[14] Earlier, Black women, such as Dean and Wright, found a way to carefully mediate their multiple identities as African Americans, as working-class women, and as reformers to improve the lived experiences of others through a kind of *community-based feminist pragmatism*.[15]

Recent advances in Black intellectual history regarding normal and industrial schooling suggest that "black consciousness and cognition" help move us beyond the binary between academic achievement and practical, manual labor. The late nineteenth-century attack on classical education by "accommodators, conservatives, or anti-intellectuals" and investment in industrial education among Black progressives, radicals, and intellectuals should be seen as one of the most significant intellectual transformations in African American history.[16] Historian James Levy maintains that by the early 1880s, declining enthusiasm on the part of the Black intelligentsia for classical education on the one hand, and interest in the sciences and technology on the other hand, was propelled by the desire to find more "rigorous modes of intellectual cultivation, not less, and to cultivate black independence and autonomous consciousness."[17] Similarly, the all-Black social, political, cultural, and eventual economic autonomy permitted on Black industrial school campuses was made most manifest through the built environment and was effective in forwarding their new "Black consciousness" and vision of the nation. Levy maintains that this new push to assert Black intellect and consciousness might be an ethos of pragmatic Black consciousness where racial identity was not dependent on Anglo-Saxon culture and traditions.

An Architecture of Education contends that women such as Dean and Wright were involved in their own intellectual project of race uplift to build their industrial schools that leveraged resources culled both from their local African American communities along with those of white Northern philanthropy. Elizabeth Wright and Jennie Dean negotiated community politics, and tested the boundaries of social and gender norms through the community-based agency of their local churches. Again, women formed a reliable constituency in their historically Black churches, and were in the ranks of leadership. Their identities, as Black working-class women and school founders, provided them with a unique vantage point from which to have students apply the social and real-world aspects of industrial school curricula and manual training. With respect to their own industrial school efforts, Wright and Dean insisted that their institutions would be coeducational and, acting as clients as they retained professional architectural designers to execute their visions, determined how to allocate gendered design in space, and how genders would interact within their campus walls. (For example, one might see shared spaces in the lecture hall and dining hall and in corridors, much more specific gendering in the various trades shops and classrooms, and gender-specific spaces such as dormitories.) These two women traversed the different categories of gender, race, class, and different stakeholder communities effectively: from slavery to freedom, from inspecting monolithically male workshops and construction sites, and meeting with elite Northern architects (both Black and white) and white Northern philanthropists.

Early Postbellum African American Schooling

In the postbellum era, the goal of basic literacy for all recently freed men and women became the most important agenda for social reformers. Mission societies had already established schools in the South in 1862 and remained involved in Black education well into the twentieth century with the American Missionary Association being the largest society. Mission schools were soon followed by the Freedman's Bureau, which in 1865 taught some 250,000 students in some

4,000 schools before disbanding in 1870. Many of the teachers at the Bureau were from prosperous white New England families that had been involved in abolitionist and antislavery societies before the war. Few of the early teachers were African American, as Black faculty cohorts were still lacking formal educational credentials. When Black teachers were hired, they were often assigned to segregated housing and to the more remote schools. However, many observers recognized that Black teachers were far more effective than whites in all-Black schools. One such example is Charlotte Forten, who had been born into a prosperous Black Philadelphia family and who taught at South Carolina's Penn School in the Sea Islands.[18] Another Black female teacher, Mary Peake, established one of the earliest schools on her own at Fortress Monroe, Virginia, in September 1861. Elsewhere, Black female educators also founded institutions to educate Black youth: Cornelia Bowen, founder of Mount Meigs Institute in Alabama (1888); Lucy Lainey, founder of Haines Normal Institute in Atlanta, Georgia (1886); and Emma J. Wilson, founder of the Mayesville Institute in Mayesville, South Carolina (1896).[19] Faculty in Progressive era institutions such as these would soon be overwhelmingly of color—recent institution graduates were rolled over into the ranks of the faculty—unlike the mixed faculty back in the day of the Freedman's Schools.

Many of these institutions shared a similar fate, with few surviving into the first half of the twentieth century, hampered by their often limited financial resources, low student enrollments, and the struggle over their control with white Northern philanthropists and their religious affiliates. Some Southern HBCUs have been absorbed into state systems of higher education. Some continue to have viable missions. For example, in 1904 Mary McLeod Bethune founded her own school, the Daytona Educational and Industrial Institute in Daytona Beach, Florida, which survives as Bethune-Cookman University, and today possesses a solid endowment and a growing number of students and programs. The school's roots can be attributed to Bethune's involvement in the Progressive era Black women's club movement and, like many educated, "genteel" African American clubwomen, Bethune distanced herself from the achievements and efforts of working-class women—unlike Wright and Dean, who saw themselves as no different from other women with a common goal of racial reform.[20]

It is estimated that in 1860 only 5–10 percent of the adult Black Southern population, both free and slave, were literate. By the 1830s, every Southern state, except for Tennessee, had prohibited the instruction of slaves, yet some education of African Americans continued to take place in the South before the Civil War in direct violation of state laws there.[21] Advocates of Black education included slave owners, who wanted a more efficient workforce, and missionaries, who insisted that slaves be able to read the Bible.[22] Interestingly, according to his great-great-great grandsons, Stonewall Jackson himself, the legendary Confederate general, had taught Sunday School in Lexington, Virginia, to slaves there, a "potentially criminal activity at the time."[23]

In the period immediately after the Civil War, churches served dual roles as religious and social centers, helping to search and reunite those Black families that had been sold and dispersed under slavery. Recently emancipated people now freely took part in church services, and the church also became the central focal point of the community as the first and only totally Black-owned institution.[24] Schools supported by the Freedman's Bureau often occupied Black churches or were built on Black-owned property. Church ministers also encouraged rural Black farmers to purchase new school property.[25] Purchasing land for schools was deeply rooted in the cooperative activities of rural life. As one teacher suggested to the local community, "We advise you to educate your children, give them trades and thereby qualify them for any position in life. For if ever we are raised to that elevated summit in life for which we are striving, it must be done by our individual exertion; no one can do it for us."[26] Grassroots educational planning was significant because so few African American farmers as yet owned their own land or could afford to purchase property.

With the support of the Freedmen's Bureau and Northern freedmen's aid societies, free Blacks were now able to create some autonomy in the face of white hostility. The Bureau encouraged the development of more schools, provided teachers for them, and, in general, helped shape Southern education. It was anticipated that in the short term, schooling would provide African Americans with basic literacy skills and hence citizen participation at the ballot box. In the long term, for the Black nation there would be intellectual and moral development that would, in turn, foster a responsible leadership class organizing the masses into full equality. These institutions also brought an educated class into rural areas whose charge was to grow the educated classes in heretofore largely illiterate regions.[27] One longtime supporter of Black education wrote, "This was no thought of white people or of philanthropists carried to them, nor even from an outsider did the suggestion come. It came from the people themselves. No one said, you ought to have an industrial school. The colored people themselves, said we ought to have an industrial school, and bravely they set to work to gain it."[28]

Denied schooling under enslavement and later oppressed by a legal system based on a white-supremacist ideology, Black women reformers felt that the industrial school, like no other institution, could secure the promise of Emancipation and the nation's new founding, something that became pivotal in the development of women's employment and activism. At the industrial school there existed a place where African Americans could secure knowledge of and practice in the latest innovations in the emerging industrial society. A painful past under enslavement had left many with memories that would forever shape their relationships with the newly reunified nation.[29] Lingering questions concerning their involvement in preserving and reinventing the American nation would soon be answered by their efforts at institution building and nation making. Institutions founded by these women reformers on behalf of the Black community were based on different cultural values, attitudes, and perceptions.

Drawing African American youth from the poor and rural South, and dressing their students in neat school uniforms as if in one stroke to erase any trace of the students' class and background, these industrial schools provided the training necessary for their graduates to join the educated working classes as skilled tradesmen or normal school teachers of both genders. Gendered education persisted at these training schools. Documenting overwhelmingly male classes and disciplines, photographs from the period show woodworking, masonry, and ironworking as gendered and male. And yet there are fascinating exceptions to these monolithically gendered classrooms and settings. The cover art for this book, a photograph by Frances Benjamin Johnston, shows an African American mixed-gender mathematics class—using the example of the Tuskegee Office Building, then under construction, as both a mathematics problem in surface area of a complex volume, and a building trades case study for calculation of surface area of bricks necessary to build it.

Historian Glenda Gilmore maintains that one widespread perception of the postbellum era then in circulation was that allegedly, Black home life was debased. African American reformers believed it imperative to address this debate in defense of the African American home and coupled this with their arguments in favor of industrial education. Gilmore has essayed on gendered industrial education and home economics for women during this period. She maintains that African American women were in essence training to be servants in domestic economies, as the only strictly industrial positions available to women were as laundresses or tobacco factory workers.[30]

By the most outward of metrics, the project of the African American nation was well underway and a Black educated class continued to take root. A powerful intersectional analysis is applied here with respect to the racial/gendered/classed significance of these campuses. Simply put, Black women were now among institutional leaders and were conspicuous as public-facing fund-raisers. Wright and Dean were, to all appearances, setting educational agenda, taking leadership roles in the design of their respective campuses, and acting as hosts to representatives from white communities when they entered their spaces. At both their campuses, Wright and Dean were also interacting regularly with elite northerners for external funding.[31] Indeed, there was competition for the dollars of both Northern philanthropists and local communities across these industrial schools and HBCUs, with Gilmore suggesting that there were the phenomena of "overnight wonders" in Black education that had sprung up to meet the growing demand.[32] By 1890, the number of HBCUs rose to over forty.[33]

Elizabeth Evelyn Wright: Tuskegee Race Woman

Inspired by the Tuskegee Institute model, Elizabeth Evelyn Wright became the very first African American woman to serve as principal of an autonomous, all-Black private school in the state of South Carolina. The school she founded and headed, Voorhees Industrial School, provided an opportunity for a growing body of race leaders in education and, more specifically, in the mechanical and industrial arts to carry Tuskegee's approach to uplift strategies into regions outside of Washington's powerful sphere of influence in the state of Alabama. Curiously, Elizabeth Wright herself only learned of Tuskegee in a rather happenstance way.[34]

Wright's first biographer recounts how, at age fourteen, this young Georgia girl initially learned of the opportunities to be had at Tuskegee: "A gentle wind arose from the southeast and was blowing briskly, when it lifted a ragged piece of newspaper from the shallow trench that separated the sidewalk from the street ... when it rose and circled and fell at her feet [Wright] became mildly curious to find out what message this strange visitor had brought."[35] When she picked up the paper, Wright was soon reading an advertisement describing the work underway at the Tuskegee Industrial School. The advertisement "told briefly how poor colored boys and girls could get an education by working their way through school. And as [sic] a picture of one of the early campus buildings was a part of the advertisement."[36] Had it not been for that strange occurrence, Wright might have never learned of Tuskegee and Booker T. Washington's important accomplishments in rural Alabama, and American history may have been deprived of the educational efforts of a pioneering race woman.

Elizabeth Evelyn Wright was born on August 18, 1872, on the William Rolfe farm some three miles from the courthouse in Talbotton, Georgia.[37] She was the seventh child of a blended family of twenty-one children—nineteen of whom were fathered by John Wesley Wright, a successful Black carpenter.[38] Wright's mother, Virginia Rolfe, was a full-blooded Cherokee described as "a beautiful Indian woman about five feet tall with long black hair and a light copper complexion." Virginia's first husband, Stephen Fowlkes, with whom she had two children, had died while working in Columbus, Georgia, during the Civil War. Virginia then married John Wesley Wright.

Talbotton, one of the oldest towns in Georgia, was infamous for its cruel treatment of Blacks and Indigenous peoples, especially from the late eighteenth century onward. The Cherokee had by then established a fully functioning and well-organized nation with its own school system and native houses of worship. They had built a capital city, New Echota, where they even printed their own newspaper. Unfortunately, at the beginning of the nineteenth century gold was discovered in the area, and by 1834 the Cherokee were given two years to vacate the land and abandon the homes they had long called their own. Several Cherokee families, including the family of Virginia Rolfe, did manage to elude the invading federal troops.[39]

The county had relied heavily on its enslaved population for cotton production during the antebellum era. After Emancipation, Talbotton remained a backwater farming community dependent on the sharecropping system. Wright herself was born in a small, unpainted three-room cabin that her father had purchased shortly after the Civil War. The family farm was located adjacent to Smith Hill, a neighborhood containing most of Talbotton's Black population. Maj. Ezekiel B. Smith, a local planter, had owned much of the area that was resettled by recently freed Blacks. Smith Hill was originally the plantation's slave quarters and later became the center of African American life in Talbotton.[40]

Education for whites had been a priority in Talbot County since its founding in the early nineteenth century. In 1830 Talbot's General Assembly helped establish the Talbotton Female Academy, later renamed the LeVert College. In succeeding years, its example was quickly followed by some twenty new schools and academies of instruction. A school for boys, Collinworth Institute, was also founded in the late 1830s. By 1870, the Georgia General Assembly passed the first law requiring public school education for all children, regardless of race. Prior to the law, Black schooling had been traditionally underserved because of a lack of qualified teachers, places of instruction, and materials. St. Philip's Church, home to Smith Hill's Black congregation, was used as a school when available for the three-month per-year period that was required by law.[41]

At age either seven or eight, Wright attended the district school held in St. Philip's Church. The church structure itself was an unfinished weatherboard structure covered with oak boards and was almost impossible to heat sufficiently in winter. The coldest months were often the most poorly attended, and were especially hard on small children such as Wright, who owned very little outerwear. That first year, Wright and her classmates attended fewer than twelve full days of instruction over the three-month period. The uncomfortably tall benches made it difficult for Wright to begin learning her ABCs, the mechanics of writing, or even basic arithmetic.[42]

When Wright was ten years old, her uncle helped move Wright and her grandmother into town, where school facilities were better. There, lessons were given by a white woman from outside the South. The school year was considerably longer than at St. Philip's, and Wright quickly excelled in her studies. By age fourteen, Wright had completed much of her education at the town school and was eager to push her studies even further, planning to become a teacher for the race. After that fateful encounter with the newspaper advertisement— and her subsequent outreach to the Institute—Wright learned more about Tuskegee's race-work efforts from the brochures and application materials sent to her at the local post office. Upon reviewing the literature, she understood that the school had helped to improve conditions in eastern Alabama through industrial and manual school training—assistance of the sort that had been most desperately needed there since the earliest years post-Emancipation.[43]

At fourteen, Wright broke the news to her family—specifically, her uncle and grandmother, Jus W. Tolge and Lydia Rolfe—that she wanted to attend the Tuskegee State Normal School in Alabama. They strongly discouraged her from even applying. They believed that it was impossible for a girl of mixed-race heritage, especially African American and Indigenous, to succeed in a world outside her own immediate, unique community. Wright's teacher, a Northern white woman, helped her to convince her family to support her decision to attend Tuskegee. The family relented, and Wright took on odd jobs to help pay for her expenses and transportation costs to Alabama from Georgia.[44]

Washington's efforts at Tuskegee left an indelible mark on Wright, one that led her to recognize the unique opportunities ahead for African American women who wished to better the race. Wright recalls, "I was at Tuskegee only a short time before I made up my mind to try and be the same type of woman as Mr. Washington was of a man.... The talks which he gave us on Sundays evenings in the Chapel did more to mold my character than anything else. His talks influenced me to try to help my fellow men to help themselves, and if a way was not opened for me, I must open it myself."[45]

At Tuskegee, Wright forged critical relationships with key race women who encouraged her education and solidified her resolve to contribute to this emerging social movement. Davidson must have seen a great deal of potential in Wright despite the young woman's physical frailties. Wright learned much from her mentor, especially concerning Blacks' immediate need for adequate housing to improve their living conditions. However, Wright was able to work with her for only a short period of time before Davidson, her own lifelong battle with tuberculosis exacerbated by injuries from a house fire, died in May 1889. Davidson's keen interest in Wright's cause had already helped the young woman to remain at Tuskegee to realize her dream. Of this period in Wright's life, her biographer J. F. B. Coleman writes:

> [she] lived even now in the school her mind had framed; and for this reason was least annoyed by adverse circumstances. She was already helping her people to the extent of her longings and felt not the thankless drudgery of her present labors. Among strangers and along the weary way she toiled, but to her it was not toil, because it anticipated an industrial school, affording educational opportunities for her neglected people.[46]

After Davidson's death, Wright befriended Booker T. Washington's third wife, Margaret Murray, who presumably introduced Wright to the assortment of women activists who often visited the Washingtons' home, The Oaks.[47] Murray, much like Davidson, was actively involved in the struggle over race uplift and was similarly committed to women's rights issues. Murray proved to be a close mentor and friend during Wright's remaining years at Tuskegee.[48]

Despite all her industrial training, Wright's education at Tuskegee had not prepared her to deal with the realities of racial discrimination and violence against African Americans. In the face of several failed attempts to found her all-Black school in South Carolina, Wright also survived acts of arson perpetrated against her by white terrorist militia groups. Documentation exists of a night in June 1894, in Varnville, South Carolina, when Wright, intending to erect a new school building there, awoke to witness two loads of lumber (delivered the previous day) that were now suspiciously ablaze. Little could be done to save the costly building materials, which had been set aside for work the next morning. This particular act of arson, believed to be the work of the local Ku Klux Klan, was not an isolated one—terror such as this was rampant throughout the New South.

Incidents such as these would ultimately not deter her dream of an independent and autonomous school for Africans Americans in South Carolina. Wright was well aware that white resistance to Black educational achievement was based, in part, on the belief that it undermined the economy of the South and threatened the supply of cheap agricultural labor.[49] An educated and informed Black working class would also further threaten an already contested white power structure. Although whites considered Booker T. Washington a moderate for publicly advocating vocational training over a more classically based education for African Americans, many of his students understood how a more radical social agenda could be achieved by establishing schools modeled after Tuskegee.[50]

Wright continued her search for a permanent site in South Carolina, where she could establish an industrial school modeled after her alma mater, Tuskegee. In Denmark, South Carolina, Wright wrote to Booker T. Washington: "since I have seen the condition of the people here, I feel that nothing would do them more good than an 'industrial school' and I am working very hard to that effect. I have a [new] tract in view containing nine hundred acres, two stores which may be turned into school rooms and a six-room cottage."[51] Located in Bamberg County, Denmark was a flourishing rural town with a population of about five hundred in 1897. Denmark was originally known as Graham's, named after the Z. G. Graham family, who owned property there and who in 1837 sold some seventeen acres to the Charleston-Hamburg Railroad. Graham's name was changed in 1891 after a local family of railroad promoters renamed it Denmark. By 1900, the population of Denmark was 739, comprising 379 whites and 360 African Americans. Many more African Americans lived in the surrounding rural areas. Only five Black families owned their own farms and ten others rented property. The town could boast two lawyers, two physicians, a dentist, and eight telegraph operators along with several shops, a restaurant, and a local newspaper office. Denmark's most prominent citizen, Stanwix Mayfield, a white member of the State Constitutional Convention and a successful lawyer in Denmark who often assisted African Americans through legal counsel, believed strongly in Wright's cause. Mayfield, along with Rep. J. E. Ellerbe, had also been influential in establishing a uniform school law for South Carolina. Wright could not have found a more supportive advocate and financial supporter than in Mayfield, especially among those Southern whites holding political office.[52]

Reports from the State Superintendent's Office of Education listed no graded public school for either Blacks or whites, and no public high school or even local academy in the Denmark region. Locally, only 108 one-room schoolhouses existed for African Americans—15 of which were constructed of partially hewn logs; the remaining 93 were wood-frame buildings. Only some 50 of those total structures were considered in good condition. Black teachers numbered only 104, often earning little more than $14 a month, while white teachers earned more than double at almost $35. White parents who could afford to do so provided private tutors for their children. The illiteracy rate in South Carolina exceeded 45 percent, the second highest in the United States. By comparison, illiteracy in the North Atlantic states was just below 7 percent.[53] In the face of circumstances such as these, Wright, supported by several other Black teachers, was determined to open a school and begin a program similar to that of Tuskegee.

Wright told Booker T. Washington that she had her sights on a property of some 20 acres in Denmark, South Carolina, owned by Mayfield. The tract was adjacent to a Black church and already held an old two-story frame plantation house and two smaller structures that could be used as temporary facilities.[54] Wright was confident she could raise some of the purchase money from local Black congregations. In a letter to Washington, she writes, "I have been visiting the churches in the counties in which I labor and the people would give small sums toward the work."[55] In hindsight, the property she purchased from Mayfield would not allow for a school with ambitions similar to Tuskegee's— that is, one that accommodated both school buildings along with a sizable tract of land to be set aside for agricultural work. In 1901, after occupying several temporary locations in and around the Denmark area, Wright determined she would purchase some 280 acres of land from Dr. S. M. Guess, a local physician. Wright was, however, left to face the final challenge of raising the $3,000 asking price for the Guess property. Fortunately, several lengthy letters of introduction induced New Jersey philanthropist Ralph Voorhees within a month to provide a substantial contribution of $5,000 for the purchase of the Guess property and for the erection of its first permanent structure—Kennerly Hall (figure 30).[56] Thus, over the years, she had finally secured her school's future with the financial backing of both the local Black community and, ultimately, Northern philanthropists.

Wright felt strongly that the school—originally named the Denmark Industrial School and renamed in 1904 as the Voorhees Industrial School for Colored Youths in Ralph Voorhees's honor—should follow Tuskegee's example in all its efforts. Unfortunately, Voorhees's typically straitened finances were such that it was difficult to implement development for all its programs. Describing the school's various programs, Wright suggested:

Our industrial work is not what we want it to be, for the lack of means. Our students are taught dairying on a small scale, some are taught cooking, laundering and house-keeping. Our boys are taught farming, the care of stock and the dignity of labor in general. One of our students has charge of our small shoe shop and is doing satisfactory work. We carry out the Tuskegee idea as far as possible and this is the only school in the state on a similar order.[57]

Boarding students numbered about 100, with roughly 280 day students. Wright's teaching staff included 15 teachers, 8 of whom, by 1905, were graduates of Tuskegee.[58] Of her teaching faculty, those responsible for carpentry and drawing were also from Tuskegee.[59]

Suffering from a series of chronic illnesses, Elizabeth Evelyn Wright was eventually admitted to the Battle Creek Sanitarium in Michigan in October 1906. She appeared to be recovering from her surgery for chronic gastritis, but suffered a relapse and died on December 14, 1906, only thirty-four years old. Her lifelong battle with chronic illness, a legacy of her early years living under hardship conditions, had finally claimed the last of her body and will. By 1923, the local Black population, the Protestant Episcopal Church, and the American Church Institute for Negroes were providing financial support so that Voorhees could remain open. The school, struggling to maintain its operations, managed to secure state support by 1948 as the only school for Blacks in the Denmark area. In 1967, the school began offering a four-year program and was renamed Voorhees College. Today, the school continues to serve the needs of its largely African American student population. The school retains its affiliation with the Episcopal Church, remains modest in size with a student body of six hundred, and has a restricted operating budget. To date, no period in the school's history has duplicated the rapid expansion and change experienced during Wright's effective leadership.

Through her many efforts, Wright was able to secure a future for the school and the local Black community. The school's central mission was to promote political, economic, and social autonomy for Blacks. Voorhees was seen as the "product of a consecrated life, built in the midst of the people who need it most." This is much like another female-led Black vocational school that had been founded just a few years prior, but without any direct connection to the Tuskegee Institute: the Manassas Industrial School for Colored Youth.[60]

Jennie Dean, Former Slave and Reformer

Not only did the founder of the Virginia-based Manassas Industrial School for Colored Youth lack the benefit of a Tuskegee education, Jennie Serepta Dean was born a slave on April 15, 1848, in Loudon County, Virginia. She would die too soon, worn out from disease and the stresses of a backbreaking life at the age of sixty-five in 1913.[61] Dean's father, Charles Dean, was born in Prince William County, Virginia, as was her mother, Annie Stewart. Both Charles Dean and Annie Stewart were slaves who apparently lived in close proximity to one another within the county. By all accounts, Annie Stewart was a cook and so was probably held in some respect by both Blacks and whites, as were most cooks for their ability to manage a household. As the property of a nearby farming family, Charles might have conceivably met Annie if he had been farmed out as a hired hand by his owner at the Newman plantation,[62] since, as the antebellum era progressed, many farmers solved their labor problems by employing other people's slaves.[63] Catherine (or Miss Kitty) Newman is believed to have owned Charles Dean for some thirty years, beginning in 1820, when Thomas Newman willed Charles's parents and their seven children to his daughter. In 1850, at her death, Miss Kitty willed Charles Dean and his brother Reuben to her nephew Crawford Cushing.[64] Jennie Dean and her sisters, Ella, Nettie, and Mary, were all born on the Cushing farm.

Dean, like all enslaved children, probably began her working life at the age of six or even earlier, depending on her size and maturity level. On large plantations, gender distinctions were established early on by both masters and overseers, with boys learning to herd sheep and cattle while girls watched over small children or worked in the kitchen. Owners did not often spare women from field labor unless they were talented seamstresses, weavers, midwives, or cooks. As one Virginia slave described a typical workday, "We wuked f'om four o'clock in de mornin' 'till midnight. At night slaves would build bon fiahs to wuk by. Effen you only wuk 'till leven o'clock, you had to pick cotton after dat. De little boys an' ev'ybody had to wuk. No res' fer niggers 'till God he step in an' put a stop to de white folks meanness."[65] Children often began their agricultural training on the plantations by picking up trash or loose stones in the field. As children grew older, they eventually helped stack and bind wheat, pull weeds, care for livestock, pick fruit, and carry water.[66]

As E. Franklin Frazier noted as far back as 1930 in his article in *The Journal of Negro History*, "The Negro Slave Family," slaves struggled to maintain a coherent family structure against masters who often broke up slave families: "social interaction within their own world on the plantation created a social life among them with nearly all the features of any society."[67] Luckily, the Deans were able to remain together as a family along with several members of their extended family. Of her experiences growing up under slavery, Dean might have reflected as former slave Tempie Cummins did in the 1930s:

> I slep' on a pallet on the floor. They give me a homespun dress onct a year at Christmas time. When company come, I had to run and slip on that dress. At other time, I wore white chillens' cast-off clothes, so wore [worn] they was ready to throw away. I had to pin them up with red horse thorns to hide my nakedness. My dress was usually split from hem to neck and I had to wear

them till they was strings. Went barefoot summer and winter till the feets crack open.[68]

To whites in the 1840s and 1850s, the area in which Dean grew up was little more than a series of large plantations. Liberia, the largest plantation, was a tract of two thousand acres owned by Mr. William I. Weir. Nearby on the old Centreville Road was a small grocery store and the Tudor Hall post office, used primarily by slaves and locals scattered over the county. This was the very first store between the villages of Centreville and Brentsville, considered the most important villages of their respective counties. By 1860, there were 853 people living in the Manassas area: 548 whites, 260 slaves, and 45 free Blacks. Its soil exhausted after decades of cultivation, surrounding Prince William County by 1860 had 8,565 people, declining significantly from 1800, when over 12,733 people were noted on census records.[69]

The expansion of rail lines in the Manassas area was the catalyst for two significant Civil War battles there. After hostilities broke out in 1861 between North and South, Confederate Gen. Robert E. Lee foresaw that the Manassas railroad junction—the only link to Southern supplies—was vulnerable to attack.[70] At the First Battle of Manassas in July 1861, the Confederates defeated the Union Army, destroying the Union's early hopes of invading the Confederate capital of Richmond. The Union armies tried to capture the city of Richmond a second time during the Peninsular Campaign of 1862, but failed again. McClellan's many failures during the last campaign spurred federal officials to charge Gen. John Pope with orders to reorganize the troops. Leading them into the Second Battle of Manassas and a second defeat, the Confederacy then turned Manassas Junction into a store and quartermaster depot to supply the troops.[71] The battlegrounds would later comprise, in part, the land for Jennie Dean's Manassas Industrial School complex, reinscribing the site with the history of the formerly enslaved.

After the war, the Southern landscape recovered very slowly, especially in the Manassas area. Farms had been occupied by both Union and Confederate troops, leaving very little agricultural infrastructure intact. Large landholders no longer had enslaved labor to cultivate the fields and many initially reverted to subsistence crop production and the raising of livestock before sharecropping with African American tenant farmers became widespread.[72] Black families had left Virginia in the late 1880s in search of a better life with many of them moving north for improved opportunities in employment and education. Soon after Emancipation Charles Dean had settled down on a farm near Sudley Springs, Virginia, on the actual battleground of Bull Run. Accounts suggest that Charles Dean had gathered just enough money in 1886 to purchase the property from Thomas Settle, but, unfortunately, he died before the deeds were completed. Jennie Dean herself helped to purchase the farm through additional work as a domestic servant in nearby Washington, DC. She sent home her wages to help support the family and to pay off the remaining debt on the property. She also helped to finance her sister Ella's education at Wayland Seminary in Washington, DC, which prepared Ella for her later role as a minister's wife.[73] While working as a domestic in Washington, DC, Dean herself could easily have become acquainted with the Hampton Normal and Agricultural Institute (now Hampton University), as well as nearby Howard University (founded in 1869).

With the founding of Black common schools throughout the South after the Civil War, substantial efforts were being made to promote literacy. By the time Dean began her work to found an industrial school in Prince William County in the 1880s, the national literacy rate for African Americans had risen to 30 percent. In Prince William County, a number of elementary schools for Black children had already opened by the time Dean finally founded Manassas in 1893: Manley School in 1871, Macrae School in the 1870s, Brown School in 1870, Chinn School in 1874, Catharpin Colored School in 1877, Summitt School in 1883, and Thoroughfare Colored School in 1884. All of these schools received little in the way of educational supplies and were often open for fewer months in the school year than those reserved for whites.[74] Opportunities for Black children to learn at the elementary school level were few because so many were required to work on farms or at unskilled jobs to help support their families.

Dean herself received very little formal education. She is believed to have spent the first few years of her education in the Congregational Bible Mission School, a public school for "colored" children in Prince William County. It might only have been a very short time until she was required to work to help support her family and leave school. On Sunday afternoons in Washington, Dean attended the colored Sunday School of the Nineteenth Street Baptist Church. She soon became a member of the church; its minister, Rev. Walter H. Brooks, encouraged her to continue her missionary work back home.[75] She returned to Virginia and spent Saturday afternoons conducting classes in cooking and sewing. On Sunday afternoons, she held classes for the young.[76] Dean's first mission church, Mt. Calvary Chapel, was a product of these initial meetings and informal gatherings.[77] Dean's earliest community-building efforts began with the founding of several churches organized at Conklin, Wellington Mission, Prosperity, and Burkes. Pilgrim's Rest was a Black settlement in the mountains of Loudon County, Virginia, settled sometime shortly after Emancipation.[78]

However, Dean was not interested simply in helping to build churches; she wished to create social settlements—whole communities—that promoted uplift. Describing her missionary work, Reverend Brooks recalled that "when the opportunity came, she returned to the area of her birth where she had conceived the vision of actual need and then went far and near, on horseback or in her little old sulky, planting Sunday Schools and otherwise laboring to make Christ known and to teach his Gospel."[79] Despite her early status as chattel in the eyes of whites, Dean never wavered in the belief that she possessed self-worth before her God. Her exposure to folk religion as a slave also laid the foundations of a nationalist consciousness and spiritual understanding to preach the fundamentals of an African-descended faith at churches and other communities.[80] In Virginia, surviving African values, especially those expressed in the context of spirituals and folktales, helped reinforce Dean's commitment to her race and community.[81] A nationalist consciousness such as Dean's, which promoted racial uplift strategies and the continued growth of the all-Black institutions that had emerged since Emancipation, would soon physically alter the Southern landscape.

Social conditions in the New South did not easily promote Black advancement, especially in education, and Jennie Dean believed that if the industrial school were to be built, she would have to turn to Northern philanthropists for financial support. Whites regarded the education of African Americans as a means of openly questioning the legitimacy of white supremacy, thereby enabling Blacks to challenge the power of Jim Crow legislation.[82] The outward symbolism of these signs of nation building was not lost on local white constituencies; a "suspicious" fire—arson targeted against African Americans—was not uncommon. Church and school burnings were attacks on the Black community's ability to buy land and organize schools. Describing a blaze that destroyed her school, one teacher wrote, "Some malicious person or persons set fire to the church in which we have been holding our school. . . . Of course, nothing could be done to save the building. It is a great loss to the people here, as they are very poor, and will not be able to build another, perhaps for years."[83] White fears of Black land ownership and subsequent empowerment were in tandem with their fears of political enfranchisement.

Dean sought support outside of the South, preferably among progressive-minded Northern reformers and religious leaders.[84] She turned to her friend, Reverend Brooks of the Nineteenth-Street Baptist Church in Washington, DC. A former slave, Brooks had been educated at Wilberforce Institute in Ohio and Lincoln University in Pennsylvania, both Northern HBCUs. Brooks was a strong believer in the necessity for Black educational advancement and assisted Dean with her missionary endeavors.[85] Serving as a choir member and pianist at his church, she had often confided in Brooks about her plans to fund the ever-growing independent church movement and to help establish a school in northern Virginia for Blacks.

In 1888 Dean shared her vision for the school with Rev. Marshall D. Williams of the First Baptist Church in Manassas, and her brother-in-law, Rev. Lewis H. Bailey. Both men supported her idea and began preaching from their pulpits about the benefits of such an ambitious plan.[86] Soon interested parents and individuals formed committees and solicited financial support from the community. Dean encouraged local parents to work and save money for the school, even promoting a Fourth of July dinner as a charity fund-raiser.

Reverend Brooks was well connected with both Northern Black and white religious leadership, and he introduced Dean to Rev. Edward Everett Hale of Massachusetts, founder of the national Lend a Hand Society and a longtime supporter of Black educational reform.[87] After learning of her plans, Reverend Hale asked Dean to visit him in Boston to seek the financial support of the white Beacon Hill establishment. Following Hale's advice, Dean, almost forty, went to Boston in the summer of 1891, working as a boardinghouse cook by day in Marion, Massachusetts, and garnering support for her project through public-speaking engagements at night. Boston's African American community—famous to Blacks well outside the city's borders because its leaders were regarded as more politically radical in their attempts to fight Jim Crow—had settled in Boston's South End and Lower Roxbury districts in the late 1880s. Presumably, Dean became familiar with them.[88]

Hale's Lend a Hand Society provided Dean with a venue for her work as a singer and itinerant preacher, and further supported her with proceeds from local charity events. In Hale's own words, the Lend a Hand organization believed strongly "that every inducement possible should be held out to the colored people to acquire an education, for their own good and for the good of this country."[89] The organization was also involved heavily in promoting legislation: "To this end our statesmen should devise some means of giving to those who are qualified all the rights of citizenship in fact, as well as in law. There should be no objection to a man's voting if he can read and write. . . . "[90] Dean had chanced upon an idealistic organization that was sympathetic to her own beliefs, and she made the Lend a Hand office in Boston her headquarters. When she told them of her elaborate plans, many people were interested and supported her long-term goals. At a gathering in the autumn of 1892 at Manassas Junction, African Americans gathered from all the surrounding towns to celebrate Dean's securing a farm site for the school.[91] Dean's passion and commitment to Black education and the Sunday School movement were shaped by the same desires of many Black Virginians, who had been similarly agitating for "race uplift" since the close of the Civil War.[92]

Emily Howland, a longtime suffragist and former abolitionist living in the small upstate New York community of Sherwood, was also influential in supporting Dean's career as a public speaker promoting African American social causes.[93] Howland had founded and provided support for—in her overwhelmingly white rural town of Sherwood—her own school, the Sherwood Select School.[94] Also at that time, Howland, a white social reformer, had a track record establishing Black industrial schools, beginning with her financial support of Booker T. Washington's Tuskegee Institute. In addition, with Howland's financial support, the Howland Chapel School was built to serve the children of former slaves in Heathsville, Virginia, shortly after the Civil War.[95] Howland not only provided financial support for the Manassas Industrial School, but also helped introduce Dean to some of New York's leading suffragists. It seems probable that Howland would have provided Dean an introduction to Susan B. Anthony, legendary white suffragist, especially given the proximity of Howland's residence in Sherwood, New York, in New York's Finger Lakes, to Anthony's in the nearby city of Rochester, New York.

In 1893, the same year as the World's Columbian Exposition, Dean appealed to Susan B. Anthony to permit her to speak before the National American Woman Suffrage Association Convention in Washington, DC. As she stood at the podium before the delegation of women suffragists, Dean might have recalled the festivities at Lincoln Park in Washington in commemoration of the fourteenth anniversary of Emancipation almost two decades previously. Anthony, although committed only to advancing the causes of white women's suffrage—she had ruled out the possibility of universal suffrage as infeasible—allowed Dean to make her speech soliciting support for the Manassas Industrial School. Convention attendees ultimately pledged $2,000 in support of the school, thus helping to secure its charter.[96]

Dean's character and strength of will is attested to in a series of letters exchanged between Howland and another reformer, Jane E. Thompson of Thoroughfare Gap, Virginia. Thompson, a white woman whose family had owned slaves before the war, had helped Dean found the Manassas Industrial School and later taught, assisted with fund-raising, and served on the Board of Directors at the school. Describing Dean's efforts that helped establish a small Black church settlement, Thompson wrote, "unless she can be with them a number of times to direct and plan they cannot succeed—they look to her to do this, and she is fully capable."[97] Here is Thompson describing Dean as she endeavored to solicit funds from Howland for Dean's model communities:

> If she can't raise corn she can, with a little help, raise good deeds among her people. With all her work for the Manassas School, and all the money she has brought to it, she receives no help on salary from them except when she is actually in field, and then just enough to live on. Her living at home is derived from her few chickens, her garden she works herself.[98]

In a letter to Howland seeking additional funds, Thompson described how "Jennie Dean put her best years into it, to want to succeed, or be the highest and best that we can make it."[99]

By 1893 Dean's school was officially chartered as the Manassas Industrial School for Colored Youth. In October 1894 the school opened and six pupils were admitted; enrollment soon increased to about seventy-five. The faculty included a Dr. Clemens, acting principal; Mr. Jeff Thomas, teacher in carpentry; Mrs. Clemens, sewing teacher; and Miss M. E. Vernon, cooking teacher, matron, housekeeper, and literary teacher.[100] During its lifetime from 1893 to 1938, the Manassas Industrial School grew from a bare one hundred–acre site to a two hundred–acre campus. The school held classes in sewing, carpentry, laundry, blacksmithing, wheelwrighting, cooking, dairying, and poultry husbandry; its eight instructors also assumed the teaching of strictly academic subjects. Faculty at Manassas had graduated from historically Black colleges and universities such as Howard and Hampton.

As the kind of curriculum once promoted for African Americans was now widely believed to be unable to critically transform the material circumstances of a family's life, a school modeled after Hampton or Tuskegee was assumed to better target their needs.[101] Nonetheless, Dean exposed her students to a curriculum that included course work in traditional academic subjects as well as in industrial training. The academic subjects taught over the course of four years included spelling, arithmetic, drawing, hygiene, geography, and grammar. Students were also required to take reading, penmanship, United States and Virginia history, elementary physics and chemistry, English and American literature, and government.[102] As the course catalog made clear, "Every effort is made to have the studies of the course constantly and closely related to the actual work which the student will have to do, and to the actual life which he will have to live."[103] Interestingly, Dean also felt that the course in English was useful for the "training of the imagination . . . the imagination which will quicken the boy or girl returning to his home in the country to see the possibilities of worthy service to his people right where he is."[104] The English course would also highlight the "worthy productions by Negro writers," inevitably examining the literary works of African women writers and reformers.[105] The course in history began in the second year to study the life stories of "great Americans" with a focus on the genre of American biography. In the third year of study the course focused on race history and the influences African Americans had on the industrial, political, and social changes taking place in the United States since their arrival as slaves. Despite her probable borderline literacy and lack of formal education, Dean saw to it that that third-year students in the history course also studied the Old Testament story of the Hebrews for comparison with the life story of African Americans.[106]

As an active fund-raiser for the school, Dean also emphasized the importance of expanding the physical campus through the promotion of various building campaigns. In her efforts to raise funds for new construction, she often sent letters to potential donors and friends of the school.[107] Each of her successful trips and endorsements of the school meant more work for her students engaged in the expansion of the physical plant at Manassas and the industrial programs there. For example, the course of study in carpentry provided its students with the training necessary to become craftsmen and artisans. Throughout the four-year program, students were engaged in various aspects of building construction such as framing, sizing studs, shingling, stairway building, setting window and doorframes, and house building.[108]

Although we may never know her specific reasons for choosing to work with white philanthropists, benefactors, architects, and planners, it is clear that she remained singularly committed to promoting race history and community revitalization. In part, she may have simply chosen to "follow the money." She may have also been useful to white Northern liberals who wished to capitalize on her image as an itinerant preacher and former slave, working to garner support for Black education. As a pious and God-loving woman, she was so invested in the Black social project of race uplift that the record of her personal life outside that mission remains obscure and seemingly purposefully elusive.

And, indeed, it is often the case that the history of African American institutions is easier to reconstruct than the personal histories of their founders. Jennie Dean's personal life was largely overshadowed by the story of the institution she founded, as she solicited funds for campus projects and campaigned for other support. A 1901 account suggests that "the story of the building of Manassas Industrial School is almost the life story of Jennie Dean."[109] A second account of Dean's life, *Undaunted Faith: The Story of Jennie Dean, Missionary, Crusader, Builder*, published in 1942 and written by longtime family friend Stephen Johnson Lewis, suggests that Dean had "the life story of a woman whose sacrifices and vision matched well with those of Douglass, Lincoln, and Booker T. Washington."[110] Lewis tells how "[she had] faith in her power to make better the living conditions of her people and to save its youth from lives of wanton lust, idleness, degradation and servility to the influence of poverty."[111] Despite these personal descriptions from family and friends, Dean's inner life remains difficult to assess, with little documentation extant vis-à-vis her personal biography. No doubt, Dean lacks documentation in part because, as an enslaved woman denied formal schooling, she may have been for all intents and purposes borderline "literate."[112] But, I would argue, this lack of personal documentation is also a critical part of the construction of the legend of her identity and the traditions surrounding oral history, and the recording of the African American past. A description of Dean, written shortly after the founding of the school, maintains that "her brightness and quick powers of observation soon placed her in the position of a leader among her people. Added to this was an honesty, self-sacrifice and tender regard for others that own the love and respect of all that knew her."[113]

The most problematic of historical sources on Dean's life as a reformer survives as part of a fund-raising tool, *The Beginning of the Manassas Industrial School for Colored Youth and Its Growth*, published in 1900.[114] It is narrated in the first person, but, keeping in mind her likely limited ability to read or write, she probably recounted much of the text to a ghost writer. The school charged twenty cents for the purchase of this narrative. Despite the narrative's attribution to Dean as its author, it is difficult to determine her place in the spectrum of literacy from existing sources.[115] Scholars of adult education and literacy maintain that access to power and knowledge attainment determine and shape literacy access and available opportunity. Anderson argues that literacy among African Americans "differed sharply from the white experience . . . [and fails to] prepare one to understand the distinct experience of African Americans or to gauge the impact of their experiences on the nation's complex and contradictory attitudes regarding the rights of individuals to literacy."[116] Universal literacy was never favored by Southern whites, who felt strongly that illiteracy among slaves, free people of color, and tenant farmers was essential for continued white racial domination. For former slaves such as Dean, literacy development might have been restricted through limited instruction during childhood or through activity in the Black church.[117]

The letters and published accounts of Dean that do survive offer up a heroic portrayal of her and the events that shaped her seemingly tireless efforts in support of educational reform. In light of the difficulty inherent in the historical recovery of Dean's life, one must think more expansively about the methods of finding and interpreting historical evidence and sources,[118] developing, meanwhile, new methodologies that challenge the myth of invisibility surrounding African American women. The buildings once found at Dean's school site are a part of a "material truth" subject to physical decay and changing meaning caused by shifting political or cultural contexts as the viewer turns to the built environment for answers and new forms of evidence.

The very absence of materials personally related to Dean might also indicate an ongoing commitment to an oral tradition, including testimony and witness that had begun under enslavement, and that continued in her postbellum public speeches and orations as an itinerant preacher. It may seem a speculative leap, but for Black women, storytelling was a primary medium through which cultural preservation and the exchange of beliefs could occur. Language was used as a means of instructing listeners in ways of promoting faith and practice for the betterment of the larger community. Women such as Dean who emerged from a history of slavery and faith constructed larger meanings about the world around them through speech, and maintained a dual role as interpreters and reinterpreters of the world around them. When comparing Dean to another orator like Sojourner Truth, it is clear that oral tradition was not simply a social act, but also one invested with political meaning and self-definition as a Black woman.[119]

Dean's institutional work can be, and has been, compared to that of male counterparts such as Booker T. Washington and Frederick Douglass. But she remains obscure largely because she did not leave behind volumes of correspondence, or even personal artifacts. Unfortunately, the demolition of the last of Dean's campus in the 1960s and 1970s—due, in part, to the white anxiety of the era that would manifest itself through the monolithic "urban renewal" or destruction of African American space—further wiped her efforts from the historical record. This is certain: her revolutionary campaigns to build the Manassas Industrial School and to fight for social justice marked her as a woman who defied the gender, race, and class conventions of her time. Frederick Douglass would speak at the dedication ceremonies of the Manassas Industrial School in 1894, honoring the tireless efforts of Jennie Dean, a former slave, who, like himself, had similarly struggled to advance the causes of the race through education. Dean understood that she could draw on her own experiences under enslavement, as did Douglass, to forge a radical religious and social agenda for uplifting her race with her work at the school.

Jennie Dean would not live to see the entire vision for her school realized—she died at the age of sixty-five at her home near Catharpin, Virginia, on May 3, 1913. Dean's death certificate lists her occupation as missionary worker. She died of three consecutive strokes and a massive cerebral hemorrhage after enduring eight long years of chronic pneumonia, a result of her many years of enslavement as a child and the debilitating activities of her later life as an educator and social activist.[120] Jennie Dean's obituary in the local Manassas paper stated how she "had an abiding faith in Christian religion, and it was this, her friends say, that upheld her and helped her win success."[121] Religion had also provided Dean with the ability to endure the cruelties of enslavement and the strength to promote education for African Americans despite local white hostility. In a letter dated several months after Dean's death in 1913, Jane Thompson reminds Emily Howland of Dean's good works: "The founder of this [the Sunday School] Convention, and indeed the Sunday School movement in northern Virginia among the colored, and in all her work for the Manassas School, she never forgot or neglected her Sunday Schools. She believed in them so heartily . . . Great noble, beautiful Jennie Dean—what a grand life hers was. God bless her, living or dead."[122]

Shortly after her death, the school faced mounting difficulties as it raised the funds necessary for its continued operations. White involvement, and eventual white control over the school after Dean's death, had for too long kept the Black community from fully participating in raising funds for its support. By the 1930s, the school faced massive debts and was plagued with its white management's internal strife and indifference to the school's original mission. School officials eventually approached Prince William County with an offer to sell the school to the county. Unfortunately, the county could not afford sole ownership of the property and, in 1938, instead converted the remaining buildings into a regional high school for African Americans after consolidation with two neighboring counties. After almost four decades of operation, the Manassas Industrial School had finally closed its doors. With no meaningful efforts forthcoming from the nascent historic preservation community, the old industrial school buildings were torn down in the 1960s—the last one in 1968—ostensibly because of their unsafe condition. Others, however, now believe that the school was leveled as a kind of token payback for the many African American advances gained through the larger civil rights movement. As historian Sabine Offe has written, "these places had to be rendered invisible, because they would have recalled the omnipresence of responsibility, not for the crimes committed elsewhere in seemingly isolated locations far from the center of civilization, but for what had been done, omitted, and overlooked in one's own neighborhood."[123] The symbolic meaning of the school site was still highly contested long after Dean's passing.

Slavery's Shadow

Despite Emancipation, the shadow of slavery had persisted in the decades following the Civil War. Slavery had been particularly traumatic, inflicting gender violence upon African American women—rape, torture, beatings, and forced infanticide—but inadvertently sensitizing African Americans to other forms of social injustice after Emancipation. Slavery imposed itself in an absolute and inescapable way on the psyche of people such as Dean, who had experienced its impact from childhood.[124] Such trauma is not easily healed. Yet the Manassas Industrial School—its grounds once a Civil War battlefield site—could not help but represent a people once enslaved, and would be a monumental effort to reinscribe enslavement, resignify its collective trauma, and depict its eventual transcendence. In his dedication address at the opening of Dean's school, Frederick Douglass is quoted as having said, "a more fitting location for the battle of enlightenment against ignorance could not have been selected than the battlefield of Manassas and Bull Run, where occurred the first conflict of American freedom against the institution of slavery."[125]

The impact of enslavement could not be forgotten by these African American women, who, as former slaves, and others as first-generation "Americans," felt the devastating effects of chattel slavery and its long-standing impact on the larger Black community. The triple burden of race, class, and gender for African American women meant that they would articulate an alternative spatial discourse where they could define their own sense of nationhood, despite living in a society that professed the need for "separate but equal," and instead promised only further segregationist policy under the protection of Jim Crow legislation. African Americans responded to crimes of racial hatred and ignorance primarily through the founding of all-Black institutions, particularly in education. They collectively recalled how whites had feared slave literacy throughout the antebellum South with its potential to spread the gospel of social equality. Now freed but in no way equal, Black women were determined to challenge the Victorian preoccupation with the realm of domesticity by creating an autonomous "woman's sphere" predicated on race uplift.

Figure 1. Contemporary United States South: location of former Manassas Industrial School and Voorhees College today. Map created by Greg Lord and the author.

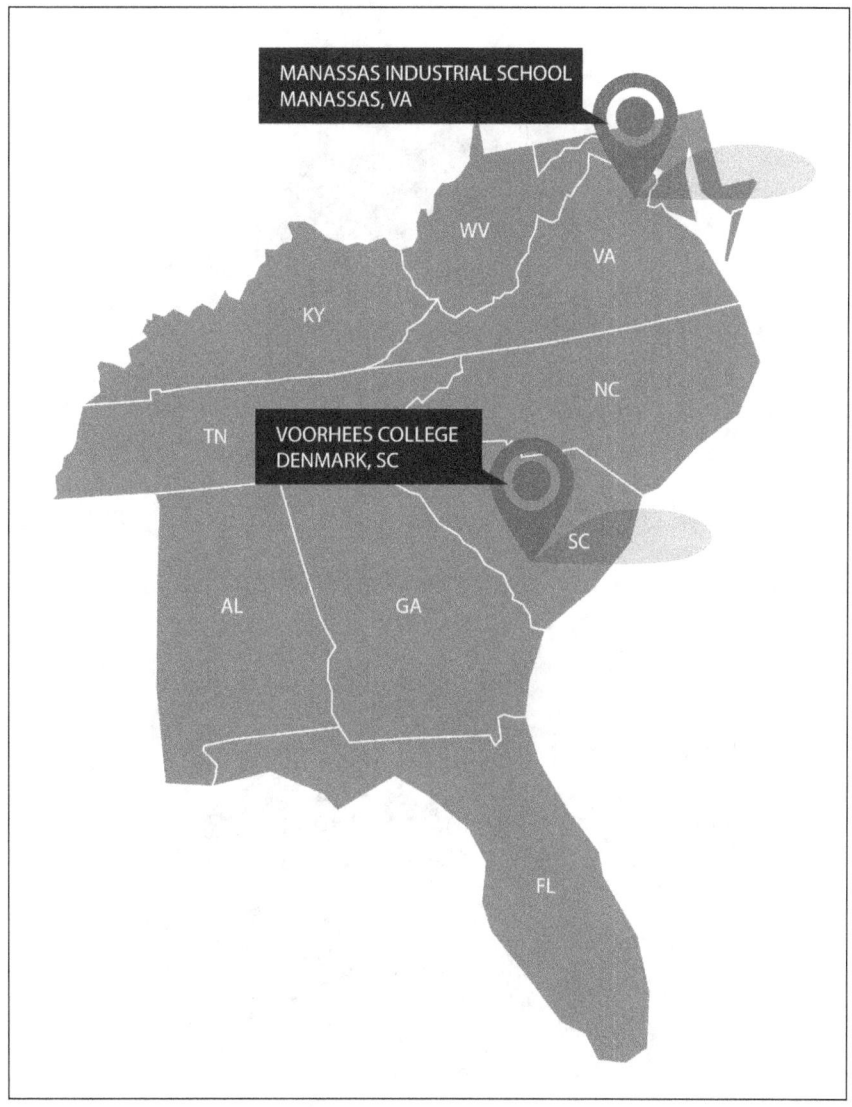

Figure 2. Elizabeth Evelyn Wright. From *Remarkable Career of a Remarkable Woman* (Denmark, SC: Vorhees Industrial School, [1919?]). Courtesy of the South Caroliniana Library, University of South Carolina, Columbia, South Carolina.

Figure 3. Jennie (Jane Serepta) Dean, Manassas Industrial School. Courtesy of the Manassas Museum System, Manassas, Virginia. Photographer: W. Fred Dowell.

Figure 4. Voorhees Industrial School (early buildings in white); Voorhees College (contemporary buildings in gray). Map created by Greg Lord and the author.

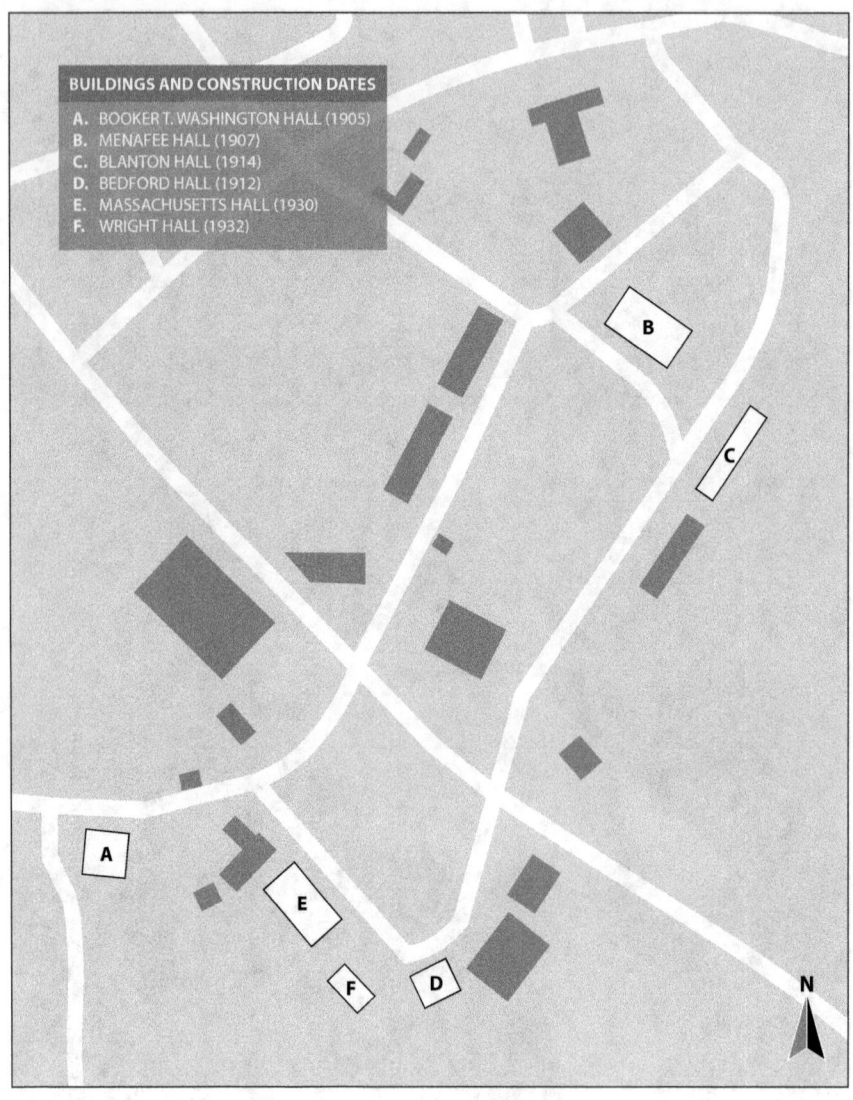

Figure 5. Manassas Industrial School (former building foundations in dotted line). Map created by Greg Lord and the author.

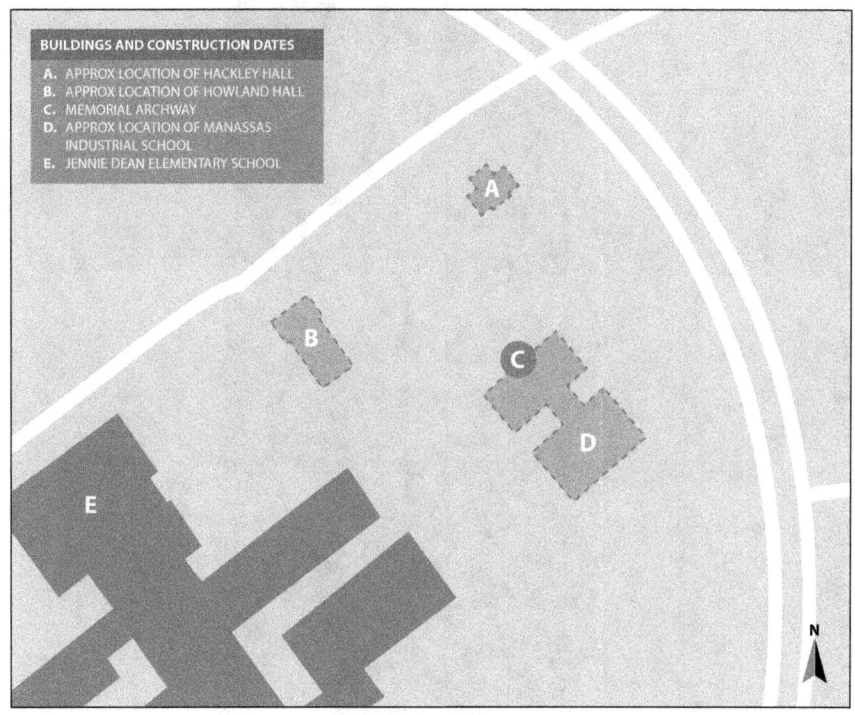

Figure 6. World's Fair, Chicago, 1893. Courtesy of the Prints and Photographs Division, Library of Congress, Washington, DC. Photographer unknown.

Figure 7. Jefferson's Lawn, University of Virginia, Charlottesville, ca. 1909. Courtesy of the Prints and Photographs Division, Library of Congress, Washington, DC. Photographer: Haines Photo Co.

Figure 8. Manassas Industrial School before 1907. Courtesy of the Manassas Museum System, Manassas, Virginia. Photographer unknown.

Architectural Description

Site: The Manassas Industrial School in Manassas, Virginia, built on the site of a Civil War battlefield, was founded by Jennie Dean in 1893. Three academic buildings were at the center of campus, with secondary buildings beyond these. The campus was razed in the 1960s, but is listed on the National Register of Historic Places as a site of archaeological significance.

Figure 9. *The Lost Cause*, Currier and Ives, ca. 1872. Courtesy of the Prints and Photographs Division, Library of Congress, Washington, DC.

Figure 10. Statue of Abraham Lincoln, Lincoln Park, Washington, DC, 2010. Courtesy of The George F. Landegger Collection of the District of Columbia Photographs in Carol M. Highsmith's America, Prints and Photographs Division, Library of Congress, Washington, DC. Photographer: Carol M. Highsmith.

Figure 11. U. S. J. Dunbar, June 27, 1923. Courtesy of the Prints and Photographs Division, Library of Congress, Washington, DC. Photographer: National Photo Company Collection.

Figure 12. Afro-American monument, composite of thirteen scenes pertaining to Afro American history, 1897. Courtesy of the Prints and Photographs Division, Library of Congress, Washington, DC. Artist unknown.

Figure 13. Ida B. Wells-Barnett, head-and-shoulders portrait, facing slightly right, 1891. Illustration in *The Afro-American Press and Its Editors*, by I. Garland Penn., 1891. Courtesy of the Prints and Photographs Division, Library of Congress, Washington, DC. Artist unknown.

Figure 14. Woman's building, World's Columbian Exposition, Chicago. View from across water. Courtesy of the Prints and Photographs Division, Library of Congress, Washington, DC. Photographer: Souvenir Photo Co.

Figure 15. Exposition grounds, World's Columbian Exposition, Chicago, 1893. Courtesy of the Prints and Photographs Division, Library of Congress, Washington, DC. Photographer: Frances Benjamin Johnston.

Figure 16. The court of honor, Chicago Day, World's Fair, Chicago, 1893. Courtesy of the New York Public Library Digital Collections, New York, New York. Photographer: Benjamin West Kilburn.

Figure 17. Midway Plaisance and balloon, World's Columbian Exposition, Chicago, 1893. Courtesy of the Prints and Photographs Division, Library of Congress, Washington, DC. Photographer unknown.

Figure 18. Souvenir map of the World's Columbian Exposition at Jackson Park and Midway Plaisance, Chicago, 1893. Courtesy of the Prints and Photographs Division, Library of Congress, Washington, DC. Artist: Hermann Heinze, A. Zeese & Co, Engravers.

Figure 19. Street of Cairo section of the Midway at the World's Columbian Exposition, Chicago, 1893. Courtesy of the Prints and Photographs Division, Library of Congress, Washington, DC. Photographer: Weber.

Figure 20. The scene outside a recreated West African village, one of many ethnographic exhibits featured on the Midway Plaisance, Dahomey Village, on the Midway. *Official Views of the World's Columbian Exposition Issued by the Department of Photography*, C. D. Arnold and H. D. Higinbotham, official photographers (Chicago: Press Chicago Photo-Grayure Co., 1893), plate 110. Courtesy of the New York Public Library Digital Collections, New York, New York. Photographer unknown.

Figure 21. Lynching, 1925. Courtesy of the Prints and Photographs Division, Library of Congress, Washington, DC. Photographer unknown.

Figure 22. The lynching problem. Print shows a Southern vigilante holding a rope with a noose and a sheriff holding a paper that states "2000 dollars must be paid by the county, for each lynching. Law of South Carolina." An African American man cowers behind the sheriff. A large building, labeled "Courthouse," is in the background. Illustration from *Puck* 45, no. 1164 (June 14, 1899), cover. Courtesy of the Prints and Photographs Division, Library of Congress, Washington, DC. Artist: Louis Dalrymple.

Figure 23. Palace of mechanical arts and lagoon at the World's Columbian Exposition, Chicago, 1892. Courtesy of the Prints and Photographs Division, Library of Congress, Washington, DC. Photographer: Frances Benjamin Johnston.

Figure 24. Booker T. Washington, half-length portrait, seated, 1895. Courtesy of the Prints and Photographs Division, Library of Congress, Washington, DC. Photographer: Francis Benjamin Johnston.

Figure 25. A class in sloyd (woodworking). Courtesy of the Prints and Photographs Division, Library of Congress, Washington, DC. Photographer: Francis Benjamin Johnston.

Figure 26. Tuskegee undergoing massive expansion in 1904, digging foundation for a new building on the institute grounds. Courtesy of the New York Public Library Digital Collections, New York, New York. Photographer: Frances Benjamin Johnston.

Figure 27. Roof construction by students at Tuskegee Institute, Tuskegee, Alabama, 1902. Courtesy of the New York Public Library Digital Collections, New York, New York. Photographer: Francis Benjamin Johnston.

Figure 28. Greenwood Village, view of buildings and grounds at the Tuskegee Normal and Industrial Institute, Tuskegee, Alabama, ca. 1905–15. Courtesy of the Prints and Photographs Division, Library of Congress, Washington, DC. Photographer unknown.

Architectural Description

Building(s): Booker T. Washington, along with his wife, Olivia A. Davidson, believed that middle-class lifestyles should be accessible to African Americans as they were to whites. Greenwood Village, a model community just outside of Tuskegee Institute and west of the campus, was founded to secure good housing and schools for the Tuskegee community and their families. Greenwood Village, built at the end of the nineteenth century, was made up of a number of small, vernacular dwellings, many with their own yards and white picket fences, at a time when the school was growing rapidly, but before it was accredited as a college (there was not a college-level department until 1925). Greenwood sat on either side of a public road that led straight to the college quadrangle. The village was further integrated into the 1904 campus plan when another two hundred acres were added and platted into a grid.

Site: Greenwood Village was located just west of Tuskegee Institute, and sat on either side of a road running to the campus quadrangle. The village was laid out in a grid, and was integrated into the plan of the larger Tuskegee Institute.

Features: The village was almost flat, with only a gentle slope to its topography. Each house boasted a grass lawn, divided from the neighboring properties by a white picket fence. Small shrubs and trees dotted the landscape around the houses.

Figure 29. View of buildings and grounds at the Tuskegee Normal and Industrial Institute, Tuskegee, Alabama, 1916. Courtesy of the Prints and Photographs Division, Library of Congress, Washington, DC. Photographer: Haines Photo Co.

Figure 30. Kennerly Hall, Voorhees Industrial School, Denmark, South Carolina, ca. 1901–2. Courtesy of the South Caroliniana Library, University of South Carolina, Columbia, South Carolina, and the Wright-Potts Library, Voorhees College, Denmark, South Carolina. Photographer unknown.

Architectural Description

Building(s): Kennerly Hall, designed by Tuskegee faculty of color, William Sidney Pittman, was built on the Voorhees Industrial School campus in 1902 in Denmark, South Carolina. This vernacular building, one of the very first structures to be built on the campus, was a symmetrical, two-story, six-bay, frame building housing offices, classrooms, and a chapel. The Hall was adjacent to the school's dormitory buildings, and overlooked the school's quad.

The base of the building and the porch base were masonry, as were the four steps leading to the porch. The porch has one square column at each front corner, and a simple balustrade running between the columns and the main structure. The porch was topped by a large triangular pediment with an overhanging cornice and no decoration in the tympanum. The porch surrounded a large double entrance door, and two narrow, two-over-two double-hung sash windows, one on either side of the door. Wood clapboard siding covered all facades of the building. Kennerly Hall's hipped roof was complemented by a cupola seemingly Italianate in style that sat above the building's entrance.

Site: The property was located within a group of campus buildings that included two matching dormitories: one for girls, and one for the male students and teachers. One of these buildings sat on either side of this property and were separated by the campus quadrangle.

Figure 31. Drawing at Voorhees was modeled after programs at Tuskegee; mechanical drawing class at Tuskegee Institute, Tuskegee, Alabama, ca. 1902. Courtesy of the Prints and Photographs Division, Library of Congress, Washington, DC. Photographer: Francis Benjamin Johnston.

Figure 32. School grounds, Voorhees Industrial School, Denmark, South Carolina, ca. 1901–2. Courtesy of the South Caroliniana Library, University of South Carolina, Columbia, South Carolina. Photographer unknown.

Architectural Description

Site: Elizabeth Evelyn Wright founded the Voorhees Industrial School in 1897 (later Voorhees College) as an institution of higher education for African Americans. While the first buildings constructed on campus were frame and vernacular, later buildings were often brick and Colonial Revival in style. Many of the campus buildings were built by Voorhees students as they were instructed in carpentry, masonry, and other building trades. The 1930s saw another wave of campus building, with a majority of buildings from this time built at the southwest end of campus. Several modern structures, including the Elizabeth E. Wright Memorial Library, which today still sits apart at the center of the quad, were added later in the century. Today, the campus remains the home of Voorhees College.

Figure 33. Booker T. Washington Hall, Voorhees Industrial School, Denmark, South Carolina, 1905. Courtesy of the South Caroliniana Library, University of South Carolina, Columbia, South Carolina. Photographer unknown.

Architectural Description

Building(s): Booker T. Washington Hall is one of the earliest buildings constructed on the Voorhees College campus (then Voorhees Industrial School) and is within the Voorhees College Historic District in Denmark, South Carolina. Designed by Wilson Cooke (a professor at Claflin College), it was originally built as Booker T. Washington Hospital in 1905. The Hall now serves the College as an administration building, housing the offices of the president. The building is symmetrical, two stories, and brick, boasting seven bays across the front facade. It is in the Colonial Revival style with a recessed central block and two flanking wings of two bays each. A set of wide stone steps leads up to the first-floor wooden portico, which runs the length of the front facade. The porch is topped by a simple entablature, and is supported by evenly spaced Tuscan columns with balustrade running between the columns. Distinctive brick quoins mark each corner on the front facade, including the end corners, as well as the inside corners at the recessed central block.

Site: The property is located in the most southwest corner of the Historic District, and is placed at a diagonal with the northeast corner closest to the rest of the District. It is part of a cluster of buildings in the southwest of the campus, but is slightly outside the main circle of buildings. Today, the building faces a small campus road, and there are a track and playing fields to the south of the building. The closest buildings to the Hall are the Jessie Dorsey Green Infirmary to the north, and the T. H. Moore Student Center and St. James building to the east.

Features: The building is on a slight grassy slope, and is surrounded by a scattering of bushes. There are some trees nearby, but not directly next to the building.

Figure 34. Menafee Trades Building, Voorhees Industrial School, 1907. Courtesy of the South Caroliniana Library, University of South Carolina, Columbia, South Carolina. Photographer unknown.

Figure 35. Blanton Hall, Voorhees Industrial School, Denmark, South Carolina, 1914. Courtesy of the South Caroliniana Library, University of South Carolina, Columbia, South Carolina. Photographer unknown.

Architectural Description

Building(s): Blanton Hall is a Colonial Revival–style building with an unusual Dutch gable–style parapet, perhaps a nod to college benefactor Ralph Voorhees's own Dutch colonial pedigree. Built in 1914, the Hall sits within the southwest semicircle off the main quad, and is one of the earlier buildings constructed on the Voorhees College campus (then Voorhees Industrial School). Intended to be the administration building, it now serves as faculty offices and classrooms. Blanton Hall's front facade is seven bays across with a three-bay first-floor portico of arched brick piers. First-floor windows have transom lights above, and white keystones emerging from the lintels atop the transom lights. A belt-course datum runs through the first-floor keystones at the same elevation as the lower datum of the portico entablature. Windows on the second floor have similar keystones, which in turn merge with the fascia of the lower roof cornice. The hipped roof has a wide, overhanging cornice with dentils, and there are two symmetrical Dutch gable–style roof parapets at either end of the front facade. Three tall, corbelled chimneys protrude from the roof; one is in the center, and one is on either end of the building. The building is a key feature of the Historic District.

Site: The property is located in the southwest section of the Historic District, and overlooks an open, grassy space. This building helps make up the semicircle of buildings at the southern end of the campus. Its nearest neighbor is the St. Philip's Episcopal Chapel, built some twenty years after Blanton Hall. Currently, a campus road runs around the sides and back of the building, and a parking lot sits at the rear of the property.

Figure 36. School grounds, Manassas Industrial School, Manassas, Virginia, 1908. Courtesy of the Manassas Museum System, Manassas, Virginia. Photographer: W. Fred Dowell.

Architectural Description

Building(s): Bailey Hall, built of clapboard in the Colonial Revival style, was a residential hall and print shop in the central part of the Manassas Industrial school campus adjacent to Howland Hall, Hackley Hall, and the Carnegie Library. The Hall's facade was dominated by a two-story entry porch covering the central doors on the first and second floors. With its honorific front doors and entry porches, Bailey Hall is in keeping with other buildings in the style, but instead of placing a full entry porch on the front of the building, the architect adds an overhang over the front door. A two-story entry porch on the right side of the building creates a balcony at both floors. Beyond the overhang over the front door, the only other detailing is a row of transom lights above the door, but lacking the detailing of higher-style Colonial Revival buildings. Porches are supported at the foundation level by brick piers, with slim, wooden columns supporting the porch on the first and second floors. A delicate balustrade runs between the building and the columns on both levels. There is a small, hipped roof above the upper porch, which connects to the building. Above the porches there is a lunette-type, semicircular louvered window in the gable of the building. There are two, two-over-two double-hung sash windows on either side of both the first- and second-floor porches. The side-gabled roof is made of standing seam metal and a corbelled chimney sits at the ridge of the building. The building was demolished between 1924 and 1943, years before the rest of the campus buildings were demolished. The Manassas Industrial School campus is now listed on the National Register of Historic Places as a site of archaeological significance.

Site: The property sits on the Manassas Industrial School campus, and is near the main campus buildings such as Hackley Hall, Howland Hall, and the Carnegie Library. Currently, archaeological remains of Bailey Hall have been identified, but no evidence of the building survives above ground. Early photographs show a temporary sidewalk leading to the front of the Hall, with woods behind. A few shrubs are dotted around the exterior of the Hall, but most of the landscape directly near the building is open grass.

Figure 37. Andrew Carnegie Library (far right), Manassas Industrial School. Courtesy of the Manassas Museum System, Manassas, Virginia. Photographer: W. Fred Dowell.

Architectural Description

Building(s): The Carnegie Library, also known as the Library and Trades Building, was one of the three central buildings on the Manassas Industrial School campus. Built after 1907, the massive brick structure was representative of the emerging industrial scale of trades buildings found at schools and college campuses of the era. In particular, its severe brick elevations recalled design strategies that architect Robert Taylor had employed at the Tuskegee Institute. The front of the Carnegie Library faced the quadrangle, with a hyphen at the back connecting the main structure to the Industrial Building behind it. The building was organized into a central hipped-roof pavilion of three bays with flanking end pavilions of one bay each, the symmetrical gabled parapets at either end helping to break down the structure's overall mass. The hipped roof was made of standing seam metal roof. There were three large shed dormers with three, six-light awning windows that sat above the windows on the first and second floors. Two small air vents projected from the ridge of the roof line. Along with the rest of the Manassas Industrial School campus, the Carnegie Library was demolished in the 1960s, and it is now listed on the National Register of Historic Places as a site of archaeological significance.

Site: The property was one of three main buildings on the Manassas Industrial School campus, and it formed a triangle with Howland Hall and Hackley Hall. The library is the central building and faces the campus quadrangle. The building is also connected by a hyphen to the Industrial Building to the south.

Features: A wide sidewalk ran across the front facade of the Carnegie Library, with grass planted adjacent to the building on either side of the door. A number of small shrubs line the side of the sidewalk across from the building. The archaeological remains of the Carnegie Library have been identified, but no evidence of the building survives above ground.

Figure 38. Charles Wellford Leavitt Plan, 1908, Manassas Industrial School, Manassas, Virginia Redrawn by Greg Lord and the author.

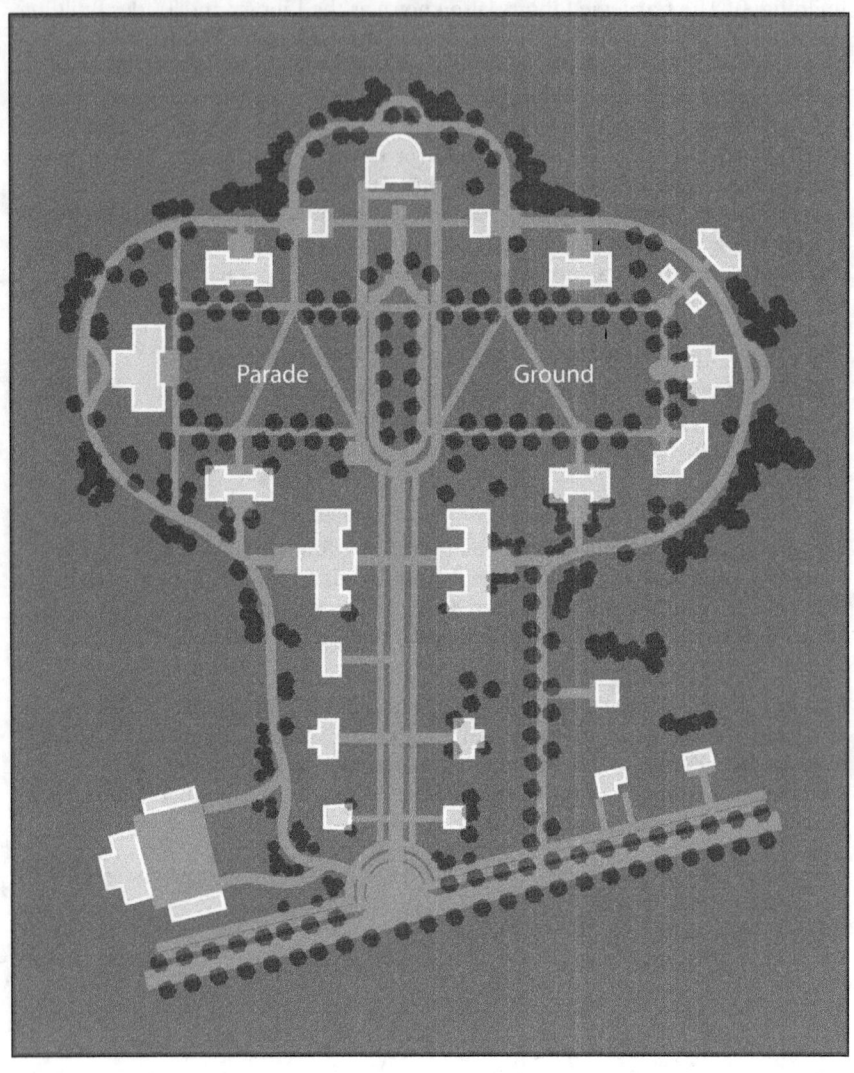

Architectural Description

Setting: Leavitt's plan at Manassas, never realized, had as its main design element the creation of a long mall intended to run along a north-south axis that began at the entrance to the school site and terminated at a Christian chapel. In the Manassas plan, ten pavilion-like structures are interspersed along a series of one-story dormitories arranged around a terraced "great lawn" with the chapel at its head. Along the main axis, Leavitt proposed the placement of administration buildings and residences for various school officials. The incorporation of a secondary axis, a cross, suggests both religious intention—literally inscribing the body of Christ, the savior of the race, onto the landscape—and the Manassas Industrial School's commitment to provide its students with an education both in the liberal arts and the manual trades (both head and hand).

Figure 39. Howland Hall, Manassas Industrial School. Courtesy of the Manassas Museum System, Manassas, Virginia. Photographer: W. Fred Dowell.

Architectural Description

Building(s): Howland Hall, one of the first structures on the Manassas Industrial School campus, was built in 1894 as a girls' dormitory and dining hall. In 1901 the structure was rebuilt after the original building was destroyed by fire. The rebuilt Howland Hall was a symmetrical, rectangular, three-story Colonial Revival structure with a gabled roof and tower at the front. After 1907, photographs show that a large, three-story addition with a gambrel roof was built perpendicular to the original structure. The addition took the place of the tower, and led to a T-shaped or cruciform building footprint that substantially altered the orientation of the building.

Front facade prior to 1907: The front facade was at the gable end of the building and was dominated by a central tower, with a double-front door topped with a transom light on the first floor, and a set of two-over-two paired double-hung sash windows on the second and third floors. A flight of stone steps led from the ground level to the front door, with the entry tower topped by a steeply pitched hipped roof. In addition, one window sat on either side of the projecting walls of the tower on the first and second floors. On each floor of the front facade on either side of the tower there were four, two-over-two double-hung sash windows.

Front facade and addition after 1907: After 1907 the building boasted a large, three-story gambrel roof addition built perpendicular to the original structure. At the rear of the building was a wooden porch with six Tuscan columns running the length of the first floor, with four wooden steps leading to the portico. A back door sat in the center of the first floor, with two, two-over-two double-hung sash windows on either side. Windows on the second floor mimicked those on the first, and the thick cornice line ran along the back facade as it ran around the sides. Even with its later addition, Howland Hall remained domestic in scale, possessing familiar Colonial Revival–style elements, such as simple Tuscan-style columns at the front portico, and a small fanlight over its door. The building had a raised foundation made of reddish-brown siltstone, with basement windows. The building was clad in white clapboard, and the roof was made of standing seam metal. Currently, archaeological remains of Howland Hall have been identified, but no evidence of the building survives above ground.

Site: The property was one of three main buildings at the Manassas Industrial School along with Hackley Hall and the Carnegie Building, facing north toward Prince William Drive. Howland Hall, Hackley Hall, and the Carnegie Building sat in a triangle with Hackley Hall to the north and east of Howland Hall, and the Carnegie Building located to the south and east.

Features: A sidewalk led from the back door of Howland Hall to join with the sidewalk from Hackley Hall to connect to Carnegie Hall and other campus buildings. The landscape around the Hall was largely grassy, with a few decorative shrubs and small trees.

Figure 40. Hackley Hall, Manassas Industrial School. Courtesy of the Manassas Museum System, Manassas, Virginia. Photographer: W. Fred Dowell.

Architectural Description

Building(s): Hackley Hall, built as a men's dormitory, was constructed prior to 1894, but after a fire in the later 1890s, it was rebuilt in 1901. The two-story Hall, one of the original buildings on the Manassas Industrial School campus, was brick, built in the Colonial Revival style, with a central gable, a one-story entry portico, and prominent cupola. The entire building was cruciform in plan. The Hall was in close proximity to neighboring Howland Hall and the Carnegie Library until the entire campus was razed in the 1960s. The foundation was made of rough-cut, rusticated stone, with basement windows puncturing the foundation stones. A set of four stairs with a wooden balustrade and decorative newel posts led from the ground to an entry portico with four slim classical columns supporting a cornice and balustrade above. The entryway centered in the projecting central block consisted of a double wooden door with transom light above. Windows were typically double-hung sash with six-over-two lights, with rusticated stone lintel overhead. Oval attic windows nestled inside the gable building elevations. An octagonal cupola sat atop the building, rising another full story from the juncture of the cruciform ridgelines, and had louvered windows, a steep roof, and a flagpole protruding from the top. The roof itself was made of standing seam metal. There were two brick corbelled chimneys, one on either side of the cupola.

Site: The property was one of three main buildings on the Manassas Industrial School campus. It faced north toward Prince William Drive, and sat on the campus quadrangle with Howland Hall and the Carnegie Library. Hackley Hall sat east of Howland Hall and to the north and east of the Carnegie Library.

Features: A sidewalk led from the back door of Hackley Hall to join with the sidewalk from Howland Hall. This sidewalk ran across the front of the Carnegie Library, and connected Hackley Hall to the other campus buildings. The landscape around the Hall was largely grassy, with a few decorative shrubs and small trees. Currently, archaeological remains of Hackley Hall have been identified, but no evidence of the building survives above ground.

Figure 41. Students at Tuskegee Normal and Industrial Institute, Tuskegee, Alabama, ca. 1902–6. Courtesy of the Prints and Photographs Division, Library of Congress, Washington, DC. Photographer: Frances Benjamin Johnston.

Chapter Five

Manassas and Voorhees

Models of Race Uplift

While the practice of American architecture was becoming professionalized during the Progressive era of the late nineteenth century, its ranks remained overwhelmingly racialized and gendered—in other words, white and male. Nonetheless, the first white female graduate from an accredited American school of architecture was Mary Louisa Page at the University of Illinois in Urbana Champaign in 1878, with Margaret Hicks of Cornell University following her the next year, graduating from the Cornell University School of Architecture in 1879. The Massachusetts Institute of Technology, the oldest school of American architecture founded in 1865, was able to claim its first white female graduate, Sophia Hayden, in 1890, and its first African American graduate, Robert R. Taylor (who would become the first accredited African American architect), in 1892. Almost fifty years would pass before Beverly Greene, believed to be the first female African American architect, received a bachelor's degree in architectural engineering in 1946 from, once again, the University of Illinois at Urbana Champaign.

Architectural production in the United States in the decades immediately before and after the Civil War was premodern, eclectic, and produced out of commercial offices and ateliers. Neoclassicism had run its course by the 1840s and, according to the American academic canon, was quickly succeeded by versions of the Gothic Revival, the High Victorian Gothic, the Second Empire, and, by the 1880s, the Richardsonian Romanesque. Proponents of the English Gothic, such as John Ruskin, had gone so far as to reject on principle the notion of further classical production. Even those American architects trained at the Ecole des Beaux-Arts in Paris and inculcated in neoclassicism returned to the United States to produce an eclectic architecture customized for American needs. Architectural historian Richard Longstreth suggests that this period can be described as academic eclecticism "fostering the art of design through a scholarly knowledge of the past."[1] During the "style wars" of the later nineteenth century, Richard Morris Hunt, the first American architect to attend the Ecole, returned to the United States in 1855, where he opened his influential architectural practice in New York City. His production, along with that of a steady stream of Beaux-Arts–trained and influenced architects, helped contribute to the professionalization of American architectural practice and the dominance of the Beaux-Arts.

The work of the Ecole des Beaux-Arts had particularly appealed to Americans. Architectural historian Richard Longstreth has written on the subject of Charles McKim, principal of McKim, Mead, and White, founded in the late nineteenth century, the large New York–based architectural firm boasting armies of draftsman. McKim had singled out the Ecole, believing it equipped its practitioners to work within the Western architectural design canon "with a facility, freedom, and correctness, a grace and an elegance, beyond the reach of any who have not enjoyed similar advantages."[2]

Teachers trained at the state-run Ecole des Beaux-Arts in Paris influenced the monumental works of many of the first generation of African American architectural students. For his thesis at MIT in 1892, Robert Taylor had designed a home for disabled ex–Civil War soldiers under the guidance of his professor, Eugène Létang, a respected graduate of the Ecole, who would be the first in a long line of French educators to teach architecture in the United States.[3] Létang, an advocate of classical French design and design strategies, would seize the opportunity afforded by the Columbian Exposition and, by promoting the design of buildings at the Exposition in his design studios in Massachusetts, both he and his students hoped to secure a place for the newly transplanted architectural methodologies of the Ecole.[4]

Taylor's work clearly provides a model as to how this accomplished African American practitioner ingeniously adapted the Beaux-Arts models, sometimes deflecting the traditional architectural language (and iconography) of the Beaux-Arts generally for reasons of budget. In the text of his thesis Taylor writes, "In view of the number of soldiers who fought in the late war now suffering from the infirmities of old age and thereby incapable of supporting themselves, the government purposes erecting a home where about two hundred may be cared for comfortably."[5] Taylor's choice of topic for his thesis suggests the importance of the Civil War to African Americans, and a personal commitment to civic design and social welfare work. In hindsight, the soldier's home can be seen as an early step in the development of an institution-building archetype for the Black nation, while also commemorating Black involvement in the Civil War.

Robert Taylor's thesis design for the veteran's home contained a series of large courtyards bounded by dormitories set symmetrically about a domed central block. The overall size, composition, and organization of the soldier's home make clear that Taylor adopted the planning style of large-scale French institutions in the Beaux-Arts tradition. However, the absence of canonical classical orders—Doric, Ionic, Corinthian, etc.—in Taylor's thesis project underlines the pragmatic approach to building problems that was transferred to MIT from the Beaux-Arts in Paris.[6] Taylor had been an outstanding student at the Massachusetts Institute of Technology, and he reapplied the lessons he had learned at MIT as he directed engineering and architecture programs at the Tuskegee Institute, where he spent most of his career. Eventually, most of Tuskegee's first-generation building program was designed by Taylor and built by student labor on campus.

An African American architect such as Robert Taylor would have been aware that African Americans in their roles as artisans, craftsmen, and laborers—both enslaved or free—had literally built much of the antebellum South. There is this allusion to preprofessional practice in the postbellum South when Taylor first arrived at Tuskegee: "There was no drawing attempted . . . and the mechanical work was largely in the hands of men trained in the old way, who did their work usually without definite plans or drawings."[7] As such, African Americans were the vessels of a living vernacular tradition indebted to a reconstituted African past.

However, this vernacular legacy, along with his immersion in Beaux-Arts pedagogy and methodology, would have left Taylor eminently well qualified to design the built environment in the emerging African American communities of the new South. African Americans eventually constructed a unique built environment: influenced by the Western canon, they would also draw heavily from vernacular and regional influences in the design of their campus buildings in the segregationist era of Jim Crow.

Soon after graduating from MIT, Robert Taylor started an architectural practice, designing both public and private commissions, before accepting Washington's offer in 1892 to teach at Tuskegee. By drawing on his experiences as a student at MIT, architect Taylor experimented with the Tuskegee campus, exploring the confluence between the Ecole's design methodologies, developments in American architectural education, and Washington's race-uplift work. Ultimately, he is credited with designing at least forty-five buildings at the Institute: these were apart from another dozen or so of his designs built throughout the South.[8] Here, Taylor attests to how he had combined his education at MIT and his teaching experience at Tuskegee to promote Black nationalist material culture:

> Some of the methods and plans of the Institute of Technology have been transplanted to the Tuskegee Institute and have flourished and grown there; if not the plans in full, certainly the spirit, in the love of doing things correctly, of putting logical ways of thinking into the humblest task, of studying surrounding conditions . . . and of using them to the best advantage in

contributing to build up the immediate community in which the persons live, and in this way increasing the power and the grandeur of the nation.[9]

Architectural training was considered one of the "most important divisions of Tuskegee's work," providing the basis for the erection of some twenty-three buildings under faculty supervision at the school site by 1901.[10] Architectural and mechanical drawing were, in particular, a critical component in the industrial training program at Tuskegee, a program of study that many of the other schools founded by Tuskegee graduates soon adopted.[11] Architectural education became an important part of the industrial school movement among African Americans, emphasizing the dual "training of the head and hand" in the service of the race.[12] Emmett J. Scott, Booker T. Washington's personal secretary and chief adviser at Tuskegee, elaborated on this, famously suggesting that "The mind is trained even as the hand is trained, and as the heart is trained, and as all are at Tuskegee."[13]

Taylor at Tuskegee

Taylor's design for Tuskegee's Thrasher Hall—originally a science building—would incorporate much of its design from his own MIT thesis.[14] Taylor's designs comprise an overt and carefully considered monumentality, particularly in the detailing of such humble materials as the Tuskegee brick. As architectural historian Ellen Weiss has noted, Taylor's designs included "a celebration of the Tuskegee brick in window surrounds, cornices, belt courses, and watertables; a sensitivity in scale; a sense of the power of sharply cut walls; and inventive massing."[15] For Weiss, each of Taylor's buildings is direct and clear, yet different from one another despite their similarities. Taylor's designs for the four Emery dormitories and Rockefeller Hall at Tuskegee reflect a kind of "Shaker-like dignity" in the articulation of their surfaces, massing, and proportions.[16] By locating the workshops of the industrial arts classrooms at the periphery and the most public face of the campus, a casual passerby might witness how Tuskegee's preference for manual training over the liberal arts was embodied in its building program and physical plant, and, as such, Taylor's architecture assuaged white fears as to Washington's intentions. Buried deeper within the campus, however, more monumental design was made manifest where the training of both the "head and heart" continued apace.

The scale and complexity of Tuskegee's buildings changed dramatically under Taylor's leadership.[17] Warren Logan, a colleague and Institute treasurer, remarked on the success of the building program under Taylor's direction: "The buildings of the Institute show a steady progression in quality of workmanship, materials, and architectural design and efficiency."[18] Logan continued: "Introducing plans, blueprints and specifications as a part of every mechanical job, however small, and instructing the students in making and using drawings, led to changes which inevitably follow newer and better ways of doing things."[19] The Beaux-Art's emphasis on monumental planning, combined with Black race-uplift doctrines, provided these early African American architects with an opportunity to apply programs and design strategies—at emerging mass and industrial scales—to the social reformist curricula at these institutes. Proponents of the Beaux-Arts have promoted its flexibility with respect to culture and region with Arthur Drexler, one-time curator of the Department of Architecture and Design at New York's Museum of Modern Art, noting that the "Ecole's capacity for deflecting, transforming, or absorbing heresies was not the least of its institutional accomplishments."[20] It must be noted how this empowering of both gender and race with respect to property and education outside the white Southern power structure would indeed be considered heretical. All of this must have proved compelling to African American architects and their own nation-building agenda in the face of a larger political and social environment that was largely unchanged since the Civil War.

Booker T. Washington's experiment in campus planning provided a generation of architects with an opportunity to design their own monumental Black City in microcosm and experiment with issues of urbanism.[21] Tuskegee, with its grand axes, buildings and vistas, ensured the campus design had impressive visual impact, and structures were carefully related to each other and the landscape.[22] Many of the buildings were of classical, "high style" design.[23] Architectural and mechanical drawing were believed to be so critical to the industrial training program at Tuskegee that they eventually entered almost all educational divisions.[24] Emmett J. Scott maintained that architectural training was one of the most important divisions of Tuskegee's race-uplift work because it literally provided the foundation for the building of not only the Institute itself, but of the neighboring Black model community, Washington's own Greenwood Village.[25]

Just west of the Tuskegee Institute campus—a physical embodiment of Booker T. Washington's belief that African Americans should have access to middle-class lifestyles[26]—Greenwood offered African American families the opportunity to live in a community of comfortable single-family homes, with access to good schools for their children.[27] Sitting on either side of the public road that led straight to the college quadrangle,[28] Greenwood was further integrated into the 1904 campus plan when another two hundred acres were added and platted into a grid.[29] Construction of Greenwood began toward the end of the nineteenth century, at a time when the Institute was growing, but before it was reorganized as a college (there was not a college-level department until 1925).[30] In contrast to the grand buildings of the Institute, the buildings in Greenwood Village were suburban: small, vernacular, simply planned, and simply detailed. Today, the majority of houses there remain white, clapboard-sided bungalows with small porches. The suburban village was made up of a number of these vernacular buildings—each large enough for one family—many with their own yards and white picket fences.

Wright's "Little Tuskegee"

Four years after the founding of Manassas, Elizabeth Evelyn Wright founded the Voorhees Industrial School in 1897 as a higher education institution for African Americans, and in doing so promoted architectural theory and practice directly transmitted from Tuskegee. Whereas Jennie Dean's Northern donors and philanthropists and Northern architect had enabled from the start an array of Colonial Revival buildings on the Manassas Industrial School campus, evidences of high-style Colonial Revival and Beaux Arts monumentality at the Voorhees campus would emerge later. The site plan of Voorhees itself resisted easy description, comprising as it did one long axial lawn with a separate trades quadrangle adjacent to it. The first buildings constructed at Voorhees were vernacular in appearance and construction, and made of wood. Later buildings were of grander scale in aspirational style and made of more durable materials such as brick. Much of the Voorhees campus was literally built by Wright's students as they were simultaneously being trained in carpentry and construction. Unlike Manassas, Voorhees College survives and when visiting it today, one sees landscaping and groupings of buildings that, at first glance, are indeed aspirational and fairly typical of American colleges dating from the turn of the century. Colonial Revival elements—classical orders applied to brick facades, hipped roofs, and generous porches—are in evidence. Some later buildings are modern in style and were constructed in the mid-twentieth century.

Most of the early buildings at Voorhees were built in the southwest corner of campus (figure 32). Kennerly Hall, a frame building with a cupola and built in 1902, was flanked by Elizabeth Voorhees Hall, a women's dorm, and Elizabeth Wright Hall, a men's dorm. In 1905 the prominent Booker T. Washington Hall (figure 33) was erected as a hospital, sitting slightly outside the crescent of campus buildings surrounding the quad. Like many Colonial Revival buildings of the time, Washington Hall has some pronounced details, such as quoins (projecting masonry corner blocks) and fanlights, signifying its presence as an imposing Colonial Revival university building.[31] The central section bay of the building is recessed, an ingenious twist on a more typical projecting Colonial Revival bay.[32] The Hall also boasts a hipped roof and full-width porch.[33]

Another early building at Voorhees was Bedford Hall, built in 1912 as the dining hall. Blanton Hall sat on the opposite side of the quad from Bedford Hall, and was built four years later in 1916. Blanton Hall was a notable building on campus given its massive scale; it was distinguishable from the rest of the campus design with its large parapets in a Dutch colonial or William and Mary architectural style. The Menafee Trades Building (figure 34) sat at the other end of the quad from the southwest collection of campus buildings. The building, built in 1907, was separated from the rest of the campus intending to be a part of a separate industrial trades quadrangle. This Beaux Arts–style building was imposing, with a central block with flanking wings.

With the exception of Booker T. Washington Hall, all the buildings faced inward toward the central lawn, lining an irregular campus quad surrounded by a ring road (much like the outer drives at Tuskegee) that dominated the center of the College. Small roads ran through the campus, connecting the buildings and open spaces. A series of paths and walkways ran between the buildings, and at times cut through the interior of the quads at angles. Larger trees framed some of the more prominent buildings, with smaller, newer tree plantings lining the walkways and the quads. Today, the campus continues to possess a park-like atmosphere with large, grassy areas, and small trees and plantings dotting the landscape. The 1930s saw another wave of campus building, with the majority of buildings built at the southwest end of campus. Later, a few massive modern buildings were added, including the Elizabeth E. Wright Memorial Library, which sits alone in the center of the central lawn. The campus that Wright established remains the home of Voorhees College today, integrating its historic architecture with later buildings.

Voorhees's Kennerly Hall was a large rectangular, two-story frame structure with an imposing double-entrance door. There was a small cupola topping the roof, a covered porch at the entrance, and two square columns at either corner. The building contained roughly nine thousand square feet with offices, classrooms, and a chapel.[34] Here, Wright drew directly from the Tuskegee architectural network, employing Robert Taylor's assistant, William Sidney Pittman, for its design.[35] At this time, Pittman had his own students help him with the design of Kennerly Hall. A graduate of Tuskegee and Drexel Institute of Art, Science, and Industry, and employed under Taylor's direction, Pittman soon became a key player in the design of at least seven historically Black colleges and universities throughout the South with the Tuskegee network providing a hands-on, pragmatic approach toward race-based advancement and Black institution building. Presumably because of Pittman's own ties to the Black working class, he discerned little difference between himself and the many students with backgrounds similar to his own from nearby rural areas. Pittman's career continued to flourish within the African American community, and by 1907 he was commissioned to design the Negro Building at the Jamestown Tercentenary Exposition, employing at a monumental scale the architectural vocabulary and strategies that he developed in his earlier African American campus designs.[36]

After Pittman's Kennerly Hall was completed, New Jersey philanthropist Ralph Voorhees supplied the funds for building the girls' dormitory, Elizabeth Voorhees Hall, and its matching building, Elizabeth Wright Hall (1903), for male students and teachers. Kennerly Hall was the focal point of an ensemble of buildings, which included both Voorhees Hall and Wright Hall. The two dormitory buildings were located at either side of Kennerly Hall, separated by the large green intended to be the school's main quadrangle.[37] After several other structures had burned on the Voorhees campus, Wright was compelled to rebuild, substituting less flammable brick for wood. Over time, a new generation of buildings would boast details such as leaded glass windows, curvilinear gables, dentil moldings, cupolas, and more detailed decorative brickwork, suggesting a period of relative financial stability for the school. With Wright's design team eventually in place, more ceremonial teaching and administration buildings would be arrayed along the edges of formal and symbolic quadrangles.

The few surviving early photographs of Voorhees[38] show the strong impact of Tuskegee's overall design concept, particularly in Pittman's design for the Menafee Trades Building of 1907 as part of a separate industrial trades quadrangle. The Menafee Building employs a familiar Beaux Arts strategy with the building organized into a dominant central block with flanking wings terminating in pavilion-like structures, much like the design employed in Huntington Hall at Tuskegee. However, the Menafee Building, built under obvious financial constraints, does without Huntington Hall's rusticated ground-floor brick coursing and abundance of detail. As late as 1916, we can see the Tuskegee influence persisting at Voorhees with the erection of Blanton Hall (figure 35), Voorhees's first all-brick administration building, which was conspicuously added to a core group of earlier buildings.

The most striking feature of the overall design of the Voorhees campus today is its grand scale, a clear statement of the educational authority and permanence that was intended for this institution founded by African Americans, with its central quad approaching Tuskegee's in size (astonishing to note, as today it has a fraction of Tuskegee's student population). Voorhees's surviving first generation of simple wood-frame structures has been repurposed on the Voorhees campus. The landmark second generation of buildings built on campus also survive and continue to fulfill Voorhees's aspirations to figure prominently as an educational institution.

It is conceivable that Wright requested Pittman to assist her in planning her own version of the Tuskegee model community, Greenwood Village, to be reworked for a site adjacent to her campus in Denmark, South Carolina.[39] Wright's model community would also be integrated into the daily operation of the school and its various activities. Wright encouraged African American families at Voorhees to purchase their own land, erect modern houses, and improve their overall living conditions in her community as part of the institution's program of uplift. Voorhees's strong industrial trades curriculum also helped them establish financial security and bolstered their rights as property-owning citizens.

Despite recurring illness, Wright actively promoted her campus's expansion. Testifying to the growing network of African American designers and builders in higher education, in 1905 she solicited the assistance of William Wilson Cooke (1871–1945), founder of the Department of Manual Training at nearby Claflin University (a private HBCU founded in 1869 by Methodist missionaries from Massachusetts) in Orangeburg, South Carolina. Cooke was the first Black architect in the state of South Carolina to secure professional qualifications to practice.[40] Under Cooke's supervision, Claflin's architecture program had embraced the Russian and Scandinavian Sloyd systems of manual training in the latter part of the nineteenth century, as did other African American industrial schools. The school catalog of 1897 had even quoted a Russian maxim: "Whatever you would have appear in the life of a nation you must first put into its schools."[41] Claflin was also the first African American school to offer a bachelor's degree in architecture. Earlier in his career, Cooke was architect to the Freedmen's Aid Society and helped design many of its early buildings.[42]

One catalog at Claflin had stated that "Drawing is the very soul of true technical education, and of exact intelligent workmanship. Drawing cultivates perception and stimulates invention. It often enables one to express by diagrams that which cannot be so readily and clearly expressed by language."[43] Over the years, the university catalog was replete with drawings depicting the campus, its various programs, and industrial departments. The woodcut images and drawings in the catalog, beginning as early as 1885, include plan drawings of a $200 model cottage, a perspective view of the campus, plans for the new manual training building, an interior view of the chapel, and images of the main Administration Building,[44] all of which powerfully visualized the material culture of uplift at Claflin. As early as 1890, Cooke was similarly committed to a "systematic training of the hand and the teaching of trades and industries in connection with courses of literary culture" and, as such, Cooke also understood the historical significance of the literary culture and its impact on African American nation building.[45] Cooke's Booker T. Washington Memorial Hospital at Voorhees, with its one-story portico of Tuscan columns across the front facade, is Voorhees's own monument to the "Tuskegee machine."

William Wilson Cooke's network at Claflin included fellow faculty member R. Charles Bates, who wrote the first treatise on architecture and building by an African American in 1892. In *The Elementary Principles of Architecture and Building*, Bates contends, "There are but few facts more manifest than that the architecture of a people exhibits their nature, and defines the historical place they occupy in civilization . . . the range [of the term architecture] is from the hut of a barbarian to the palace of a person of the highest civilization."[46] Well aware of the conditions of the race, Bates reflects on nationalism and its relation to architectural design: "In the earlier days each nation had its architectural peculiarities, and they have them now; but the difference to-day is that then they were fixed, now they are flexible and subject to amendment, and change is sure to follow change . . . yet the nationality of each kind of mind has been indelibly stamped."[47]

The socio-spatial complexities entailed with uplift work are more difficult to analyze from this historical distance. Today a researcher labors to determine how symbolic were the architectural choices at Manassas and Voorhees, and whether they mollified racial animosity or stirred up familiar anti-Black sentiment. It would certainly be difficult, even futile, to point to any one architectural feature as a lightning rod in particular, but certainly these institutions overall served as conspicuous targets for racial conflict. Previous scholars have demurred on this issue. In her study of Robert R. Taylor and his contributions to Tuskegee as director of mechanical industries from 1892 to 1899, Ellen Weiss has maintained that Tuskegee's adoption of the Colonial Revival style did not provoke racial violence or attacks against the campus. Weiss writes, "white Alabamians did not threaten Tuskegee for building a columnar portico, the supreme symbol of power and authority of western civilization. Architectural forms in this instance were less closely tied to political and cultural meaning than much current criticism supposes."[48]

Yet historical records certainly affirm that Tuskegee was targeted with threats of violence. In the 1920s the Ku Klux Klan marched against the campus to try to undermine Black control of the Tuskegee Veterans Hospital. Other racially motivated incidents might have gone unreported by Tuskegee at the time, as even a whisper of negative press might have impacted the amount of contributions from white benefactors.[49] Wright herself withstood harassment, threats, and insults hurled against her and her school on several occasions. The threat of future property damage was made apparent when the Harrell College for Negroes in Seneca, South Carolina, was dynamited by white supremacists—a little over a couple hours by train from Voorhees—leaving the building heavily damaged and near ruin.[50] The material culture of these Black campuses embodied a perceived threat to the Southern white agenda that sought to maintain control over the New South, politically, socially, and economically.

Historian Ellen Weiss argued that "the ironies of the elegant Ionic portico or the 'stately Southern Colonial' style [on the Carnegie Library of 1901 at Tuskegee], are enormous—the reminder of antebellum slavery being only the most obvious."[51] Weiss argued, mistakenly I would maintain, that since we know of few examples of white Alabamians threatening the campus "for building the supreme symbol of power and authority of western civilization," it might appear that these structures were not regarded as provocative.[52] Weiss wrote, "Architectural symbols, apparently, are actually fairly free of political and cultural meaning, unlike political or professional realities or social conventions."[53] Weiss fails to appreciate the architectural symbolism employed by Washington and his architects; why Weiss privileged the late twentieth century's claim to irony is unclear. The complexity of the historical experiences of African Americans in the late nineteenth century is undeniable. Perhaps whites of the Progressive era would have substituted outrage for irony after viewing the "stately Southern Colonial" style on Tuskegee's buildings.

I maintain that the use of the so-called "elegant Ionic portico" has always held a deeper meaning and is symbolic of Black attempts to express political, social, and economic advances in the New South. As such, both Booker T. Washington and Robert Taylor were clearly concerned with the visual messages that the campus might convey to outsiders. Architectural history has also reinforced beliefs once widespread in the study of material culture that it was the preserve of architects emerging from dominant culture to inscribe the symbolism of Western power and authority through built form. Rather, Cornel West has argued that "the challenge is to try and understand architectural practices as power-laden cultural practices that are deeply affected by larger historical forces."[54] Through this prism, African Americans were expressing a renewed sense of self-determination and collective community empowerment through a "transcript" hidden from dominant culture in the design of their campus buildings.

Those architects initially trained at places like Tuskegee approached the study and practice of architecture very differently from those trained only at elite Northern white schools. Community building, as the Tuskegee graduates were taught, was an essential part of architectural practice. Ideally, Booker T. Washington holds both school and community as inseparable, and Washington was outspoken against those educated at schools that "instead of working out and teaching methods of connecting the school with life, thus making it a centre and a source of interest that might gradually transform the communities about them, these colleges have too frequently permitted their graduates to go out with the idea that their diploma was a sort of patent of nobility."[55] Taylor in particular saw building and construction as an important but lost set of practices among African Americans. In 1911 he wrote:

> It is about forty-five years since the negro was emancipated and, therefore, about forty-five years in which he has had an opportunity to think for himself. Prior to that time he was subject to the master class, who were responsible for providing work for him and seeing that he performed his work according to plans and methods definitely laid out. . . . He built the houses, boats and bridges, made the wagons and buggies, did ordinary machine work. In some of the trades he developed a certain degree of skill, showing a large native capacity, but these were few and isolated cases. Where fine work was to be done . . . men were brought from other parts of the country or even European countries . . . the negroes were an unlettered people, and therefore lacked the mental training to back up the skill of hand.[56]

He went on to suggest that, in their eagerness to break away from their immediate past, African Americans were rejecting critical skills they had acquired as slaves. Taylor therefore understood his role as a kind of pioneer, attempting to revive interest in the technical trades and professions.[57]

The Colonial Revival at the Manassas Industrial School

Unlike Voorhees College, the Manassas Industrial School for Colored Youth is no longer in existence, but surviving photographs depict a Colonial Revival/vernacular composition and ensemble of generous gables, gambrel roofs, and porches (figure 36). The stripped-down Colonial Revival style employed in some buildings here were in the service of a vernacular means of construction, but many college campuses of the time used similar design strategies, presumably for the same financial and practical, as well as symbolic, reasons. Founder Jennie Dean's tireless fund-raising work enabled Manassas to be designed top-down, by preeminent white architects who had already made their mark on other (not predominantly Black) colleges and universities. Voorhees, on the other hand, went through several phases of construction: founder Elizabeth Evelyn Wright, having started from bare ground, erected her first vernacular buildings, and then, with greater resources at her command, retained male African American architects and construction professionals trained at Tuskegee, Wright's alma mater, for later work.

Three photographs by W. Fred Dowell that survive in the collections of the Virginia Historical Society provide the casual viewer tantalizing evidence of the formal compositional strategy that was being realized at the Manassas campus. The most striking of the three images was shot at a considerable distance from the school's center showing Hackley Hall, Howland Hall, and the Carnegie Library (figure 37). The bare physical landscape surrounding the three buildings remind the viewer of the site's historical significance as a former battlefield. The land itself is mostly grass, with the exception of a few trees that sparsely shade the school site. As a composition, the three buildings give witness to African Americans' growing facility in the industrial trades—the craftsmanship has been well documented in the archive of photographer Frances Benjamin Johnston at the Library of Congress, for example—while also providing a telling statement of the Civil War's destruction. The photographs help to tell not only the story of enslavement but attest to how a blasted landscape could be transformed by African Americans in the New South.

A Battlefield Campus

With the school built on a leveled battlefield site, the grounds of the campus were largely grassy, open, and flat. Small decorative shrubs and trees soon dotted the landscape; some appeared to be random, while some served to demarcate organizing lines. Sidewalks connected the three primary buildings on campus, with a large walkway running across the front of the Carnegie Library, the only one of the three main buildings that was built after a major fire that had destroyed both Howland Hall and Hackley Hall (rebuilt in 1901). Around that time, the Manassas Board of Directors retained New York City–based landscape architect Charles Wellford Leavitt to draft a new master plan for the school.[58]

Leavitt was chosen by the Manassas board, presumably because of his close association with George Foster Peabody, a native Georgian gone north to a successful career on Wall Street in New York City, and who, as a philanthropist, had promoted Black educational reform since the Reconstruction era of the late 1860s. Trained as an engineer, Charles Wellford Leavitt Jr. was a white man from the upper classes, educated at two elite private schools in the North: the Gunnery in Washington, Connecticut, and Cheltenham Academy in Cheltenham, Pennsylvania. In 1891, at the age of twenty, he began his career as the engineer in charge of construction for the Caldwell Railway. In 1897 Leavitt opened his own practice in New York City, describing himself as a "landscape engineer." He preferred this term to "landscape architect" because it made reference to his engineering background and his expertise in large-scale landscape, civil-engineering, and city-planning projects. Leavitt's professional goal was to "produce results that approach perfection . . . through matured study and skilled workmanship."[59]

Critics have noted Leavitt's competent manipulation of scale and his extensive use of site-specific landscaping throughout his works. Leavitt's civic projects, beginning at the turn of the twentieth century, included city plans for Long Beach and Garden City on Long Island, New York; New Cape May, New Jersey; and Lakeland, Florida. More important, however, were his campus designs, including plans for the University of Georgia at Athens; Lehigh University at Bethlehem, Pennsylvania; and the University of South Carolina. Other institutional work included the Berry School in Rome, Georgia (now Berry College); the Tome Institute, Port Deposit, Maryland; and plans for the presidential palace in Havana, Cuba.[60] Leavitt had modeled much of his design for the Manassas Industrial School after his plans for the University of Georgia at Athens. Once again the universe of Northern philanthropy played a key role, with George Foster Peabody introducing Leavitt to the university's eleventh chancellor, Walter Barnard Hill. Peabody had earlier met Chancellor Hill at the University of Georgia's gala centennial celebration in 1901, and presumably Peabody introduced Leavitt to the leadership at the Manassas Industrial School.

At Manassas, the main design element of the unrealized Leavitt plan of 1908 would be the creation of a long mall intended to run along a north-south axis that began at the entrance to the school site and terminated at a Christian chapel (figure 38). Thomas Jefferson's arrangement of buildings around the open "Lawn" at the University of Virginia culminates in a secularized, domed Pantheon-like structure at the focal point. In the Manassas plan, ten pavilion-like structures are interspersed along a series of one-story dormitories arranged around a terraced "great lawn," with the chapel at its head.[61] Along the main axis, Leavitt proposed the placement of administration buildings and residences for various school officials. He then divided the trades and industry programs from the academic curriculum along either side of the mall by employing their own respective quadrangles on an east-west axis, accompanied by a large dining hall. The incorporation of a secondary axis, a cross, suggests both religious intention—literally inscribing the body of Christ, the savior of the race, onto the landscape—and the Manassas Industrial School's commitment to provide its students with an education both in the liberal arts and the manual trades (both head and hand). The secondary quadrangles could also be used as parade grounds for school ceremonies and displays of educational achievements. The entire master plan was ringed by a service road that led to a series of outer farm buildings. The chapel, located prominently at the focal point of the mall, can be seen to symbolize Dean's own commitment to the religious and spiritual and her emergence from African American church culture and society. The prominent placement of the chapel also suggests the strong link between religion, educational advancement, and race progress. Although clearly influenced by Jefferson, Leavitt reimagines the secular architectural plan, and in the design of individual buildings and as a trained professional, Leavitt transcends the limits of the gentleman-architect tradition of the early North American colonies and states—architects of the kind who often designed early college campuses as little more than a collection of large houses.[62]

Not long after Jennie Dean established Manassas Industrial College in 1893, the primary structures on the campus were built. Over time, the campus grew to two hundred acres, including a model farm. Two dormitories—Howland Hall (figure 39) and Hackley Hall (figure 40)—and the Carnegie Library were the three primary buildings that dominated the campus and formed its core. These buildings were different in their detailing and components, but they related to each other stylistically and were similar in scale. These three buildings surrounded a central quadrangle (this predates the quadrangles of the succeeding Leavitt plan), although only the Carnegie Library opened onto it. Howland Hall and Hackley Hall faced the same direction as the Library.

While these three buildings formed the core of the campus, Manassas also had numerous smaller buildings, including Bailey Hall (residence), Charter Cottage (classroom and dormitory), Orchard Cottage (farmhouse), Berwind Hospital, and Roof Tree (principal's house). These buildings were smaller, built of wood with clapboard siding, and almost domestic in scale. As such, these secondary buildings contrast with the honorific and ceremonial buildings at the center of campus. At least one of the domestic-scale buildings did not face the quadrangle, reinforcing the understanding that other compositional and functional hierarchies were emerging early within the Manassas built environment.

Leavitt's plan for Manassas attempted to incorporate the necessary functional and symbolic programming required for an institution to compete in the emerging twentieth-century educational landscape, an undertaking similar to his work at the University of Georgia in Athens.[63] With the Ecole des Beaux-Arts already providing an enormous impetus to American city planning and architecture—at the World's Columbian Exposition of 1893 and elsewhere—on the emerging American campus, the Beaux Arts movement sought to create a parallel "City of Learning," correcting what were perceived as the compositional and design deficiencies of earlier American colleges.

Architectural design, as attested to in surviving photographs, was rooted in the Colonial Revival mainstream. Built to be a men's dormitory, Hackley Hall was a neo-Georgian brick institutional building with a gable-end central mass, a small portico at the entrance door, and a cupola. It was typical for Colonial Revival buildings to have honorific entrances, and Hackley Hall's, with its white wood porch, stood out against the red brick facade. During the Colonial Revival, entrances were often marked by a repertoire of standard design elements surrounding the door, such as broken pediments, fanlights, and sidelights, yet these elements were not present on this building.[64] The windows in Hackley Hall were unique six-over-two double-hung sashes. It was common for Colonial Revival windows to be multipane upper sashes over a single lower pane, but in Hackley Hall, the lower sash has two panes, making for not only a unique design but perhaps a pragmatic concession to the local availability and cost of building materials such as glass.[65]

Also built in 1894 (with a massive addition in 1907) and rebuilt after the fire, Howland Hall (named after philanthropist Emily Howland of New York) was intended to be a girls' dormitory and dining hall. The Hall continued to serve this purpose after its reconstruction. In the pre-1907 building the front facade was on the end gable and not, as was more typical, on the long facade.[66] By placing the entrance to the Hall on the gable end and by having a tower, it is even conceivable that the architect may have been drawing an allusion to the one-room schoolhouses of recent African American history with their gable-end entrances and bell towers with hipped roofs.[67] The later addition to Howland Hall had Colonial Revival–style elements, also in a stripped-down Tuscan order. An expansive fanlight is a typical element of Colonial Revival style, but in the addition to Howland, the fanlight is small-scaled and simply detailed. On the side of the building, the two third-floor windows were connected by an arch with a not-so-canonical Palladian-type window. The gambrel roof appears oversized, and the second floor cut out with the gable dormer was, again, unique.

The Carnegie Library was a symmetrical Beaux Arts–type building with a central mass and flanking wings, a hipped roof, and three large shed dormers. The use of classical ornament—one of the stylistic ties to the use of classical orders—has almost disappeared here, generally restricted to a few cornices and door surrounds. Design of the Library becomes a dignified and ingenious essay in almost pure brick masonry—no doubt as a cost-saving strategy—much like buildings at the Tuskegee Institute and the Hampton Institute. Above the front door transom was a shallow arch of bricks, and there was one unornamented brick pilaster on the outside of each of the sidelights so that the doorway seemed to be recessed. Above the arch was a masonry plaque, which also sat within the projecting brick design. On either side of the front door there were six, six-over-six double-hung sash windows. Above each window was a three-light transom awning window, and above the transoms there were splayed lintels made of brick. The front of the Library faced the quadrangle, and there is a hyphen from the back facade connecting the main structure to the Industrial Building.

Structures intended to provide community services were also an important part of Manassas. Berwind Hospital (1901–15), a two-story wooden structure (a gift from Northern philanthropist John E. Berwind, of the Berwind-White Coal Mining Company), contained a boys' ward, a girls' ward, nurses' room, isolation rooms, kitchenette, sun porches, and well-equipped bathrooms. In addition, there were three houses on the school grounds that acted as models to demonstrate advances in the domestic sciences and agriculture. Charter Cottage (1893/94) served as a dormitory after initially being used as the school's first classroom building. Orchard Cottage was a farmhouse with eight rooms and a cellar used by the school's farmer. The third house, Roof Tree, was used as the principal's home and was constructed in the summer of 1907.

From records, we can discern many features of the Manassas campus, but how Dean intended the campus to be "read" is a matter of speculation. Accepting some of the architectural stylistic conventions of the time—in particular from the Beaux Arts and Colonial Revival—and by appropriating them, the researcher asks if she knowingly subverted the white master's narrative and iconography. Again, Dean leaves no written documentation attesting to this. In any event, making a conscious decision to ally herself with the Northern white philanthropic establishment, and employing men such as Charles W. Leavitt as architects and planners, Dean certainly raised the ante, as it were, with the Southern white establishment. The humiliating childhood experiences of slavery now a generation behind her, Dean's achievements underscored that African Americans were literally transforming the landscape. Her obituary stated: "This worthy woman spent her declining years in the neighborhood in which she was born and enjoyed the fullest respect of her white neighbors. Her work will live after her and make her name for many generations an inspiration to those of her race who would emulate her difficult achievements."[68]

Slavery had stripped away the social organization that served Africans' personal and communal needs—kinship, culture, and community—with a system that advantaged white slave-owning society.[69] Later, African Americans would find themselves being physically terrorized and psychically shamed once again in the post-Reconstruction South. Dean's and Wright's built responses to enslavement and its trauma—the construction of the Manassas Industrial

School and Voorhees College—garnered them and their community authority and power over the legacy of enslavement. The buildings on these campuses serve as a form of testimony, an eyewitness account to the ravages endured by African Americans under chattel slavery and their ultimate transcendence. Acting for Dean and Wright as a counternarrative to slavery, the buildings themselves are a unique "living monument,"[70] and provided a bricks-and-mortar community for post-Reconstruction African Americans. Also, in light of her presumed borderline literacy (as was discussed earlier), while Dean's record through storytelling and preaching was that of an oral tradition, her buildings would act on her behalf as a form of material culture and archival testimony. Wright, on the other hand, well schooled and ambitious, intending to be "as much a woman as Washington was a man," would also have known too well how Southern whites would respond in outrage to her school as a "site of memory" for the Civil War, the physical immediacy of her campus all too evident.

The buildings testify to the trauma experienced by former slaves and raise important questions about the inherent tensions between enslavement and liberation.[71] The enslaved had not been seen as fully human, being little more than domestic property, but they could now, as a freed people within their own institutions, assert their humanity and recount their personal memories of the past.[72] Recalling the church mission schools that Jennie Dean had built in northern Virginia shortly after the Civil War that served as sites of reunification for the Black race, Manassas and Voorhees also demonstrated a form of communal resistance against Jim Crow, demonstrating strength in the unity of the emerging African American nation. Regardless of the many efforts by whites to rewrite the past and disavow Black contributions to the South, African Americans had secured the right and agency to create the spaces necessary for social reform. For African Americans, the emerging nation seen in microcosm at Manassas and Voorhees—one, a school founded by a formerly enslaved woman, the other by a woman representing the first generation of the post-Civil War educated classes—would continue the struggle of reformers crossing gender and racial lines as they worked toward a nationalist agenda.

Chapter Six

Historically Black Colleges and Universities

In Service to the Race

The ideal Black woman of the Victorian era was expected to be committed to the domestic sphere as a wife and mother, acting as a dutiful companion to her husband while maintaining and managing an attractive home. Yet as many scholars have argued, the ideal of the postbellum Black woman was different from what was demanded of "true womanhood" by white society: the Black woman was expected to participate fully in both the private and public spheres. By the late nineteenth century, while Black men were active and empowering themselves in public debate, African American women were involved in the founding and building of institutions for the race. But few scholars have recognized the inherent distinctions between the efforts of working-class women who struggled against the simultaneous categories of race, class, and gender within the Black community, and those elite women who were afforded social privilege. Elite Black women were expected to participate within the acceptable boundaries of the "cult of true womanhood," which espoused "piety, purity, submissiveness, and domesticity." Women were only expected to participate in public affairs through their local churches.[1] Unlike elite white women, who began to blur the distinctions between private and public only during the Progressive era, African American working-class women reformers had long been engaged in community affairs, working across the categories of race, class, and gender. The distinctions between public and private spheres, or the dichotomy between domestic and public, particularly among African American women, is unique. Black women found ways to challenge the traditional paradigms of patriarchy and hierarchy, which relegated women to separate spheres, through their efforts in race uplift. Black women reformers, because of their acknowledged duties as the mothers and wives of the race, assumed the primary responsibility for communal self-improvement, challenging the politics and power of separate spheres as the tools of male oppression.[2] African American women who broke with these gendered notions of propriety were, however, prepared to meet the challenges of their roles as bearers of culture and as agents for historical recovery, regardless of their treatment by Black male reformers.

Historically Black Colleges and Universities Today

Today, the historically Black college and university (HBCU) campus, as a standing cultural artifact, uniquely reflects the historical experiences of Southern African Americans in the decades following enslavement, the trauma of which persists and is regularly revisited even into the early years of the twenty-first century. For generations, HBCUs were the only institutions of higher education open to Southern African American students, and were, in many respects, the epicenter of any community throughout the rural South fortunate enough to host one.[3] Today, one might well wonder what significance the sites of HBCUs now hold in a "multicultural," "pluralist," and "post-racial" society.[4]

HBCUs around the country had been perceived by white southerners after the Civil War as exclusively African American institutions that attempted to radically restructure the social and political order after the abolition of chattel slavery, further confounding those efforts of the New South's elite planter class to represent their wartime defeat as a victory nonetheless. For many white southerners, the continued subjugation of Blacks through debt peonage and sharecropping was ultimately a successful revival of indentured servitude. The dominant white social order of the South had been simply recast and appropriated from the antebellum to the postwar South. Meanwhile the many failures of Reconstruction only helped to secure and bolster the continued attacks and mistreatment of African Americans under the rule of Southern mob violence. However, Black institutions founded on the basic principles of self-empowerment and political autonomy through agricultural and mechanical education, in addition to the education afforded by the liberal arts, threatened a long-established social order that persisted despite defeat on the war's battlefields.

Today, the National Center for Education Statistics reports that roughly 12.9 percent of Black undergraduate students attend historically Black colleges and universities, yet these institutions graduate a disproportionate 21.5 percent of the Black undergraduate population.[5] Despite the continued significance of HBCUs in the historical and cultural landscape of the South, there was no targeted federal effort to secure historic preservation among HBCUs until 1986, when Fisk University received a congressional appropriation of $161,000 for repairs at Jubilee Hall, a National Historic Landmark, in an attempt to provide aid to Fisk after it had fallen on hard times during the late 1970s and early 1980s. Repair work done on Fisk's Jubilee Hall helped convince potential donors and grantors to provide funding to ensure the school's future. By the end of the Clinton Administration, HBCUs across the country had received well over $10 million for preservation and community revitalization projects since those first efforts at Fisk. Yet at one point, the General Accounting Office estimated that $775 million would be required for an estimated 712 HBCU properties found to be in danger, with about half of the structures already on the National Register.[6]

The first program to distribute funds was made possible through the Secretary of the Interior's Historic Preservation Initiative for HBCUs, a program that grew out of discussions with the Department of the Interior and the United Negro College Fund. The presidents of several Black colleges and universities had expressed their concern over the fate of their most historic buildings, many of which were in danger of collapse. A second effort emerged after advocacy on the part of then-Rep. James Clyburn of South Carolina. An Omnibus Parks Bill of 1996 provided funding for twelve more school buildings eligible after an additional $21 million was approved by Congress.[7] This compares to overall federal outlays of $1.56 trillion in 1996. By 2009, twenty HBCUs had received federal stimulus money to preserve historic buildings on their campuses.[8]

Fisk, along with other HBCUs, is enjoying support from alumni who have supported preservation of physical heritage and tradition.[9] One Park Service official agreed that the colleges "have noticed increased support from alumni, foundations, and improvements in attitude among students and faculty. It also stimulates the community around the college."[10] President Marguerite Archie-Hudson of Talladega College in Alabama maintained that the HBCUs are "going to continue to make a case to the National Historic Trust that these buildings constitute American treasures and really are a story of a significant portion of American higher education, and [are] as valuable as all other artifacts. The historic stock in terms of buildings on these campuses is invaluable."[11]

Memory Sites and Naming

Starting in 1989, the Black communities of Manassas and the surrounding area have worked to commemorate the accomplishments of Jennie Dean and the Manassas Industrial School with the construction of a memorial site project on the school's former site (now adjacent to the Jennie Dean Elementary School). The Manassas Society for the Preservation of Black Heritage approached the Manassas City Council, arguing that the "Project preserves an idea, an institution, and seeks to depict the struggles and the contributions made by

Afro-Americans in the development of the Piedmont region following the Civil War."[12] The project was completed in 1995 and included the placement of outlines of several of the school's original buildings, historic markers, landscaping, an information kiosk, sculpture, and a model of the original campus.

Visitors to HBCU campuses today will find little mention of the generation of tenacious post-Reconstruction women reformers. A kind of historical amnesia prevalent at most colleges and universities manifests itself in the naming of buildings in honor of donors, faculty, administrators, and even students. Most of us take for granted that campus buildings are, more often than not, named after an institution's financial benefactors. But few among us stop to consider the sort of history lesson being played out at as one examines the names of buildings, the information provided on historical markers, or what is represented by the sort of statues and sculptural reliefs so often found around college campuses. Most interesting is the way in which institutional memory and its history is portrayed and displayed at these sites. At Mississippi Valley State University there are now streets named in honor of Medgar Evers and Fannie Lou Hamer, two of the more influential African Americans fighting for the causes of civil rights in the state of Mississippi and both of whom also attended college there. Yet one will also find a Walter Sillers Fine Arts Building named in honor of Walter Sillers Jr. (1888–1966) and a Fielding Wright (1895–1956) Science Building—both honorees being white segregationist political leaders drawn from Mississippi's recent fraught history.[13] Elsewhere, leading colleges and universities outside the South have been forced to confront dark histories: for example, after months of protests, Yale University's Calhoun College, once named in honor of U.S. vice president and Yale graduate, John C. Calhoun (a staunch defender of Southern slavery, characterizing it as a "positive good"), has been recently renamed Grace Hopper College in honor of computer scientist and U.S. Navy rear admiral, Grace Murray Hopper, awarded a PhD in mathematics from Yale in 1934.

Historical amnesia as to the origins and purpose of HBCUs can be found at the highest levels in dominant culture even today. The Trump Administration's Secretary of Education Betsy DeVos, the titular head of education in the United States—cluelessly confused the origins of HBCUs, saluting them as exemplars of choice when there was no choice at all to be had among African Americans after Reconstruction, when the penniless, formerly enslaved were cast out and their rights were suppressed. Historical amnesia of another kind can be found at HBCUs across the country that have failed to honor the important work of women reformers in the founding of these normal and industrial schools—one of the few exceptions being Elizabeth Evelyn Wright Hall at Voorhees. Making such women reformers invisible is a disservice to students. As historian James W. Loewen suggests, "When institutions of higher learning tell their history fully and honestly, they also exemplify good historical practice for their students. In the process they provide a much-needed lesson about the contentious, sometimes unpleasant, nature of truth."[14] In 2016, when the National Trust for Historic Preservation made Morgan State University in Baltimore (Maryland's largest historically Black college) one of the newest National Treasure sites, Stephanie Meeks, then president and CEO of the National Trust, wrote in her announcement that "[HBCUs] tell an important and often overlooked American story that should be told."[15]

Lincoln Park: A Living Monument

Reality itself is layered. The unveiling of a statue in Lincoln Park in 1876 did not just honor the martyred president, but in doing so acted to preserve the memory of the Civil War and the impact of the president's Emancipation Proclamation on African Americans—at the same time as Lincoln's history vis-à-vis emancipation had been called into question by Black leaders such as Douglass. The monument site itself was significant, sitting as it did on the grounds of a former Union campground and temporary war facility, the Lincoln Hospital, to further remind students of the Civil War how African Americans had fought to secure their own freedom. For former slaves such as Dean, who remembered the site as a place where escaped slaves from the Upper South sought refuge, it invoked a collective meaning.[16] The site became a kind of living monument or historical marker that changed over time. Even more importantly for the "biography of place" associated with this site were the contributions of thousands of African American soldiers and women, who helped to erect the actual monument through fund-raising activities shortly after Lincoln's death. Through this national fund-raising effort, the Black community recognized itself as participating as a collective in self-help initiatives.

In the Progressive era, African American men contended with disenfranchisement that hindered them from advancing causes for race betterment. Meanwhile, white Southerners who opposed memorials to the enslaved—such as the memorial to the Black Mammy—argued, "This is not the time for erecting monuments to the old slave—if there will ever be a time. Our country is already black with their living presence. Shall there be a black monument erected in every fair Southern city or State, when there is not a State in the South not in mourning for some beautiful woman whose life has been strangled out by some black fiend?"[17] African American women were left to respond to these slurs and stereotypes in the arenas left open to them in education, the mass media (especially newspapers), or race literature.

Hate persists. A pattern of harassment and intimidation against HBCUs was demonstrated on the eve of this century in January 2000, shortly after the New Year's festivities. Southern University in Louisiana was one of several HBCUs that tightened campus security efforts after receiving a letter threatening the impending escalation of a racial holy war. Within days of each other,

Fisk University and Meharry Medical College, both in Nashville, Tennessee, Alabama's Oakwood College (now Oakwood University) in Huntsville, A&M University, Alabama State University, and Stillman College in Tuscaloosa, Alabama, all received the same message: an unsigned one-page hate letter, decorated with a Confederate flag. It opened with the salutation, "This is to all you Niggers." At the very top of the letter, the word "RAHOWA" was scrawled in upper-case letters, an acronym for "Racial Holy War." In the first paragraph the author writes, "We hope you're getting all the education you can in your so called historical . . . colleges, and universities. You're just wasting precious time. . . . We will eventually get rid of all you niggers one way or another. The total destruction of your race is our mission in life."[18] And in closing, the letter warned that in the "Year 2000, the war escalates. . . . The White race will be preserved forever."[19] Autonomous Black institutions such as HBCUs are still lightning rods for outbreaks of racism and bigotry even in the twenty-first century.

Reinscribing Power and Agency: Wright and Dean

Pierre Nora, in "Between Memory and History: Les Lieux de Mémorie," has argued that we are in a critical moment in our own history as sites of memory continue to be destroyed in the wake of industrial growth and expansion. He suggests that "a process of decolonization has affected ethnic minorities . . . that until now have possessed reserves of memory but little or no historical capital."[20] According to Nora, "we have seen the end of societies that had long assured the transmission and conservation of collectively remembered values, whether through churches or schools, the family or the state; the end too of ideologies that prepared a smooth passage from the past to the future or that had indicated that the future should keep from the past. . . ."[21] Institutions, among African Americans of the late nineteenth century, became the most important transmitters of communal memory and collective identity. African American women's creation of a new public order involved a struggle for the control of memory—of slavery and their eventual survival as a community—that few whites were willing to acknowledge. Women reformers understood that in founding these all-Black institutions, they were not only reinscribing power and agency—something today understood as intersectional strategies—but were also promoting collective resistance and advancement, strategies that would ultimately work to transcend divisions and inequities of race and gender.[22]

Notes

Introduction

Epigraph: Dr. J. F. B. Coleman, *Tuskegee to Voorhees: The Booker T. Washington Idea Projected by Elizabeth Evelyn Wright* (Columbia, SC: The R. L. Bryan Company, 1922), v.

1. Discussions concerning industrial education or manual education began as early as the 1830s and 1840s with the New York Colored (or later, Negro) Convention Movement. Industrial education is defined as a course of instruction for students between the ages of fourteen and eighteen that prepares them to be wage earners in household arts, industry, or agriculture. Manual training is part of a general education, which teaches students the value of work, but does not train them for a specific profession. Jacqueline Jones, *Soldiers of Light and Love: Northern Teachers and Georgia Blacks, 1865–1873* (Athens: University of Georgia Press, 1992), 82, 109–10. Jones found that violence against teachers and school property was common. For further reading on Black education, see Louis R. Harlan, *Separate and Unequal* (New York: Praeger, 1970); Henry Allen Bullock, *A History of Negro Education in the South, From 1619 to the Present* (New York: Praeger, 1970); John Hope Franklin, *Schools for All: The Blacks and Public Education in the South, 1865–1877* (Lexington: University Press of Kentucky, 1974); Robert G. Sherer, *Subordination or Liberation? The Development and Conflicting Theories of Black Education in Nineteenth Century Alabama* (Tuscaloosa: University of Alabama Press, 1977); Vincent P. Franklin and James D. Anderson, eds., *New Perspectives on Black Educational History* (Boston: G. K. Hall & Co., 1978); Donald Spivey, *Schooling for the New Slavery: Black Industrial Education, 1868–1915* (New York: Greenwood Press, 1978); Robert C. Morris, *Reading, 'Riting, and Reconstruction: The Education of Freedmen in the South, 1861–1870* (Chicago: University of Chicago Press, 1981). See also "Negro Public Schools," Tuskegee Institute Clippings File, Tuskegee University Archives, Tuskegee, AL.

2. Race uplift work involving literacy, broad social and economic betterment, enfranchisement, school building, and children's health were the primary areas of concern and advocacy. Mary L. Lewis, "The White Rose Industrial Association, the Friend of the Strange Girl in New York," *The Messenger: World's Greatest Negro Monthly* 7, no. 4 (1925): 158; Virginia Matthews, "The Redemption of Our City," *Federation* 2 (July 1902): 57. Traditionally, *race uplift* attempted to regulate the actions and behaviors of African Americans in order to appeal to whites in positions of power and privilege. Wolcott argues that race uplift was in many ways evolutionary in that the road to "freedom" would be a long one and would require moral uprightness to be widely successful—a politics of respectability. Victoria Wolcott, *Remaking*

Respectability: African American Women in Inter-War Detroit (Chapel Hill: University of North Carolina Press, 2001), 13–14.

3. Coleman, *Tuskegee to Voorhees*; "Death of the Founder of the Manassas Industrial School," *Manassas Journal*, n.d., 2; "Industrial School Founder Succumbs," *Manassas Democrat*, May 8, 1913, 1. The only full-length studies or biographies of African American women educators of the late nineteenth and early twentieth centuries in recent years include works on Mary McLeod Bethune, Charlotte Hawkins Brown, and Eugenia Burns Hope. Recent edited collections still make no mention of Wright or Dean. Karen A. Johnson, Abdul Pitre, and Kenneth L. Johnson, eds., *African American Women Educators: A Critical Examination of Their Pedagogies, Educational Ideas, and Activism from the Nineteenth to the Mid-twentieth Century* (New York: R&L Education, 2014), 1–22; Bobby L. Lovett, *America's Historically Black Colleges and Universities: A Narrative History, 1837–2009* (Macon, GA: Mercer University Press, 2015). For a discussion of the ways in which landmarks help us understand our past, see James Oliver Horton, *Landmarks of African American History* (New York: Oxford University Press, 2005), 8–10.

4. Mia Bay, "The Battle for Womanhood Is the Battle for Race: Black Women and Nineteenth-Century Racial Thought," in *Toward an Intellectual History of Black Women*, ed. Mia Bay and Farah J. Griffin (Baltimore: Johns Hopkins University Press, 2015), 79–80.

5. Kimberlé Crenshaw, "Mapping the Margins: Intersectionality, Identity Politics, and Violence Against Women of Color," *Stanford Law Review* 43, no. 6 (1991): 1241; Jennifer C. Nash, "re-thinking intersectionality," *Feminist Review* 89, no. 1 (2008): 2; Bonnie Thornton Dill and Ruth Enid Zambrana, "Critical Thinking About Inequality: An Emerging Lens," in *Emerging Intersections: Race, Class, and Gender in Theory, Policy, and Practice*, ed. Bonnie Thornton Dill and Ruth Enid Zambrana (New Brunswick, NJ: Rutgers University Press, 2009), 7; Sumi Cho, Kimberlé Williams Crenshaw, and Leslie McCall, "Toward a Field of Intersectionality Studies: Theory, Applications, and Praxis," *Signs: Journal of Women and Culture in Society* 38, no. 4 (2013): 785–810.

6. Carol Faulkner and Alison M. Parker, *Interconnections: Gender and Race in American History* (New York: University of Rochester Press, 2012), 1–4.

7. An intersectional feminist framework (or IFF) also looks to ways of fostering social justice and empowering communities. Although a slightly later period, Matthews-Gardner found that the National Association of Colored Women (NACW) was one of the few remaining autonomous Black organizations that could be called civic that remained politically active in the public sphere. They struggled with how to address their collective identities that defined their race and gender. A. Lanethea Matthews-Gardner, "The Postwar Black Women's Club Movement: The Intersection of Gender, Race, and American Political Development, 1940–1960," *Journal of Women, Politics and Policy* 31, no. 3 (2010): 260.

8. Here I draw heavily on Sara Ahmed, *Living a Feminist Life* (Durham, NC: Duke University Press, 2017), 4–5.

9. Patricia Hill Collins and Sirma Bilge, *Intersectionality* (Cambridge, MA: Polity Press, 2016), 27; Bonnie Thornton Dill, Amy McLaughlin, and Angel David Nieves, "Future Directions of Feminist Research: Intersectionality," in *Handbook of Feminist Research: Theory and Praxis*, ed. Sharlene Nagy Hesse-Biber (New York: Sage Publications, 2007), 629–37.

10. The monumental can include architecture, sculpture, painting, and other forms of material cultural production. Ellen Daugherty, "Negotiating the Veil: Tuskegee's Booker T. Washington Monument," *American Art* 24, no. 3 (Fall 2010): 52–77.

11. Carter G. Woodson, *The Education of the Negro Prior to 1861* (Washington, DC: The New Era Printing Company, 1919), 25; *Freedmen's Record* 4 (October 1867): 160.

12 Luther P. Jackson, "The Educational Efforts of the Freedmen's Bureau and Freedmen's Aid Societies in South Carolina, 1862–1872," *The Journal of Negro History* 8, no. 1 (January 1923): 1–40.

13. Ronald E. Butchart, "Remapping Racial Boundaries Teachers as Border Police and Boundary Transgressors in Post-Emancipation Black Education, USA, 1861–1876," *Paedagogica Historica: International Journal of the History of Education* 43, no. 1 (2007): 61.

14. Manning Marable, "Tuskegee and the Politics of Illusion in the New South," *Journal of Black Studies and Research* 8, no. 7 (1977): 13; Pero Gaglo Dagbovie, "Exploring a Century of Historical Scholarship on Booker T. Washington," *The Journal of African American History* 92 no. 2 (2007): 239–40.

15. W. E. B. Du Bois, *The Souls of Black Folk* (New York: Random House, 1993), 38, 44–45. Du Bois was very public about his disdain for Washington and propelled through the press (even at the time of his death) rhetoric about his accommodationist policies. W. E. B. Du Bois, "The Late Booker T. Washington," *The Crisis* 11, no. 2 (December 1915): 82.

16. Booker T. Washington, "A Sunday Evening Talk," *Tuskegee Student*, June 2, 1900, 3–4; Coleman, *Tuskegee to Voorhees*, 31.

17. J. O. Midnight, "Thousands Crowd to Hear Booker T.," *Afro-American*, March 27, 1909, 1. Recent scholarship on Washington rejects the notion that he was an "Uncle Tom" or a "sellout." Rebecca Carroll, ed., *Uncle Tom or New Negro? African Americans Reflect on Booker T. Washington and Up from Slavery One Hundred Years Later* (New York: Broadway Books, 2006), 3, 9–163.

18. Bertha La Branche, Tuskegee-educated, and her husband, Jonas Edward Johnson, cofounded the Prentiss Normal and Industrial School. Graces Morris Allen Jones cofounded the Piney Woods School. Mary Paterson Holtzclaw and her husband cofounded the Utica Normal and Industrial Institute. See Neil R. McMillen, *Dark Journey: Black Mississippians in the Age of Jim Crow* (Urbana: University of Illinois Press, 1990), 96–98.

19. *Tenth Annual Report of the Principals of the Calhoun Colored School, of Calhoun, Lowndes County, Alabama, with the Reports of the Heads of Departments* (Boston: Geo. H. Ellis Co., Printers, 1902), 1–18.

20. Kate Dossett, *Bridging Race Divides: Black Nationalism, Feminism, and Integration in the United States, 1896–1935* (Gainesville: University Press of Florida, 2008), 8.

21. Jane Rhodes, *Mary Ann Shadd Cary: The Black Press and Protest in the Nineteenth Century* (Bloomington: Indiana University Press, 1998), xiv, 22, 42.

22. Dossett, *Bridging Race Divides*, 9.

23. Ibid., 8; James Levy, "Forging African American Minds: Black Pragmatism, 'Intelligent Labor,' and a New Look at Industrial Education, 1879–1900," *American Nineteenth Century History* 17, no. 1 (2016): 46.

24. V. P. Franklin and Bettye Collier-Thomas, "Biography, Race Vindication, and African-American Intellectuals: Introductory Essay," *Journal of Negro History* 81,

no. 1–4 (1996): 1. For a compilation of primary documents and essays on Black nationalism, see John H. Bracey Jr., August Meier, and Elliott Rudwick, eds., *Black Nationalism in America* (New York: The Bobbs-Merrill Company, Inc., 1970); Wilson Jeremiah Moses, ed., *Classical Black Nationalism: From the American Revolution to Marcus Garvey* (New York: New York University Press, 1996).

25. Collective destiny, for Wilson J. Moses, is grounded to a "classical" Black nationalist tradition. See Michele Mitchell, *Righteous Propagation: African Americans and the Politics of Racial Destiny after Reconstruction* (Chapel Hill: University of North Carolina Press, 2004), 252–53; William J. Moses, "National Destiny and the Black Bourgeois Ministry," *The Wings of Ethiopia: Studies in African American Life and Letters* (Ames: Iowa State University Press, 1990), 159–77, 160, 174. The religious undertones to uplift were pervasive, but biblical references to nation were important to any understanding of race advancement.

26. Pero Gaglo Dagbovie, "Black Women Historians from the Late Nineteenth Century to the Dawning of the Civil Rights Movement," *Journal of African American History* 89, no. 3 (Summer 2004): 243. As in Dagbovie's assertion of "historians without portfolio," it might be useful to use "designers without portfolio" for the work of these Black women reformers.

27. Some recent works include Gerri Bates, "The Hallowed Halls: African American Women College and University Presidents," *The Journal of Negro Education* 76, no. 3 (2007); Ashley N. Robertson, *Mary McLeod Bethune in Florida: Bringing Social Justice to the Sunshine State* (Mount Pleasant: Arcadia Publishing, 2015); Audrey Thomas McCluskey, *A Forgotten Sisterhood: Pioneering Black Women Educators and Activists in the Jim Crow South* (New York: Rowman & Littlefield Publishers, 2014); Carroll L. L. Miller and Anne S. Pruitt-Logan, *Faithful to the Task at Hand: The Life of Lucy Diggs Slowe* (Albany: SUNY Press, 2012).

28. bell hooks, "Choosing the Margin as a Space of Radical Openness," in *Yearnings: Race, Gender and Cultural Politics* (London: Turnaround Press, 1989); bell hooks, *Feminist Theory from Margin to Center* (Cambridge, MA: South End Press, 2000). See also Nancy A. Naples, *Feminism and Method: Ethnography, Discourse Analysis, and Activist Research* (New York: Routledge, 2003), 3. Gail Lee Dubrow, "Restoring a Female Presence," in *Architecture: A Place for Women*, ed. Ellen Perry Berkeley and Matilda McQuaid (Washington, DC: Smithsonian Institution Press, 1989); Gail Lee Dubrow, "Preserving Her Heritage: American Landmarks of Women's History" (PhD diss., University of California–Los Angeles, 1991); Leonie Sandercock, "Feminist and Multicultural Perspectives on Preservation Planning," *Making the Invisible Visible: A Multicultural Planning History*, ed. Leonie Sandercock (Berkeley: University of California Press, 1998), 57–77. Also see Richard Schein, "Race and Landscape in the United States," in *Landscape and Race in the United States*, ed. Richard Schein (New York: Routledge, 2006), 15.

29. Steven Hahn, *A Nation under Our Feet: Black Political Struggles in the Rural South from Slavery to the Great Migration* (Cambridge, MA: The Belknap Press of Harvard University Press, 2003), 279. This work is significant because it moves the historiography of the period away from a "liberal integrationist framework" to a more critical understanding of slaves and freed people as political agents or actors. Education in the postwar South would not have been possible without the efforts of freed people during the Civil War. Heather Andrea Williams, *Self-Taught: African*

American Education in Slavery and Freedom (Chapel Hill: University of North Carolina Press, 2007).

30. Joseph Heathcott, "Review," *Winterthur Portfolio* 46, no. 4 (Winter 2012): 309–10; Craig Barton, ed., *Sites of Memory: Perspectives on Architecture and Race* (Princeton, NJ: Princeton Architectural Press, 2001); Randy Mason, *The Once and Future New York: Historic Preservation and the Modern City* (Minneapolis: University of Minnesota Press, 2009); Max Page, *The Creative Destruction of Manhattan, 1900–1940* (Chicago: University of Chicago Press, 2001).

31. Dianne Harris, "Social History: Identity, Performance, Politics, and Architectural History," *Journal of the Society of Architectural Historians* 64, no. 4 (December 2005): 422.

32. Tom Snyder, *120 Years of American Education: A Statistical Portrait* (Washington, DC: National Center for Education Statistics, 1993), 9.

33. Frances Ellen Watkins Harper, "Woman's Political Future," in *World's Congress of Representative Women*, ed. May Wright Sewall (Chicago: Rand McNally, 1894), 433–37; Manning Marable, "Introduction," *Souls* 2, no. 4 (Fall 2000): 6.

34. Carol Faulkner, *Women's Radical Reconstruction: The Freedmen's Aid Movement* (Philadelphia: University of Pennsylvania Press, 2007), 151–52.

35. Thomas J. Brown, *Civil War Canon: Sites of Confederate Memory in South Carolina* (Chapel Hill: University of North Carolina Press, 2015), 132. Few works consider the actual space or site of ritual lynchings in any detail; see Amy Louise Wood, *Lynching and Spectacle: Witnessing Racial Violence in America, 1890–1940* (Chapel Hill: University of North Carolina Press, 2011), 8–9.

36. James West Davidson, *"They Say": Ida B. Wells and the Reconstruction of Race* (New York: Oxford University Press, 2008), 171, 197; Mia Bay, *To Tell the Truth Freely: The Life of Ida B. Wells* (New York: Hill and Wang, 2010), 131–32.

37. Ellen Weiss, "Robert R. Taylor of Tuskegee: An Early Black Architect," *ARRIS: Journal of the Southeastern Society of Architectural Historians* 2 (1991): 3–19; Ellen Weiss, *Robert R. Taylor and Tuskegee: An African American Architect Designs for Booker T. Washington* (Montgomery, AL: New South Books, 2012), 30, 79, 129, 228.

38. The Inter Ocean, *Centennial History of the City of Chicago. Its Men and Institutions. Biographical Sketches of Leading Citizens* (Chicago: Inter Ocean, 1905), 45.

39. Robert W. Rydell, "The City as Playground: The World's Fair Midways," in *Going Out: The Rise and Fall of Public Amusements*, ed. David Nasaw (Cambridge, MA: Harvard University Press, 1993), 62–79.

40. Abraham Flexner, *Universities: American, English, German* (New York: Oxford University Press, 1930), 14, 19.

41. Paul Venable Turner, *Campus: An American Planning Tradition* (Cambridge, MA: The MIT Press, 1987), 4.

42. Patricia C. Sherwood and Joseph Michael Lasala, "Education and Architecture: The Evolution of the University of Virginia's Academical Village," in *Thomas Jefferson's Academical Village: The Creation of an Architectural Masterpiece*, ed. Richard Guy Wilson (Charlottesville: University of Virginia Press, 1993), 9; Gary Wills, *Mr. Jefferson's University* (Washington, DC: National Geographic Society, 2002), 9. Jefferson drew on these two books for his pavilion design: James Gibbs, *Rules for Drawing the Several Parts of Architecture: In a More Exact and Easy Manner Than Has Heretofore Practised* (London: W. Innys, etc., 1753); Charles Errard, *Parallele of the Ancient*

Architecture with the Modern One, According to the Ten Main Authors Who Wrote of the Five Orders (Paris: Library of the King for Artillery & Genius, 1766).

43. Booker T. Washington, *Up from Slavery: An Autobiography* (New York: A. L. Burt Company, Publishers, 1900), 149.

44. Anna Julia Cooper, *A Voice from the South* (Xenia, OH: The Aldine Printing House, 1892), 27.

45. Ibid., xlv.

46. Voorhees Industrial School, *Voorhees Industrial School, Denmark, South Carolina* (Bamberg: A. W. Knight, 1907), 9.

47. Mary N. Woods, "Thomas Jefferson and the University of Virginia: Planning the Academic Village," *Journal of the Society of Architectural Historians* 44, no. 3 (October 1985): 268.

48. Booker T. Washington, *My Larger Education: Being Chapters from My Experience* (New York: Doubleday, 1911), 299.

49. Hazel Carby, *Reconstructing Womanhood: The Emergence of the Afro-American Woman Novelist* (New York: Oxford University Press, 1987), 120; Pier Gabrielle Foreman, *Activist Sentiments: Reading Black Women in the Nineteenth Century* (Urbana: University of Illinois Press, 2009), 10. Foreman uses the term *histotextuality* to describe the unique nature of race literature.

50. Edward W. Soja, *Postmodern Geographies: The Reassertion of Space in Critical Social Theory* (New York: Verso, 1997), 1. We must also keep in mind the work of Arturo Escobar, Ernesto Laclau, Chantal Mouffe, John Urry, and Bob Jessup that made space an important part of their theorizing about social movements. Race has been largely overlooked, with some arguing that it would be impossible for any sociologist (in classical social theory) to consider "*all relevant dimensions*" of social life." Harry F. Dahms, "Retheorizing Global Space in Sociology: Towards a New Kind of Discipline," in *The Spatial Turn: Interdisciplinary Perspectives*, ed. Barney Warf and Santa Arias (New York: Routledge, 2008), 90. The works of Gillian Rose, Setha Low, Denise Lawrence-Zuniga, Laura Pulido, and Katherine McKittrick have deeply influenced my work on spatial history and place.

51. Dubrow's pioneering work, especially with the *Power of Place* in Los Angeles, opened new areas of preservation scholarship about people of color (POC). Gail Lee Dubrow and Jennifer B. Goodman, *Restoring Women's History Through Historic Preservation* (Baltimore: Johns Hopkins University Press, 2002), 5. Sarah Deutsch, *Women and the City: Gender, Space and Power in Boston, 1870–1940* (New York: Oxford University Press, 2002), 43. Deutsch is one of the few feminist historians to look critically at the influence of women reformers on the American built environment beginning in the late nineteenth century. Recent scholarship that considers place as an active agent and "sentient co-presence and kin to human life" supports my emphasis on place as containers of "trauma narratives." Kearney writes, "what is needed is a fully operational methodology that epistemologically grasps at place-meaning from a new direction." Amanda Kearney, *Violence in Place, Cultural and Environmental Wounding* (New York: Routledge, 2016), 1. Violence "in place" requires "a phenomenological approach [that] offers a way to deal with the 'richness' of place, where the ecological and the cultural, the human and non-human, the local and the global, and the real and the imaginary all become bound together in particular formations in particular places" (19). Paul Cloke and Owain Jones,

Tree Cultures: The Place of Trees and Trees in Their Place (New York: Bloomsbury Academic, 2002), 8, 64–66.

Chapter One

Epigraph: William E. Curtis, "Jennie Dean's School," *Washington Star*, February 5, 1907. Echoing similar sentiments by a noted race leader and newspaper editor, T. Thomas Fortune, "Tribute Paid the Founder of Manassas," *Norfolk Journal*, March 15, 1919.

1. "The Lincoln Monument: Unveiling of the Statue in Lincoln Square," *New York Times*, April 15, 1876, 1. For a more detailed account, see *Inaugural Ceremonies of the Freedmen's Memorial Monument to Abraham Lincoln* (Saint Louis, MO: Levison & Blythe, 1876). See also "Editor's Easy Chair," *Harper's New Monthly Magazine*, 34, no. 201 (1867): 389–90; "Editor's Easy Chair," *Harper's New Monthly Magazine*, 34, no. 204 (1890): 804; Kirk Savage, "Race, Memory, and Identity: The National Monuments of the Union and the Confederacy" (PhD diss., University of California–Berkeley, 1990), 50–52.

2. See Benjamin Quarles, *The Negro in the Civil War* (1953; repr., Boston: Little, Brown and Company, 1969), 340–47.

3. Constance McLaughlin Green, *The Secret City: A History of Race Relations in the Nation's Capital* (Princeton, NJ: Princeton University Press, 1967), 74; Eric Foner, *Reconstruction: America's Unfinished Revolution, 1863–1877* (New York: Harper & Row, Publishers, 1988), 5–6. See also James M. McPherson, *The Struggle for Equality: Abolitionists and the Negro in the Civil War and Reconstruction* (Princeton, NJ: Princeton University Press, 1964), 72–124, 336–40.

4. Green, *The Secret City*, 74.

5. Sandra Fitzpatrick and Maria R. Goodwin, *The Guide to Black Washington* (New York: Hippocrene Books, 1990), 68–70, 59–61.

6. For a more complete description of the memorial campaign, see Kirk Savage, *Standing Soldiers, Kneeling Slaves: Race, War, and Monument in Nineteenth-Century America* (Princeton, NJ: Princeton University Press, 1997), 89–128; Kathryn Allamong Jacob, *Testament to Union: Civil War Monuments in Washington, D.C.* (Baltimore: The Johns Hopkins University Press, 1998), 24–27; Wesley Moody, *Demon of the Lost Cause: Sherman and Civil War History* (Columbia: University of Missouri, 2011), 117. See Rubil Morales-Velazquez, "Imagining Washington: Monuments and Nation Building in the Early Capital," *Washington History* 12, no. 1 (2000). See also Elizabeth Clark-Lewis, ed., *First Freed: Washington, D.C. in the Emancipation Era* (Washington, DC: A. P. Foundation Press, 1998). On African Americans and memorial making, see Dennis P. Ryan, "The Crispus Attucks Monument Controversy of 1887," *Negro History Bulletin* 40, no. 1 (1977): 656–57; Patricia West, "'The Bricks of Compromise Settle into Place': Booker T. Washington's Birthplace and the Civil Rights Movement," in *Domesticating History: The Political Origins of America's House Museums*, ed. Patricia West (Washington, DC: Smithsonian Institution Press, 1999), 128–57. A very similar statue sits on the Tuskegee campus, except Booker T. Washington is cast "lifting the veil of ignorance from the face of a black slave." Marable, "Tuskegee and the Politics of Illusion in the New South," 13–24.

7. Confederated Southern Memorial Association, *A History of the Confederated Memorial Associations of the South* (New Orleans: The Graham Press, 1904), 282–88; James W. Loewen and Edward H. Sebesta, eds., *The Confederate and Neo-Confederate Reader: The "Great Truth" about the "Lost Cause"* (Jackson: University Press of Mississippi, 2011), 312.

8. George C. Round, "History of Manassas" (Manassas, VA: N.p., 1897). See also Ruth Round Hooff, *Glimpses of George Carr Round* (Manassas, VA: George C. Round Elementary School, 1986).

9. "The Lincoln Monument: Unveiling of the Statue in Lincoln Square," 1; *Inaugural Ceremonies of the Freedmen's Memorial*, 4.

10. W. Stuart Towns, "Honoring the Confederacy in Northwest Florida: The Confederate Monument Ritual," *The Florida Historical Quarterly* 57, no. 2 (1978): 205; Kathleen Ann Clark, *Defining Moments: African American Commemoration and Political Culture in the South, 1863–1913* (Chapel Hill: University of North Carolina Press, 2006), 54.

11. Philip S. Foner, "Oration in Memory of Abraham Lincoln, Delivered at the Unveiling of the Freedmen's Monument in Memory of Abraham Lincoln," *The Life and Writings of Frederick Douglass* (New York: International Publishers, 1955), 309.

12 David W. Blight, "'For Something Beyond the Battlefield': Frederick Douglass and the Struggle for the Memory of the Civil War," *The Journal of American History* 75, no. 4 (1989): 1158.

13. Historians continue to argue that Black attempts at redefining nationalism was largely due to their perceived failures during the American Revolution. African Americans argued that the republican ideology of natural rights was a way in which they could continue their quest for citizenship. I instead would argue that their appeals for citizenship are nationalist and continue to appear as they agitate for civil rights. That nationalist fervor continues well into the late nineteenth century, although I believe that they are no longer invested in rebuilding the larger "American nation" but are instead committed to the race and seeking reform through their own nation-building process—taking shape in the built environment. For discussion of the meaning of the American Revolution to African Americans, see Benjamin Quarles, *The Negro in the American Revolution* (New York: Collier Books, 1961); Michael Lee Lanning, *Defenders of Liberty: African Americans in the Revolutionary War* (New York: Birch Lane, 1999). See especially Sylvia R. Frey, *Water from the Rock: Black Resistance in a Revolutionary Age* (Princeton, NJ: Princeton University Press, 1991).

14. *New National Era*, November 24, 1870.

15. Foner, "Oration in Memory of Abraham Lincoln," 312. For the first thorough look at Lincoln and his relationship with African Americans, see Benjamin Quarles, *Lincoln and the Negro* (New York: Oxford University Press, 1962). A more recent discussion of Lincoln and his views on African American freedom, see William C. Harris, *With Charity for All: Lincoln and the Restoration of the Union* (Lexington: University Press of Kentucky, 1997), 229–75.

16. Savage, "Race, Memory, and Identity," 119–20.

17. The term *New South* suggested an idealized white supremacy as the basis for racial and economic progress. Historian Tera Hunter writes, "African Americans in the New South would be closely defined by the Old—in cotton fields or in servile labor in private homes, rather than in factory, managerial, or professional positions.

Black workers would serve a visible and integral, yet subservient, role in the modern economy." Tera Hunter, *To 'Joy My Freedom: Southern Black Women's Lives and Labors After the Civil War* (Cambridge, MA: Harvard University Press, 1997), 83–84.

18. Harris, *With Charity for All*, 319.

19. "Efforts of Copperhead Teachings," *Daily Missouri Democrat*, May 2, 1865.

20. Arthur Lloyd Hunter, "The Sacred South: Postwar Confederates and the Sacrilization of Southern Culture" (PhD diss., Saint Louis University, 1978), 1. For a discussion of masculinity and manhood prior to the 1850s, see Dana D. Nelson, *National Manhood: Capitalist Citizenship and the Imagined Fraternity of White Men* (Durham, NC: Duke University Press, 1998).

21. Hunter, "The Sacred South," 1.

22. Richard D. Starnes, "Forever Faithful: The Southern Historical Society and Confederate Historical Memory," *Southern Cultures* 2, no. 2 (1996): 177. For a more in-depth discussion, see Foner, *Reconstruction*, 412–17.

23. "State Pride," *Our Living and Our Dead* 1, no. 1 (1874): 46–47; W. Stuart Towns, *Enduring Legacy: Rhetoric and Ritual of the Lost Cause* (Tuscaloosa: University of Alabama Press, 2012), 22, 64.

24. John A. Simpson, "The Cult of the 'Lost Cause,'" *Tennessee Historical Quarterly* 34, no. 4 (1975): 350–51.

25. Gaines M. Foster, *Ghosts of the Confederacy: Defeat, The Lost Cause, and the Emergence of the New South 1865–1913* (New York: Oxford University Press, 1987), 4–5; Caroline E. Janney, *Burying the Dead But Not the Past: Ladies' Memorial Associations and the Lost Cause* (Chapel Hill: University of North Carolina Press, 2008), 2.

26. James E. Young, *The Texture of Memory: Holocaust Memorials and Meanings* (New Haven, CT: Yale University Press, 1993), 177.

27. "To the Patrons of the Land We Love," *The Land We Love* (N.p.: N.d., n.p.).

28. Susan Speare Durant, "The Gently Furled Banner: The Development of the Myth of the Lost Cause, 1865–1900" (PhD diss., University of North Carolina–Chapel Hill, 1972).

29. "Recollections of the 'Lost Cause' by a Southern Cavalry Officer," *The Land We Love* 4, no. 1 (1867): 38–49. For a biased analysis of this magazine, see Ray M. Atchinson, "The Land We Love: A Southern Post-Bellum Magazine of Agriculture, Literature, and Military History," *The North Carolina Historical Review* 37, no. 4 (1960): 506–15.

30. Anne Sarah Rubin, "Redefining the South: Confederates, Southerners, and Americans, 1863–1868" (PhD diss., University of Virginia, 1999), 75.

31. Ibid., 76.

32. Blight, "'For Something Beyond the Battlefield,'" 229.

33. Edward L. Ayers, *The Promise of the New South: Life After Reconstruction* (New York: Oxford University Press, 1992), 334.

34. Ibid.

35. Karen L. Cox, "Women, the Lost Cause, and the New South: The United Daughters of the Confederacy and the Transmission of Confederate Culture" (PhD diss., University of Southern Mississippi, 1997), 6.

36. Ibid., 1–2. For a discussion on historical texts, see Fred Bailey, "The Textbooks of the 'Lost Cause': Censorship and the Creation of Southern State Histories," *Georgia Historical Quarterly* (Summer 1991): 507–33; AnnMarie Brosnan,

"Representations of Race and Racism in the Books Used in Southern Black Schools During the American Civil War and Reconstruction Era, 1861–1876," *Paedagogica Historica: International Journal of the History of Education* 52, no. 6 (2016): 718–33.

37. Eugene D. Genovese, *Roll, Jordan, Roll: The World the Slaves Made* (New York: Vintage Books, 1976), 353. A rich and recent literature has emerged on the Black Mammy, see also Joan Marie Johnson, "'Ye Gave Them a Stone': African American Women's Clubs, the Frederick Douglass Home, and the Black Mammy Monument," *Journal of Women's History* 17, no. 1 (2005): 62–86; Psyche A. Williams-Forson, *Building Houses Out of Chicken Legs: Black Women, Food and Power* (Durham, NC: University of North Carolina Press, 2006); Micki McElya, *Clinging to Mammy: The Faithful Slave in Twentieth-Century America* (Cambridge, MA: Harvard University Press, 2007); Kimberly Wallace-Sanders, *Mammy: A Century of Race, Gender, and Southern Memory* (Ann Arbor: University of Michigan Press, 2009); Patricia Davis, "Memories in Transition: Black History Museums, New South Narratives, and Urban Regeneration," *Southern Communication Journal* 78, no. 2 (2013): 107–27.

38. Jacquelyn Dowd Hall, "'You Must Remember This': Autobiography as Social Critique," *The Journal of American History* 85, no. 2 (September 1998): 450.

39. Thomas Nelson Page, "Pen Picture of Yourselves, Your Mothers, and Grandmothers," *Confederate Veteran* 25, no. 7 (1917): 340.

40. W. Fitzhugh Brundage, "White Women and the Politics of Historical Memory in the New South, 1880–1920" (Unpublished paper, University of Florida, 2000), 1–2. I would like to thank Professor Brundage for sharing a copy of his insightful work on elite white women and constructions of historical memory in the New South.

41. Ibid., 3.

42. Drew Gilpin Faust, *Mothers of Invention: Women of the Slaveholding South in the American Civil War* (New York: Vintage Books, 1996), 252. See also Brundage, "White Women and the Politics of Historical Memory," 3.

43. Confederated Southern Memorial Association, *A History of the Confederated Memorial Associations*, 29.

44. Faust, *Mothers of Invention*, 253.

45. Brundage, "White Women and the Politics of Historical Memory," 3. Although these women challenged Southern mythology through their own literary genre, they should not be overlooked.

46. Carby, *Reconstructing Womanhood*, 120.

47. See Claudia Tate, *Domestic Allegories of Political Desire: The Black Heroine's Text at the Turn of the Century* (New York: Oxford University Press, 1992); John Ernest, *Resistance and Reformation in Nineteenth-Century African-American Literature* (Jackson: University Press of Mississippi, 1995).

48. Fanny Fielding, "Southern Homesteads," *The Land We Love* 1, no. 6 (1870): 410.

49. Ibid.

50. Thomas Bender, *New York Intellect: A History of Intellectual Life in New York City, from 1750 to the Beginnings of Our Own Time* (Baltimore: The Johns Hopkins University Press, 1987), 268.

51. Ibid., 269.

52. Lawrence Ray Drinkwater, "Scholarship, Honor, and the Lost Cause: A History of McCabe's University School, 1865–1901" (PhD diss., Virginia Commonwealth University, 1994), 116–17.

53. Troy Dean Howell, "William Gordon McCabe, Headmaster: The 'Old Boy' Academy in Transition" (MA thesis, University of Virginia, 1989), 9.

54. The Confederate monuments in honor of Stonewall Jackson and Robert E. Lee have been disavowed by several of their descendants. After white nationalists attacked demonstrators in Charlottesville in August 2017, two of Stonewall Jackson's great-great grandsons, Jack and Warren Christian, addressed open letters to the public as to why these memorials should be taken down, tapping as they did, in their words, into "pre-existing iconography for racists." The Lee family is apparently divided over Robert E. Lee statues surviving from the "Lost Cause," with Blair Lee IV, a "distant cousin," speaking in favor of their retention, and Karen Finney, biracial and a great-great-great grandniece of Lee, maintaining that "It's time to bring the statues down." Jack Christian and Warren Christian, "The Monuments Must Go: An Open Letter from the Great-Great-Grandsons of Stonewall Jackson," *Slate*, August 16, 2017; Drew Schwartz, "Even Robert E. Lee's Descendants Don't Like White Nationalists," *Vice*, August 16, 2017, https://www.vice.com/en_us/article/evvzzj/even-robert-e-lees-descendants-dont-like-white-nationalists-vgtrn; Mike Semel, "Robert E. Lee V: What It's Like to Carry Around This Name," *Washington Post*, August 19, 2017; Simon Romero, "'The Lees Are Complex': Descendants Grapple with a Rebel General's Legacy," *New York Times*, August 22, 2017.

55. *The Confederate Home and School, Charlestown, S.C.* (Charleston: The News and Courier Book Presses, 1886); Drinkwater, "Scholarship, Honor, and the Lost Cause," 117; *Confederate Veteran* 2, no. 8 (1894): 224; "A South Carolina College for Women," *Woman's Tribune*, April 30, 1892.

56. "Memorial to Stonewall Jackson's Army," *Confederate Veteran* 25, no. 6 (1917): 246. Although this advertisement appears much later in the pages of the *Confederate Veteran*, it is one of many that emphasize efforts to honor Southern manhood in the built environment.

57. Rev. C. D. Waller, "A Living Monument," *Confederate Veteran* 8, no. 7 (1900): 334.

58. Drinkwater, "Scholarship, Honor, and the Lost Cause," 117.

59. Genovese quoted in June O. Patton, "Moonlight and Magnolias in Southern Education: The Black Mammy Memorial Institute," *The Journal of Negro History* 65, no. 2 (1980): 149.

60. For a broad discussion on the historical implication of the "Mammy" figure, see M. M. Manring, *Slave in a Box: The Strange Career of Aunt Jemima* (Charlottesville: University of Virginia Press, 1998). See also "Mrs. Longstreet Pleads for Monument to Slaves," N.p., n.d., Division of Behavioral Science Research (reel 1), Tuskegee University Archives, Tuskegee, AL; "In the Movement for Black Mammy Memorial," 4; "The Black Mammy Memorial," *Savannah Tribune*, September 23, 1911; "The 'Black Mammy' Monument," *New York Age*, January 6, 1923, 4; "Will Oppose a Monument to Negro Mammies," *Washington Tribune*, February 3, 1923; "Voice Protest Against 'Mammy' Statue," *Washington Tribune*, February 10, 1923; "That 'Black Mammy' Monument," *Christian Index*, February 22, 1923, 2.

61. "The Monumental Spirit of the South," *Confederate Veteran* 22, no. 8 (1914): 344. See also "G.A.R. Encampment," *Woman's Tribune*, October 1, 1892, 177.

62. "Proposed Monuments by Colored Citizens," *Cleveland Daily Leader*, October 10, 1865, 2.

63. National Lincoln Monument Association, *Constitution of the Educational Monument Association to the Memory of Abraham Lincoln* (Washington, DC: McGill & Witherow, 1865).

64. Ibid., 1; "Freedom's Memorial," *National Freedman*, August 15, 1865, 231–32; James E. Yeatman, "The Freedmen's Monument to Lincoln," *National Freedman*, October 15, 1865, 304; "A National Monument," *Independent*, December 27, 1866, 1.

65. "Proposed Monuments by Colored Citizens," 2.

66. Bender, *New York Intellect*, 266.

67. "The Lincoln Monument," 1.

68. Ibid.

69. Ibid.

70. Letter from Frederick Douglass to W. J. Wilson, *Anglo-African*, September 3, 1865.

71. Rev. Henry Highland Garnet, "Frederick Douglass' Letter in Opposition to the Colored People's Lincoln Monument Institute," *Anglo-African*, September 16, 1865, 2.

72. Ibid.

73. Booker T. Washington, *The Negro Problem* (New York: James Pott & Company, 1903), 75.

74. *Freedman's Journal*, January 1, 1865, 3; Henry L. Swint, *Dear Ones at Home: Letters from Contraband Camps* (Nashville: Vanderbilt University Press, 1966), 4.

75. *Freedman's Journal*, January 1, 1865, 3.

76. Booker T. Washington, "Address," *Exercises at the Dedication of the Monument to Colonel Robert Gould Shaw and the Fifty-Fourth Regiment of Massachusetts Infantry* (Boston: Municipal Printing Office, 1897), 59–61; emphasis added.

77. See Nina Silber, *The Romance of Reunion: Northerners and the South, 1865–1900* (Chapel Hill: University of North Carolina Press, 1993).

78. Kenneth A. Breisch, *Henry Hobson Richardson and the Small Public Library in America: A Study in Typology* (Cambridge, MA: The MIT Press), 48, 216; Mark Girouard, *Sweetness and Light: The "Queen Anne" Movement, 1860–1900* (New York: Oxford University Press, 1977), 5. See also T. J. Jackson Lears, *No Place for Grace: Antimodernism and the Transformation of American Culture, 1880–1920* (Chicago: University of Chicago Press, 1991), passim.

79. Mrs. T. P. O'Connor, *My Beloved South* (New York: G. P. Putnam's Sons, 1914), iii.

80. Glenda Elizabeth Gilmore, *Gender and Jim Crow: Women and the Politics of White Supremacy in North Carolina, 1896–1920* (Chapel Hill: University of North Carolina Press, 1996), xvi.

81. Cooper, *A Voice from the South*, 145.

82. Foner, *Reconstruction*, 26–27. See also Frederick Cooper, "Elevating the Race: The Social Thought of Black Leaders 1827–1850," *American Quarterly* 24 (December 1972): 604–26; Benjamin Quarles, *Black Abolitionists* (New York: Oxford University Press, 1969).

83. Jones, *Soldiers of Light and Love*, 61.

84. Ibid., 5.

85. Jennifer Fleischner, "Memory, Sickness, and Slavery," in *Mastering Slavery: Memory, Family, and Identity in Women's Slave Narratives* (New York: New York University Press, 1996), 399.

86. For a discussion of the "democratic college" model, see Turner, *Campus*, 129–62.

87. Hilary Winchester, "The Construction and Deconstruction of Women's Roles in the Urban Landscape," in *Inventing Places: Studies in Cultural Geography*, ed. Kay Anderson and Fay Gale (Melbourne: Longman Cheshire, 1992), 140.

88. James C. Scott, *Domination and the Arts of Resistance: Hidden Transcripts* (New Haven, CT: Yale University Press, 1990), 4–5. See also Janet Hoskins, *Biographical Objects: How Things Tell the Stories of People's Lives* (New York: Routledge, 1998), 1–2.

89. Scott, *Domination and the Arts of Resistance*, 4–5. See also Hoskins, *Biographical Objects*, 120. For works that begin to examine the role of memory, history, and imagination in placemaking, see Kay J. Anderson, "The Idea of Chinatown: The Power of Place and Institutional Practice in the Making of a Racial Category," *Annals of the Association of American Geographers* 77, no. 4 (1987): 580–98; David Harvey, "Between Space and Time: Reflections on the Geographical Imagination," *Annals of the Association of American Geographers* 80, no. 3 (1990): 418–34; Steven Hoelscher and Derek H. Alderman, "Memory and Place: Geographies of a Critical Relationship," *Social and Cultural Geography* 5, no. 3 (September 2004): 347–55.

90. Hare as quoted in Louis R. Harlan, *Booker T. Washington: The Wizard of Tuskegee, 1901–1915* (New York: Oxford University Press, 1983), 169.

91. James W. Fernandez, "Architectonic Inquiry," *Semiotica* 89, no. 1/3 (1992): 216.

92. Marvin Trachtenberg, *The Statue of Liberty* (New York: Viking, 1976), 15. Also see Alan Trachtenberg, *Brooklyn Bridge: Fact and Symbol* (Chicago: University of Chicago Press, 1979).

Chapter Two

Epigraphs: Cooper, *A Voice from the South*, 131–32; Frederick Douglass and Ida B. Wells, *The Reason Why the Colored American Is Not in the World's Columbia Exposition, The Afro-American's Contribution to Columbian Literature* (Chicago: Ida B. Wells, 1893).

1. Several leading Black publications highlighted her efforts and brought attention to the work of countless numbers of other African American women reformers who struggled to end mob violence. *Noted Negro Women* by Monroe Majors, *Women of Distinction* by L. A. Scruggs, and *The Work of the Afro-American Woman* by Gertrude Mosell, all published in 1893, were influential in highlighting the causes for race betterment. Recent works on Wells have broadened our understanding of her work, including Patricia A. Schechter, *Ida B. Wells-Barnett and American Reform, 1880–1930* (Chapel Hill: University of North Carolina Press, 2001), 94–96; Davidson, *"They Say": Ida B. Wells and the Reconstruction of Race*, 170, 196; Bay, *To Tell the Truth Freely*, 131–32, 154–57; Sarah L. Silkey, *Black Woman Reformer: Ida B. Wells, Lynching, and Transatlantic Activism* (Athens: University of Georgia Press, 2015), 62, 63, 71, 89.

For a recent study that looks to commemorate lynchings in America, see Bryan Stevenson, *Lynching in America: Confronting the Legacy of Racial Terror* (Montgomery, AL: Equal Justice Initiative, 2015).

2. Ida B. Wells, *Southern Horrors. Lynch Law in All Its Phases* (New York: The New York Age Print, 1892). Her later publications include *A Red Record* (Chicago: Miss Ida B. Wells, 1895); *Mob Rule in New Orleans* (Chicago: Miss Ida B. Wells, 1900).

3. Anna R. Paddon and Sally Turner, "African Americans and the World's Columbian Exposition," *Illinois Historical Journal* vol. 88 (Spring 1995): 22–23.

4. Christopher Robert Reed, *"'All the World Is Here'": The Black Presence at White City* (Bloomington: Indiana University Press, 2000), 32. Also see Bruce G. Harvey, *World's Fairs in a Southern Accent: Atlanta, Nashville, and Charleston, 1895–1902* (Knoxville: University of Tennessee Press, 2014).

5. "The Women and the World's Fair," *New York Age*, October 24, 1891, 4; Clara Doty Bates, "Woman's Part at the World's Fair," *Review of Reviews* 7 (May 1893): 422–23; Jeanne Madeline Weimann, *The Fair Women* (Chicago: Academy, 1981), 47.

6. For a detailed discussion of the Black experience at MIT, see Clarence Williams, *Technology and the Dream: Reflections on the Black Experience at MIT, 1941–1999* (Cambridge, MA: The MIT Press, 2001).

7. Bertha Palmer as quoted in Robert Muccigrosso, *Celebrating the New World: Chicago's Columbian Exposition of 1893* (Chicago: Ivan R. Dee, 1993), 132–39. See "Mine and Mining Building," *Woman's Tribune*, October 29, 1892, 211; "Diagram of the World's Fair and Grounds and Buildings," *Woman's Tribune*, October 22, 1892, 205.

8. May Wright Sewall, ed., *The World's Congress of Representative Women* (Chicago: Rand, McNally, 1894), 703–5. See also Reed, "'All the World Is Here,'" 122–23.

9. Carby, *Reconstructing Womanhood*, 3.

10. "Work of Colored Women: Some Excellent Exhibits Made by Them at the World's Fair," *New York Times*, June 10, 1893, 5; *Report of the Board of General Managers of the Exhibit of the State of New York at the World's Columbian Exposition* (Albany, NY: James B. Lyon, State Printer, 1894). See also Reed, "'All the World Is Here,'" 110–14.

11. Reed, "'All the World Is Here,'" 113–14.

12 Thomas J. Bell, "The Chicago Fair," *Bulletin of Atlanta University*, July 1893, 3.

13. Paula Giddings, *When and Where I Enter: The Impact of Black Women on Race and Sex in America* (New York: Bantam Books, 1984), 85.

14. "No 'Nigger Day,' No 'Nigger Pamphlet!,'" *Indianapolis Freeman*, March 25, 1893, 4.

15. As quoted in Robert Rydell, *All the World's a Fair: Visions of Empire at American International Expositions, 1876–1916* (Chicago: University of Chicago Press, 1987), 52. See also "The Women and the World's Fair," 4; M. W. Caldwell, "World's Fair Commissioner," *New York Age*, February 14, 1891. For a more complete description of issues facing African American women, see Ann Massa, "Black Women in the 'White City,'" *Journal of American Studies* 8, no. 3 (1974): 319–37.

16. Caldwell, "World's Fair Commissioner."

17. Gail Bederman, "'Civilization,' the Decline of Middle-Class Manliness, and Ida B. Wells's Antilynching Campaign (1892–94)," *Radical History Review* no. 52 (1992): 12; Bay, *To Tell the Truth Freely*, 151–52. Interestingly, Frederick Douglass, who coauthored the pamphlet with Wells, insisted upon Black manliness as a key

component to achieving civilization. He writes, "We are men and our aim is perfect manhood, to be men among men. Our situation demands faith in ourselves, faith in the power of truth, faith in work and faith in the influence of manly character." Frederick Douglass, "Introduction," in *The Reason Why the Colored American Is Not in the World's Columbian Exposition* (Chicago: Miss Ida B. Wells, 1892), 12.

18. Campbell Robertson, "History of Lynchings in the South Documents Nearly 4000 Names," *New York Times*, February 10, 2015, https://www.nytimes.com/2015/02/10/us/history-of-lynchings-in-the-south-documents-nearly-4000-names.html?_r=0; Mark Berman, "Even More Black People Were Lynched in the U.S. Than Previously Thought, Study Finds," *Washington Post*, February 10, 2015, https://www.washingtonpost.com/news/post-nation/wp/2015/02/10/even-more-black-people-were-lynched-in-the-u-s-than-previously-thought-study-finds/?utm_term=.141ceab76049; Sarah Sullivan, "Extralegal Violence: The Ku Klux Klan in the Reconstruction Era," *Elements* 12, no. 2 (2016): 35–46.

19. Muccigrosso, *Celebrating the New World*, 144. See also Paddon and Turner, "African Americans and the World's Columbian Exposition," 27–28.

20. Elliott M. Rudwick and August Meier, "Black Man in the 'White City': Negroes and the Columbian Exposition, 1893," *Phylon* 26, no. 4 (1965): 27–28.

21. Ida B. Wells-Barnett, *The Reason Why the Colored American Is Not in the World's Columbian Exposition: The Afro-American's Contribution to Columbian Literature*, ed. Robert W. Rydell (Urbana-Champaign: University of Illinois Press, 1999), 67.

22. "Goodbye to the Fair," *Chicago Tribune*, November 1, 1893, 4; Blair Kamin, "The Dream City: This Town Could Learn a Thing or Two from Burnham's Bold Utopia," *Chicago Tribune*, May 2, 1893, 1; John J. Flinn, *The Best Things to Be Seen at the World's Fair* (Chicago: Columbian Guide Co., 1893), 12.

23. Robert Rydell, *All the World's a Fair: Visions of Empire at American International Expositions, 1876–1916* (Chicago: University of Chicago Press, 1987), 39. See also James Gilbert, *Perfect Cities: Chicago Utopias of 1893* (Chicago: University of Chicago Press, 1991); Donald L. Miller, *City of the Century: The Epic of Chicago and the Making of America* (New York: Touchstone Books, 1997), for discussion of city ideology.

24. Frances Hodgson Burnett, *Two Little Pilgrims' Progress: A Story of the City Beautiful* (New York: Charles Scribner's Sons, 1895), 4.

25. David Schuyler, Gregory Kaliss, and Jeffrey Schlossberg, eds., *The Papers of Frederick Law Olmsted: The Last Great Projects, 1890–1895* (Baltimore: The Johns Hopkins University Press, 2015), 20–21; Bederman, "'Civilization,' the Decline of Middle-Class Manliness, and Ida B. Wells's Antilynching Campaign (1892–94)," 10; "The World's Fair of 1892," *Scientific American*, January 4, 1890, 2. See also Stanley Appelbaum, *The Chicago World's Fair of 1893: A Photographic Record* (New York: Dover Publications, Inc., 1980), 15–52; Robin F. Bachin, *Building the South Side: Urban Space and Civic Culture in Chicago, 1890–1919* (Chicago: University of Chicago Press, 2004), 171.

26. Frederick Starr, "Anthropology at the World's Fair," *Popular Science Monthly* 43, no. 5 (1893): 621; Rydell, *All the World's a Fair*, 40–41; David Schuyler, "Frederick Law Olmsted and the World's Columbian Exposition," *Journal of Planning History* 15, no. 1 (2016): 9. See especially David Nasaw, "The City as Playground: The World's Fair Midways," in *Going Out: The Rise and Fall of Public Amusements*, ed. David Nasaw (Cambridge, MA: Harvard University Press, 1993), 62–79. For a discussion

on the place of anthropology in America's public life and culture, see Micaela di Leonardo, *Exotics at Home: Anthropologies, Others, American Modernity* (Chicago: University of Chicago Press, 1998).

27. David R. Wilcox, "Going National: American Anthropology Successfully Redefines Itself as an Accepted Academic Discipline," in *Coming of Age in Chicago: The 1893 World's Fair and the Coalescence of American Anthropology*, ed. Curtis M. Hinsley and David R. Wilcox (Lincoln: University of Nebraska Press, 2016), 63, 414; Norman Bolotin, *Chicago's Grand Midway: A Walk around the World at the Columbian Exposition* (Urbana-Champaign: University of Illinois Press, 2017), 20.

28. Linda O. McMurry, *To Keep the Waters Troubled: The Life of Ida B. Wells* (New York: Oxford University Press, 1998), 200; Mariann Shaw, *World's Fair Notes, a Woman Journalist Views Chicago's 1893 Columbian Exposition* (Chicago: Pogo Press, 1992), 25, 56.

29. Shawn Michelle Smith, *American Archives: Gender, Race, and Class in Visual Culture* (Princeton, NJ: Princeton University Press, 1999), 160.

30. Andrea Oppenheimer Dean, "Revisiting the White City," *Historical Preservation* 45, no. 2 (1993): 42. Dean argues that the Exposition halted the development of a "modern and functional American architecture." See especially John W. Reps, *The Making of Urban America: A History of City Planning in the U.S.* (Princeton, NJ: Princeton University Press, 1965), 497–502; Leland M. Roth, *McKim, Mead & White, Architects* (New York: Harper & Row Publishers, 1983), 184–99.

31. Neil Harris, Wim de Wit, James Gilbert, and Robert W. Rydell, eds., *Grand Illusions: Chicago's World's Fair of 1893* (Chicago: Chicago Historical Society, 1993), 44.

32. Mardges Bacon, "Toward a National Style of Architecture: The Beaux-Arts Interpretation of the Colonial Revival," in *The Colonial Revival in America*, ed. Alan Axelrod (New York: W. W. Norton & Company, 1985), 92–93.

33. Ibid., 95.

34. Alex Krieger, "Civic Lessons of an Ephemeral Monument, Monumentality and the City," *The Harvard Architecture Review* 4 (Spring 1984): 149.

35. Lewis Mumford, *The Brown Decades: A Study of the Arts in America, 1865–1895* (New York: Dover Publications, Inc., 1931), 56; David F. Burg, *Chicago's White City of 1893* (Lexington: University Press of Kentucky, 1976), 49–53; James O'Gorman, "Marshall Field Wholesale Store," *Journal of the Society of Architectural Historians* 36 (October 1978): 180–88.

36. Victorian tensions between displays of wealth, comfort, and "high culture" were clearly visible. Katherine Grier, *Culture and Comfort: Parlor Making and Middle Class Identity, 1850–1930* (Washington, DC: Smithsonian Institution Press, 2013), 116.

37. Mumford, *The Brown Decades*, 9.

38. Ibid., 15. African Americans blurred the distinction between notions of public and private spheres. See Elsa Barkley Brown, "Negotiating and Transforming the Public Sphere: African American Political Life in the Transition from Slavery to Freedom," *Public Culture* 7, no. 1 (1994): 107–46.

39. Susan Prendergast Schoelwer, "Curious Relics and Quaint Scenes: The Colonial Revival at Chicago's Great Fair," in *The Colonial Revival in America*, ed. Alan Axelrod (New York: W. W. Norton & Company, 1985), 184–85.

40. Steven Conn, *Museums and American Intellectual Life, 1876–1926* (Chicago: University of Chicago Press, 1998), 121.

41. Krieger, "Civic Lessons of an Ephemeral Monument," 153; Alan Trachtenberg, *The Incorporation of America: Culture and Society in the Gilded Age* (New York: Hill and Wang, 1982), 211–18.

42. Neil Harris, *Building Lives: Constructing Rites and Passages* (New Haven, CT: Yale University Press, 1999), 42.

43. Mary N. Woods, "Henry Van Brunt: The Historic Styles, Modern Architecture," in *American Public Architecture: European Roots and Native Expressions*, ed. Craig Zabel and Susan Munshower (College Park: The Pennsylvania State University, 1989), 88–89.

44. Krieger, "Civic Lessons of an Ephemeral Monument," 155.

45. John Coleman Adams, "What a Great City Might Be—a Lesson from the White City," *The New England Magazine* 14, no. 1 (1896): 4; Rossiter Johnson, *A History of the World's Columbian Exposition Held in Chicago in 1893*, vol. II (New York: D. Appleton and Co., 1898), 316.

46. E. George Payne, *Principles of Educational Sociology: An Outline* (New York: New York University Press, 1928), 28; Thomas Nast, "'The Nigger Must Go,' 'The Chinese Must Go,' and 'The Poor Barbarians Can't Understand Our Civilized Republication Form of Government,'" *Harper's Weekly: Journal of Civilization* 23, no. 1185 (September 13, 1879): 1. *Harper's Bazaar* and *Puck* routinely published degrading caricatures.

47. Bridget R. Cooks, "Fixing Race: Visual Representations of African Americans at the World's Columbian Exposition, Chicago, 1893," *Patterns of Prejudice* 41, no. 5 (2007): 435–36.

48. Lee D. Baker, *From Savage to Negro: Anthropology and the Construction of Race, 1896–1954* (Berkeley: University of California Press, 1998), 22. Baker argues that biology dominated the study of race in the early twentieth century.

49. Ibid., 23–24. The U.S. Supreme Court's decision on the case, *Plessy v. Ferguson* (1896), created the doctrine of separate but equal, which persisted for fifty-eight years. It allowed for whites to adopt a racially conceived nativism against incoming foreigners and African Americans.

50. *The Chicago Manual of Style* allows capitalization of *black* if an author or publication prefers to do so. For a recent editorial discussion, see Merrill Perlman, "Black and White: Why Capitalization Matters," *Columbia Journalism Review*, http://www.cjr.org/analysis/language_corner_1.php.

51. Reed, "'All the World Is Here,'" 144–46.

52. Robert W. Thurston, *Lynching: American Mob Murder in Global Perspective* (New York: Routledge, 2016), 112. A 1908 poem was printed on a postcard entitled "The Dogweed Tree" with a photo of five lynched men from Texas.

53. Robert Rydell, "Editor's Introduction," *The Reason Why the Colored American Is Not in the World's Columbian Exposition: The Afro-American's Contribution to Columbian Literature*, xiii. See also Robert Rydell, "A Cultural Frankenstein? The Chicago World's Columbian Exposition," in *Grand Illusions: Chicago's World's Fair of 1893*, ed. Neil Harris et al. (Chicago: Chicago Historical Society, 1993).

54. Ida B. Wells, *United State Atrocities: Lynch Law* (London: Lux, 1893), 1–3; Ida B. Wells, "Lynch Laws in All Its Phases," *Our Day* 11 (May 1893): 333–37.

55. "Editorial," *Kansas City American Citizen*, July 1, 1892; also see David M. Tucker, "Miss Ida B. Wells and Memphis Lynching," *Phylon* 32, no. 2 (1971): 117.

56. Bederman, "'Civilization,'" 5.

57. Ibid., 7–8.

58. Numerous lynchings took place in civic spaces, including courthouse squares. James Allen, *Without Sanctuary: Lynching Photography in America* (Santa Fe, NM: Twin Palms Publishers, 2000), 176, 179, 184, 193; Amy Louise Wood, *Lynching and Spectacle: Witnessing Racial Violence in America, 1890–1940* (Chapel Hill: University of North Carolina Press, 2011), 39, 45–47, 61, 81, 211. Also see Ray Stannard Baker, "What Is a Lynching? A Study of Mob Justice, South and North," *McClure's Magazine* 24 (January 1905): 299–314.

59. Hall as discussed in W. Fitzhugh Brundage, ed., "Introduction," in *Under Sentence of Death: Lynching in the South* (Chapel Hill: University of North Carolina Press, 1997), 11. Slaves from the 1712 Rebellion in New York City were executed and left hanging to convince Blacks that their bodies and souls had not returned to Africa as often believed. See Kenneth Scott, "The Slave Insurrection in New York in 1712," *The New York Historical Society Quarterly* 45, no. 1 (1961): 43–74.

60. Leon Litwack, *Trouble in Mind: Black Southerners in the Age of Jim Crow* (New York: Alfred A. Knopf, 1998), 286–87; J. A. Hobson, "'Lynching' in the Southern States," *Speaker* 8 (August 29, 1903): 498–99. See also Crystal N. Feimster, *Southern Horrors: Women and the Politics of Rape and Lynching* (Cambridge, MA: Harvard University Press, 2011); Michael J. Pfeifer, *Lynching Beyond Dixie: American Mob Violence Outside the South* (Urbana-Champaign: University of Illinois Press, 2013); James H. Cone, *The Cross and the Lynching Tree* (Ossining, NY: Orbis Books, 2013); Manfred Berg, *Popular Justice: A History of Lynching in America* (New York: Rowman & Littlefield Publishers, 2015); Mattias Smangs, "The Lynching of African Americans in the U.S. South: A Review of Sociological and Historical Perspectives," *Sociology Compass* 11, no. 8 (2017): 1–13.

61. Carby, *Reconstructing Womanhood*, 5.

62. For a similar discussion like Robin D. G. Kelley's, see Sara M. Evans and Harry C. Boyte, *Free Spaces: The Sources of Democratic Change in America* (New York: Harper & Row Publishers, Inc., 1986), 17 and esp. 18. Evans and Boyte contend that "a focus on free spaces at the heart of democratic movements aids in the resolution of polarities that have long and bitterly divided modern observers and critics—expressive individualism versus ties of community; modernity versus tradition; public and private values, and so forth—by highlighting the living environments where people draw upon both 'opposition' to create new experiments." For a compelling look at utopian movements and their failures, see David Harvey, *Spaces of Hope* (Berkeley: University of California Press, 2000).

63. Jane Dailey, "Deference and Violence in the Postbellum South: Manners and Massacres in Danville, Virginia," *The Journal of Southern History* 63, no. 3 (1997): 557–58.

64. Ghassan Hage, *White Nation: Fantasies of White Supremacy in a Multicultural Society* (Annandale: Pluto Press Australia, 1998), 68–69.

65. David Sibley, "Survey 13: Purification of Space," *Environment and Planning D: Society and Space* 6, no. 4 (1988): 409–10.

66. For a discussion on the relations between history and form, as well as creating an "American style," see Woods, "Henry Van Brunt."

67. William B. Rhoads, "The Colonial Revival and the Americanization of Immigrants," in *The Colonial Revival in America*, ed. Alan Axelrod (New York: W. W. Norton & Company, 1985), 341–42.

68. Ibid., 239.

69. Trachtenberg, *The Incorporation of America*, 4–6.

70. Shawn Michelle Smith, "Photographing the 'American Negro': Nation, Race, and Photography at the Paris Exposition of 1900," in *With Other Eyes: Looking at Race and Gender in Visual Culture*, ed. Lisa Bloom (Minneapolis: University of Minnesota Press, 1999), 62.

71. Robin Bachin, "Cultural Boundaries: Constructing Urban Space and Civic Culture on Chicago's South Side, 1890–1919" (PhD diss., University of Michigan, 1996), 6.

72. For a discussion on the term *New South*, see ibid., chapter 3, note 19. See also Litwack, *Trouble in Mind*, 184–89.

73. Smith, "Photographing the 'American Negro,'" 86.

74. Sarah Deutsch, "Reconceiving the City: Women, Space, and Power in Boston, 1870–1910," *Gender and History* 6, no. 2 (1994): 208.

75. Winchester, "The Construction and Deconstruction of Women's Roles," 141.

76. See W. Fitzhugh Brundage, ed., *Under Sentence of Death: Lynching in the South* (Chapel Hill: University of North Carolina, 1997).

77. Jacqueline Jones Royster, ed., *Southern Horrors and Other Writings: The Anti-Lynching Campaign of Ida B. Wells, 1892–1900* (New York: Bedford Books, 1997), 36–37.

78. Howard F. Gillette Jr., "White City, Capital City," *Chicago History: The Magazine of the Chicago Historical Society* 18, no. 4 (1989–90): 26.

79. Michele H. Bogart, *Public Sculpture and the Civic Ideal in New York City, 1890–1930* (Chicago: University of Chicago Press, 1989), 58; Vivian Greene, "Utopia/Dystopia," *American Art* 25, no. 2 (2011): 2–3. The movement focused on tasks that governments could do unilaterally, including a focus on the civic center, the gateway railroad station, the processional boulevard, the belt parkway, the park system design, and the public playground.

80. Bogart, *Public Sculpture and the Civic Ideal in New York City*, 58.

81. Candace Wheeler, "A Dream City," *Harper's New Monthly Magazine* 86, no. 516 (1893): 836.

82. Dell Upton, *Architecture in the United States* (New York: Oxford University Press, 1999), 81–82. Upton writes, "during the half century after 1875 when the Colonial Revival was most influential, it was above all the ancestral homeland of those who defined themselves as Anglo-Saxon, Teutonic, Protestant, or simply white. The Colonial Revival was an origin myth told through landscape.... It adopted the rhetoric of a revitalization movement, harkening back to a time when people were ostensibly more virtuous, more public-spirited, more homogenous, and led simpler lives." For an interesting discussion on the consumption of the Colonial Revival, see Karal Ann Marling, *George Washington Slept Here: Colonial Revivals and American Culture* (Cambridge, MA: Harvard University Press, 1988).

83. Jon A. Peterson, "The City Beautiful Movement: Forgotten Origins and Lost Meanings," *Journal of Urban History* 2, no. 4 (1976): 415–34.

84. Rosemarie K. Bank, "Representing History: Performing the Columbian Exposition," *Theatre Journal* 54, no. 4 (December 2002): 591.

85. W. E. B. Du Bois as quoted in Sterling Stuckey, *Slave Culture: Nationalist Theory and the Foundations of Black America* (New York: Oxford University Press, 1987), 265.

86. Ibid., 265.

87. Although problematic in its reading of Black agency, it revises our understanding of Black involvement in the settlement house movement; see Elisabeth Lasch-Quinn, *Black Neighbors: Race and the Limits of Reform in the American Settlement House Movement, 1890–1945* (Chapel Hill: University of North Carolina Press, 1993). For a discussion of settlement houses and Christian activism, see Judith Weisenfeld, *African American Women and Christian Activism: New York's Black YMCA, 1905–1945* (Cambridge, MA: Harvard University Press, 1997). On the use of urban space and its impact on the shaping of democracy, see Mary P. Ryan, *Civic Wars: Democracy and Public Life in the American City During the Nineteenth Century* (Berkeley: University of California Press, 1997).

88. Valerie Gill, "Catharine Beecher and Charlotte Perkins Gilman: Architects of Female Power," *Journal of American Culture* 21, no. 2 (1998): 17–24. Although focusing exclusively on white women's cultural production, this work suggests an important way of looking to the work of women not trained as professional architects and their impact on design through domestic manuals.

89. Ben Schiller, "Learning Their Letters: Critical Literacy, Epistolary Culture, and Slavery in the Antebellum South," *Southern Quarterly* 45, no. 3 (2008): 25–26.

Chapter Three

Epigraphs: Booker T. Washington, *Up from Slavery: An Autobiography* (New York: A. L. Burt Company, 1900), 108; Samuel C. Armstrong, "General Armstrong's Memoranda," *The Southern Workman and Hampton School Record* 20, no. 12 (December 1893): 178.

1. Kevin Gaines, *Uplifting the Race: Black Leadership, Politics, and Culture in the Twentieth Century* (Chapel Hill: University of North Carolina Press, 1996), 103.

2. David Glassberg, "Monuments and Memories," *American Quarterly* 43, no. 1 (1991): 143.

3. Cooper, *A Voice from the South*, 135.

4. Mary Helen Washington, "Introduction," in *A Voice from the South* (New York: Oxford University Press, 1988), xxix.

5. Carby, *Reconstructing Womanhood*, 99, 105.

6. Frances E. W. Harper, *Iola Leroy or Shadows Uplifted* (Philadelphia: Carrigues Brothers, 1893), 172. See also Elizabeth Ammons, *Conflicting Stories: American Women Writers at the Turn into the Twentieth Century* (New York: Oxford University Press, 1991), 20.

7. Cooper, *A Voice from the South*, 144.

8. Ibid., 143.

9. Rebecca Ginsburg and Clifton Ellis, eds., *Cabin, Quarter, Plantation: Architecture and Landscapes of North American Slavery* (New Haven, CT: Yale University Press, 2010); Rebecca Ginsburg and Clifton Ellis, *Slavery in the City: Architecture and Landscapes of Urban Slavery in North America* (Charlottesville: University of Virginia Press, 2017). See also Catherine Armstrong, "Slavery and Landscape," *Slavery and Abolition* 38 no. 1 (2017): 2.

10. James E. Newton and Ronald L. Lewis, eds., *The Other Slaves: Mechanics, Artisans, and Craftsmen* (Boston: G. K. Hall & Co., 1978), xiv. See also Tia Marie Blassingame, "Breaking Through a 'Thounderous Silence': The African American in the Evolution of American Architecture" (senior thesis, Princeton University, n.d.), American Institute of Architects (AIA) Archives, Washington, DC.

11. "Architecture Among Negroes in America," *The Negro History Bulletin* 3, no. 7 (April 1940): 99.

12 Richard K. Dozier, "A Historical Survey: Black Architects and Craftsmen," *Black World* (May 1974): 5–6.

13. Ibid., 7.

14. Mary N. Woods, *From Craft to Profession: The Practice of Architecture in Nineteenth-Century America* (Berkeley: University of California Press, 1999), 100.

15. Harper, *Iola Leroy*, 219.

16. Albert J. Raboteu, *Slave Religion: The "Invisible Institution" in the Antebellum South* (New York: Oxford University Press, 1978), 240; Hans A. Baer, "The Role of the Bible and Other Sacred Texts in African American Denominations and Sects," in *African Americans and the Bible: Sacred Texts and Social Textures*, ed. Vincent L. Wimbush (Eugene, OR: Wipf and Stock Publishers, 2012), 93.

17. Eddie S. Glaude Jr., *Exodus! Religion, Race, and Nation in Early Nineteenth-Century Black America* (Chicago: University of Chicago Press, 2000), 3–5, 84.

18. Glaude, *Exodus!*, 83–84; John Gillis, ed., *Commemorations: The Politics of National Identity* (Princeton, NJ: Princeton University Press, 1994); Yael Zerubavel, *Recovered Roots: Collective Memory and the Making of the Israeli National Tradition* (Chicago: University of Chicago Press, 1995).

19. For a discussion of freedom celebrations, see Alessandra Lorini, *Rituals of Race: American Public Culture and the Search for Racial Democracy* (Charlottesville: University of Virginia Press, 1999), 28–32, 209–56. See also Geneviève Fabre, "African-American Commemorative Celebrations in the Nineteenth Century," in *History and Memory in African-American Culture* (New York: Oxford University Press, 1994), 72–91.

20. Genovese as quoted by Glaude, *Exodus!*, 6. See also Genovese, *Roll, Jordan, Roll*, 280–81.

21. Cooper, *A Voice from the South*, 57.

22. Ibid., 107. As Foreman points out, race leaders considered literature central to supporting uplift efforts. Foreman, *Activist Sentiments*, 143.

23. Cedric J. Robinson, *Black Movements in America* (New York: Routledge, 1997), 101.

24. Benedict Anderson, *Imagined Communities: Reflections on the Origin and Spread of Nationalism* (New York: Verso, 1991), 5–7.

25. Glaude, *Exodus!*, 10.

26. Ibid., 10–11.

27. John L. Mitchell, "Shall the Wheels of Race Agitation Be Stopped," *The Colored American Magazine* 5 (September 1902): 386–91.

28. Joanne P. Sharp, "Gendering Nationhood": A Feminist Engagement with National Identity," in *BodySpace*, ed. Nancy Duncan (New York: Routledge, 1996), 97.

29. Cooper, *A Voice from the South*, 28.

30. Sharp, "Gendering Nationhood," 97.

31. Richard Guy Wilson and Sara A. Butler, *University of Virginia: Campus Guides* (Princeton, NJ: Princeton Architectural Press, 1999), 11; Turner, *Campus*, 163–213. Turner gives the most complete and broad-based analysis of the City Beautiful movement and its impact on campus planning thus far. Also see Montgomery Schuyler, "Architecture of American Colleges," *The Architectural Record* 27, no. 6 (1910); John R. Thelin and James Yankovich, "Bricks and Mortar: Architecture and the Study of Higher Education," in *Higher Education: Handbook of Theory and Research*, ed. John C. Smart (New York: Agathon Press, Inc., 1987), 3:57–83; Lawrence Biemiller, "Planning the College Campus: The Evolution of a 'Distinctively American Form,'" *Chronicle of Higher Education*, May 30, 1984, 5–7.

32. Barbara Snowden Christen, "Cass Gilbert and the Ideal of the City Beautiful: City and Campus Plans, 1900–1916" (PhD diss., City University of New York, 1997), 212.

33. Ibid., 215.

34. Ashton R. Willard, "The Development of College Architecture in America," *The New England Magazine* 16, no. 5 (1897): 513, 514; Bainbridge Bunting, *Harvard: An Architectural History* (Cambridge, MA: Harvard University Press, 1998), 35.

35. George Humphrey Yetter, "Stanford White at the University of Virginia: The New Building on the South Lawn and the Reconstruction of the Rotunda in 1896" (MA thesis, University of Virginia, May 1980), 62. For example, women's colleges such as Smith and Mount Holyoke attempted to protect their female students, offering them "strict segregation from the world, constant supervision, and the intimacy of a single, all-purpose structure" from the evils of the world. See Lisa Chase, "Imagining Utopia: Landscape Design at Smith College, 1871–1910," *New England Quarterly* 65, no. 4 (1992): 562. Initially many women's colleges designed their facilities as little more than the size of a "generous house" to protect their students and confine women to domestic roles. See Helen Lefkowitz Horowitz, "Designing for the Genders: Curricula and Architecture at Scripps College and the California Institute of Technology," *Pacific Historical Review* 54, no. 4 (1985): 453.

36. David Schuyler, "Frederick Law Olmsted and the Origins of Modern Campus Design," *Planning for Higher Education* 25, no. 2 (1996–97): 2. Charles A. Prosser, "Facilities for Industrial Education," in *Proceedings of the National Education Association* (Ann Arbor, MI: National Education Association, 1912), 912.

37. Roger L. Geiger, "The Era of Multipurpose Colleges in American Higher Education, 1850–1890," in *The American College in the Nineteenth Century* (Nashville: Vanderbilt University Press, 2000), 134.

38. A. D. F. Hamlin, *A Text-Book of the History of Architecture* (New York: Longmans & Green, 1896), 357, 386, 402; Claude Fayette Bragdon, *The Beautiful Necessity: Seven Essays on Theosophy and Architecture* (Rochester, NY: Mansas Press, 1910), 87.

39. Laurence Veysey, *The Emergence of the American University* (Chicago: University of Chicago Press, 1965), 269; Frederick Rudolph, *The American College and University: A History* (Athens: University of Georgia Press, 1990), 264–86.

40. Turner, *Campus*, 164.

41. Ibid., 167. For a historical discussion of gown versus town, see Laurence Brockliss, "Gown and Town: The University and the City in Europe, 1200–2000," *Minerva* 38, no. 2 (2000): 147–70.

42. For further discussion regarding the image of a university and its relation to educational philosophy, see Albert Bush-Brown, "Image of a University: A Study of Architecture as an Expression of Education at Colleges and Universities in the United States between 1800–1900" (PhD diss., Princeton University, 1959).

43. Henry Van Brunt as quoted in Woods, "Henry Van Brunt," 88–89.

44. Christen, "Cass Gilbert and the Ideal of the City Beautiful," 217.

45. Woods, "Henry Van Brunt," 88–89; Woods, "Thomas Jefferson and the University of Virginia," *Journal of the Society of Architectural Historians* 44 (October 1985): 268. Although many works do exist on UVA's architecture and planning, two excellent places to begin are Pendleton Hogan, *The Lawn: A Guide to Jefferson's University* (Charlottesville: University of Virginia Press, 1987); Richard Guy Wilson, ed., *Thomas Jefferson's Academical Village: The Creation of an Architectural Masterpiece* (Charlottesville: Bayly Art Museum of the University of Virginia, 1993).

46. Woods, "Henry Van Brunt," 88–89.

47. Rhoads, "The Colonial Revival and the Americanization of Immigrants," 239. See also "The Columbian Exposition and American Civilization," *Atlantic Monthly*, May 1893, 577–88.

48. Mary N. Woods, "Charles F. McKim and the Foundation of the American Academy in Rome," in *Light on the Eternal City: Observations and Discoveries in the Art and Architecture of Rome*, ed. Hellmut Hager and Susan Scott Munshower (University Park: Pennsylvania State University, 1987), 307.

49. Yetter, "Stanford White at the University of Virginia," 56; Bryant F. Tolles, *Architecture and Academe: College Buildings in New England Before 1860* (Lebanon: University Press of New England, 2011), 67.

50. Schuyler, "Frederick Law Olmsted," 2.

51. Ibid., 10.

52. Alfred Morton Githens, "The Group Plan I: A Theory of Composition; The Carnegie Technical Schools," *The Brickbuilder* 15, no. 7 (1906): 134–38; Alfred Morton Githens, "The Group Plan II: The Elemental Types of Composition," *The Brickbuilder* 15, no. 9 (1906): 179–82.

53. Githens as quoted in Christen, "Cass Gilbert and the Ideal of the City Beautiful," 216.

54. Turner, *Campus*, 4; Sheldon Rothblatt, "The Writing of University History at the End of Another Century," *Oxford Review of Education* 23, no. 2 (1997): 151.

55. Edward E. Redcay, *County Training Schools and Public Secondary Education for Negroes in the South* (Washington, DC: The John F. Slater Fund, 1935), 31; Mark Auslander, "The Other Side of Paradise: Glimpsing Slavery in the University's Utopian Landscapes," *Southern Spaces*, May 13, 2010, https://southernspaces.org/2010/other-side-paradise-glimpsing-slavery-universitys-utopian-landscapes.

56. Richard K. Dozier, "Tuskegee Institute: From Humble Beginnings to National Shrine," *Historic Preservation* 33, no. 1 (1981): 42; Michael R. West, *The Education of Booker T. Washington: American Democracy and the Idea of Race Relations* (New York: Columbia University Press, 2006), 54–57. Describing his own experiences under Gen. S. C. Armstrong, Washington wrote, "The worth of work with the hands as an uplifting power in real education was first brought home to me with striking emphasis when I was a student at Hampton." See Booker T. Washington, *Working with the Hands: Being a Sequel to "Up from Slavery" Covering the Author's Experiences in Industrial Training at Tuskegee* (New York: Doubleday, Page, and Co., 1904), 3; Alphonse Heningburg, "The Relation of Tuskegee Institute to Education in the Lower South," *The Journal of Educational Sociology* 7, no. 3 (November 1933): 157.

57. Washington, *Working with the Hands*, 12.

58. Arthur M. Evans, "Working Out Race Problem at Great Tuskegee Institute, Marvel of the South," *Chicago Record Herald*, April 26, 1912, Tuskegee Institute Clippings File, Tuskegee University Archives, Tuskegee, AL. See also Arthur M. Evans, "Practical Work at Tuskegee Has Tremendous Influence in Southern States," *Chicago Record Herald*, April 25, 1912, Tuskegee Institute Clippings File, Tuskegee University Archives, Tuskegee, AL; Elizabeth E. Lane, "Tuskegee School: A Practical Solution of the Negro Problem," *Lend a Hand: A Record of Progress* 13, no. 1 (1894): 17–21. Wilson's *Biographical Dictionary* is an important intervention in this history of African American architects of the nineteenth century. Dreck Spurlock Wilson, ed., *African American Architects: A Biographical Dictionary, 1865–1945* (New York: Routledge, 2004).

59. Emmett J. Scott, "Training Head and Hand: Architectural and Mechanical Drawing at Tuskegee," *Tuskegee Student*, April 20, 1901, 1.

60. "Architectural Drawing at the Tuskegee Normal and Industrial Institute," *Architects' and Builders' Magazine* 5, no. 8 (1904): 377–78.

61. Ibid., 1.

62. Woods, *From Craft to Profession*, 74.

63. Ibid.

64. Janet Parks and Barry Bergdoll, *Mastering McKim's Plan: Columbia's First Century on Morningside Heights* (New York: Miriam and Ira D. Wallach Art Gallery, Columbia University, 1997), 41, 146.

65. Woods, *From Craft to Profession*, 75.

66. James Benson Sellers, *Slavery in Alabama* (Tuscaloosa: University of Alabama Press, 1950), 81, 264.

67. Monroe N. Work, "How Tuskegee Has Improved a Black Belt County" (1900), 1, Monroe N. Work Papers, Tuskegee University Archives, Tuskegee, AL; Monroe N. Work, "Macon County in 1881" (1900), 1–3, Monroe N. Work Papers, Tuskegee University Archives, Tuskegee, AL. See also Virginia Lantz Denton, *Booker T. Washington and the Adult Education Movement* (Gainesville: University Press of Florida, 1993), 92–94; Allen W. Jones, "The Role of Tuskegee Institute in the Education of Black Farmers," *The Journal of Negro History* 60, no. 2 (April 1975): 252–53.

68. Work, "How Tuskegee Has Improved a Black Belt County," 1, 3–4.

69. Washington, *Working with the Hands*, 32.

70. John C. Mohawk, *Utopian Legacies: A History of Conquest and Oppression in the Western World* (Santa Fe, NM: Clear Light Publishing, 2000), 206.

71. James D. Anderson, *The Education of Blacks in the South, 1860–1935* (Chapel Hill: University of North Carolina Press, 1988), 2.
72. Washington as quoted in W. E. B. Du Bois, *Black Reconstruction in America* (New York: A Touchstone Book, 1992), 641–42.
73. *St. Paul Dispatch*, July 11, 1902; *Appeal*, July 19, 1902; Emma Lou Thornbrough, "Booker T. Washington as Seen by His White Contemporaries," *Journal of Negro History* 53 (April 1968): 161–82; William H. Watkins, "Teaching and Learning in the Black Colleges: A 130-Year Retrospective," *Journal of Teaching Education* 3, no. 1 (1990): 10–25; Kevern J. Verney, *The Art of the Possible: Booker T. Washington and Black Leadership in the United States, 1881–1925* (New York: Routledge, 2014), 11. Samuel R. Spencer Jr.'s 1955 autobiography and August Meier's 1957 article "Towards a Reinterpretation of Booker T. Washington" were among the exceptions of early scholarship that did not portray him negatively. Recent works on Booker T. include: W. Fitzhugh Brundage. *Booker T. Washington and Black Progress: Up from Slavery 100 Years Later* (Gainesville: University Press of Florida, 2003); Jacqueline M. Moore, *Booker T. Washington, W. E. B. Du Bois and the Struggle for Racial Uplift* (Wilmington: Rowman & Littlefield Publishers, 2003); West, *The Education of Booker T. Washington*; Robert J. Norrell, *Up from History: The Life of Booker T. Washington* (Cambridge, MA: Harvard University Press, 2009); Kenneth M. Hamilton, *Booker T. Washington in American Memory* (Urbana-Champaign: University of Illinois Press, 2017).
74. Harlan, *Booker T. Washington*, 237. Harlan writes, "Washington was no Moses . . . the burden of his compromises and accommodations to a repressive system of white supremacy often vitiated his efforts to advance the interests of blacks, and indeed the history of his years of black leadership in American illustrates the impossibility of reforming a system while at the same time accommodating to its institutions and spirit" (237). See unpublished correspondence between Victoria Earle Matthews (as well as many other reformers) and Booker T. Washington in his papers held in the Booker T. Washington Collection, Manuscript Division, Library of Congress, Washington, DC. Noel Pearson, "White Guilt, Victimhood and the Quest for a Radical Centre," *Griffith Review* 16 (May 2007), https://griffithreview.com/articles/white-guilt-victimhood-and-the-quest-for-a-radical-centre/. It is well known that in the first decade of their relationship Du Bois and Washington corresponded on legal strategies, planned academic and community conferences, and sought ways to work with one another. Some scholars have argued that Du Bois understood and appreciated Washington's pragmatic strategy. Du Bois knew the context and the limitations of Black advancement in the face of segregation, lynchings, and white supremacy. See also Moore, *Booker T. Washington, W. E. B. DuBois, and the Struggle for Racial Uplift*.
75. Moore, *Booker T. Washington*, 144.
76. Booker T. Washington, *Tuskegee and Its People: Their Ideals and Achievements* (Freeport, ME: Books for Libraries Press, 1971), 8–9.
77. Verney, *The Art of the Possible*, 62, 69.
78. Michael Dennis, "Reforming the 'Academical Village': Edwin A. Alderman and the University of Virginia, 1904–1915," *The Virginia Magazine of History and Biography* 105, no. 1 (1997): 53.
79. Kenrick Ian Grandison, "From Plantation to Campus: Progress, Community, and the Lay of the Land in Shaping the Early Tuskegee Campus," *Landscape Journal*

15, no. 1 (1996): 6. Many guests and visitors to Tuskegee referred to it as "Booker T. Washington's City." For a thorough discussion and analysis of the architecture of the Tuskegee Institute, see Richard K. Dozier, "Tuskegee: Booker T. Washington's Contribution to the Education of Black Architects" (PhD diss., University of Michigan, 1990), 93. I have limited my discussion here to the buildings most relevant to my main argument.

80. L. Albert Scipio, *Pre-War Days at Tuskegee: Historical Essay on Tuskegee Institute, 1881–1943* (Silver Spring, MD: Roman Publications, 1987), 29. For a more thorough discussion, see Sherer, *Subordination or Liberation?*

81. Washington, *Up from Slavery*, 139.

82. Scipio, *Pre-War Days at Tuskegee*, 31.

83. Barbara Mooney as quoted in Ellen Weiss, "Booker T. Washington's Architectural Strategies," in *Space Unveiled: Invisible Cultures in the Design Studio*, ed. Carla Jackson Bell (New York: Routledge, 2015), 15.

84. Washington, *Working with the Hands*, 70.

85. Ibid., 1, 5; Monroe N. Work, "Extension Work Among the Negroes of Macon County, Alabama" (1900), 2, Monroe N. Work Papers, Tuskegee University Archives, Tuskegee, AL.

86. Dozier, "Tuskegee," 49–50. See also Blinzy L. Gore, *"On a Hilltop High": The Origin and History of Claflin College to 1984* (Spartanburg, SC: The Reprint Company, 1994).

87. For a detailed list of additional sources on campus planning, see Mary Vance, *Campus Planning: A Bibliography* (Monticello: Vance Bibliographies, 1986). Some scholars argue that the period between 1850 to 1875 was pivotal to advances in modernity. Geiger, ed., *The American College in the Nineteenth Century*, vii–viii.

88. Washington as quoted in Dozier, "Tuskegee: Booker T. Washington's Contribution to the Education of Black Architects," 41.

89. "Architecture Among Negroes in America," 99–100.

90. Ibid., 100.

91. Aurelius P. Hood, *The Negro at Mound Bayou: Being an Authentic Story of the Founding, Growth and Development of the "Most Celebrated Town in the South"* (Mound Bayou: A. P. Hood, 1909), 9; Towns and Settlements, Booker T. Washington Collection, Tuskegee University Archives, Tuskegee, AL; "Mound Bayou—Past and Present," *The Negro History Bulletin*, April 1940, 105, 107, 109. For other works on Black towns, see Nell Irvine Painter, *Exodusters: Black Migration to Kansas after Reconstruction* (New York: Knopf, 1977); Elizabeth Rauh Bethel, *Promiseland: A Century of Life in a Negro Community* (Philadelphia: Temple University Press, 1981).

92. John Brinckerhoff Jackson, *Discovering the Vernacular Landscape* (New Haven, CT: Yale University Press, 1984), 149–50.

93. H. E. Gulley, "Women and the Lost Cause: Preserving a Confederate Identity in the American Deep South," *Journal of Historical Geography* 19, no. 2 (1993): 125.

94. Ibid., 125–26.

95. O. A. Stewart, "Greenwood: A Dream Come True," *Tuskegee Messenger* 10 (July 1934): 1–4.

96. Dozier, "Tuskegee," 132–33.

97. Ibid., 134–37.

98. Harlan, *Booker T. Washington*, 171.

99. Scott as quoted by Weiss, "Booker T. Washington's Architectural Strategies," 17.

100. Ibid., 17.

101. Jackson, *Discovering the Vernacular Landscape*, xii.

102. *Testimony Taken by the Joint Select Committee to Inquire into the Condition of Affairs in the Late Insurrectionary States, Alabama* (Washington, DC: Government Printing Office, 1872), 56, 107, 279.

103. James L. LeLoudis, *Schooling the New South: Pedagogy, Self, and Society in North Carolina, 1880–1920* (Chapel Hill: University of North Carolina Press, 1996), 18.

104. Gavin Wright, *Old South, New South: Revolutions in the Southern Economy Since the Civil War* (New York: Basic Books, 1986), 18–19. See also Paul M. Gaston, *The New South Creed: A Study in Southern Mythmaking* (New York: Vintage Books, 1973); Dwight B. Billings, *Planters and the Making of a "New South": Class, Politics, and Development in North Carolina, 1865–1900* (Chapel Hill: University of North Carolina Press, 1979); Jonathan M. Wiener, *Social Origins of the New South: Alabama, 1860–1885* (Baton Rouge: Louisiana State University Press, 1978).

105. M. Christine Boyer, *The City of Collective Memory: Its Historical Imagery and Architectural Entertainments* (Cambridge, MA: The MIT Press, 1994), 343.

106. For an examination of Black experiments in building utopias, see William Pease and Jane Pease, *Black Utopia: Negro Communal Experiments in America* (Madison: State Historical Society of Wisconsin, 1972).

Chapter Four

1. The Manassas Industrial School, *The Manassas Industrial School for Colored Youth Located at Manassas, Virginia, 1902–1903 Catalog* (Manassas, VA: The Manassas Industrial School, 1902), 1; Voorhees Industrial School, *Voorhees Industrial School*, Robnett provides a way of understanding the interplay between external political events and internal collective identity sustenance and change (267), see Belinda Robnett, "External Political Change, Collective Identities, and Participation in Social Movement Organizations," in *Social Movements: Identity, Culture, and the State*, ed. David S. Meyer, Nancy Whittier, and Belinda Robnett (New York: Oxford University Press, 2002), 267–68.

2. Foner, *Reconstruction*, 26–27. See also Cooper, "Elevating the Race," 604–26; Quarles, *Black Abolitionists*; Evelyn Brooks Higginbotham, "African American Women's History and the Metalanguage of Race," in *We Specialize in the Wholly Impossible*, ed. Darlene Clark Hine, Wilma King, and Linda Reed (New York: Carlson Publishing, 1995), 3–24.

3. Jones, *Soldiers of Light and Love*, 61.

4. Ibid., 5.

5. Brittney C. Cooper, *Beyond Respectability: The Intellectual Thought of Race Women* (Urbana: University of Illinois Press, 2017), 11–13.

6. Unfortunately, the use of the term *Black nationalism* often elicits images of Black male leaders like Marcus Garvey, Malcolm X, or Louis Farrakhan instead of late nineteenth-century women reformers like Anna Julia Cooper, Frances E. W. Harper, Elizabeth Evelyn Wright, or Jennie Dean. Images of African American

women as nationalists typically appear beginning only in the 1960s with the emergence of the Black Power and civil rights movements. Angela Davis, Assata Shakur, and Kathleen Cleaver are the names of women most readily associated with Black nationalism.

7. J. Kenneth Morris, *Elizabeth Evelyn Wright, 1872–1906: Founder of Voorhees College* (Sewanee: University of the South, 1983), 1.

8. Susan M. Cruea, "Changing Ideals of Womanhood During the Nineteenth-Century Woman Movement," *American Transcendental Quarterly* 19, no. 3 (2005): 187–88, provides an excellent discussion of these changing images of women from the nineteenth into the twentieth century. Some scholars have argued that "Real Womanhood" emerged as a uniquely indigenous American ideal. Cogan quoted in Cruea, "Real Womanhood offered women a vision of themselves as biologically equal to men rationally as well as emotionally and in many cases markedly superior" (191–92).

9. Ibid., 192.

10. Martha H. Swain, "Clubs and Voluntary Organizations," *The New Encyclopedia of Southern Culture* 13 (2009): 74; Linda Rochelle Lane, *A Documentary of Mrs. Booker T. Washington* (New York: Edwin Mellen Press, 2001), 55, 229.

11. Swain, "Clubs and Voluntary Organizations," 74.

12 Mary Ellen Pethel and Sarah Wilkerson Freeman, "Lifting Every Female Voice: Education and Activism in Nashville's African American Community, 1870–1940," in *Tennessee Women: Their Lives and Times*, vol. 1, ed. Beverly Greene Bond and Sarah Wilkerson Freeman (Athens: University of Georgia Press, 2009), 241.

13. Taylor quoted in Dossett, *Bridging Race Divides*, 164.

14. Ula Taylor, *The Veiled Garvey: The Life and Times of Amy Jacques Garvey* (Chapel Hill: University of North Carolina Press, 2002), 87.

15. Although a more contemporary look at feminist pragmatism, see Judy Whipps, "Local Community: Place-Based Pragmatist and Feminist Education," *The Pluralist* 9, no. 2 (Summer 2014): 29–41.

16. Levy, "Forging African American Minds," 44–45. Levy writes, "This new vision, what might be termed the ethos of Pragmatic Black Consciousness, contained elements both modern and fundamental to evolving black ideas about racial identity: It was to be active, not passive, engaged with the real world, not abstract, and, most importantly, autonomous, not dependent on dominant 'Anglo-Saxon' culture and traditions. The vision found one of its most vital expressions in industrial education and often rejected traditional training approaches such as classical education. Industrial education in all of its various facets offered powerful tools to craft the new consciousness" (45).

17. Ibid., 45.

18. Faulkner, *Women's Radical Reconstruction*, 73. See also Brenda Stevenson, ed., *The Journals of Charlotte Forten Grimké* (New York: Oxford University Press, 1988).

19. Marva L. Rudolph, "Emma J. Wilson," in *Notable Black American Women, Book II*, ed. Jessie Carney Smith (New York: Gale Research, 1992), 723.

20. Joyce Ann Hanson, *Mary McLeod Bethune and Black Women's Political Activism* (Columbia: University of Missouri Press, 2003), 62, 64; Vickie L. Suggs, "Mary McLeod Bethune: The Significance of Rhetorical Action in the Development of Black College Leader," in *Historically Black College Leadership and Social*

Transformation: How Past Practices Inform the Present and Future, ed. Vickie L. Suggs (Charlotte: Information Age Publishing, Inc., 2014), 23–42; Robertson, *Mary McLeod Bethune in Florida*.

21. As early as 1825 an institution for the education of freed Blacks and mulatto slaves was formed in West Tennessee by Frances Wright. In November 1862, General Grant and Chaplain John Eaton began efforts to assist former slaves in the Mississippi Valley area, with Black men and women to work at the Union camps, and, in turn, receive a basic education. Alice Dana Adams, *The Neglected Period of Anti-Slavery in America* (Boston: Radcliffe College Monographs No. 14, 1908), 152; John W. Blassingame, "The Union Army as an Educational Institution for Negroes, 1862–1865," *Journal of Negro Education* 34, no. 2 (1965): 153; Warren B. Armstrong, "Union Chaplains and the Education of the Freedmen," in *The Price of Freedom, Slavery and the Civil War*, ed. Martin H. Greenberg and Charles G. Waugh (Nashville: Cumberland House, 2000), 226; Williams, *Self-Taught*, 124.

22. William Preston Vaughn, *Schools for All: The Blacks and Public Education in the South, 1865–1877* (Lexington: University Press of Kentucky, 1974), 1–2.

23. Christian and Christian, "The Monuments Must Go."

24. W. E. B. Du Bois, *Black Reconstruction in America 1860–1880: An Essay Toward a History of the Part Which Black Folk Played in the Attempt to Reconstruct Democracy in America* (Atlanta: Classic Textbooks, 1935), 226.

25. Richard Paul Fuke, "Land, Lumber, and Learning: The Freedmen's Bureau, Education, and the Black Community in Post-Emancipation Maryland," in *The Freedmen's Bureau and Reconstruction: Reconstructions*, ed. Paul A. Cimbala and Randall M. Miller (New York: Fordham University Press, 1999), 295. See also William F. Mugleston, ed., "The Freedmen's Bureau and Reconstruction in Virginia: The Diary of Marcus Sterling Hopkins, a Union Officer," *The Virginia Magazine of History and Biography* 86, no. 1 (1978): 45–102; William T. Alderson, "The Freedmen's Bureau in Virginia" (MA thesis, Vanderbilt University, 1949).

26. Fuke, "Land, Lumber, and Learning," 292–93.

27. See notes 106 and 112. Painter problematizes Truth's literacy; see Nell Painter, "Representing Truth: Sojourner Truth's Knowing and Becoming Known," *The Journal of American History* 81, no. 2 (September 1994): 465; Nell Irvin Painter, "Sojourner Truth in Life and Memory: Writing the Biography of an American Exotic," *Gender and History* 2, no. 1 (1990): 13. An earlier biographer of Truth fails to consider issues of representation, see Carleton Mabee, "Sojourner Truth, Bold Prophet: Why Did She Never Learn to Read," *New York History*, 69 (January 1988): 55–77.

28. Mrs. Bernard Whitman, "Manassas Industrial School," *Lend a Hand: A Record of Progress* 14, no. 4 (1895): 298.

29. David W. Blight, *Race and Reunion: The Civil War in American Memory* (Cambridge, MA: Harvard University Press, 2001), 310–11. See also Geneviève Fabre and Robert O'Meally, eds., *History and Memory in African-American Culture* (New York: Oxford University Press, 1994).

30. Glenda Elizabeth Gilmore, *Defying Dixie: The Radical Roots of Civil Rights, 1919–1950* (New York: W. W. Norton & Company, 2009), 108.

31. Just one example of continuing fund-raising efforts at Voorhees; "Raising Funds for Colored School," *Philadelphia Inquirer* 174, no. 160 (June 8, 1916): 10.

32. Gilmore, *Gender and Jim Crow*, 139.

33. By 1910, more than one hundred private and public Black colleges were formed. Some of these included: Morehouse College (1867), Atlanta, GA; Howard University (1867), Washington, DC; Spelman College (1881); Atlanta, GA; Shaw University (1865), Raleigh, NC; Fisk University (1866), Nashville, TN; Atlanta University (1867), Atlanta, GA; Virginia Union University (1899), Richmond, VA; Straight University (1869), New Orleans, LA; Talladega College (1867), Talladega, AL; Clark University (1870), Atlanta, GA; Meharry Medical College (1867), Nashville, TN; Morgan College (1867), Baltimore, MD; New Orleans University (1873), New Orleans, LA; Philander Smith College (1883), Little Rock, AR; Rust College (1883) Holy Spring, MS; and Samuel Houston College (1900), Austin, TX.

34. "School Founded in S.C. by Woman Has Fully Developed," *Metropolitan Post*, 9. By 1938, Voorhees included 400 acres, 28 buildings, 720 pupils, 34 teachers and helpers, and a total valuation of U.S.$258,000 (with inflation, in today's marketplace, the valuation would exceed well over U.S. $4.4 million).

35. Coleman, *Tuskegee to Voorhees*, 18–19.

36. Ibid., 19.

37. Some reports suggest that Wright was instead born on April 3, 1872.

38. Coleman, *Tuskegee to Voorhees*, 13.

39. Morris, *Elizabeth Evelyn Wright, 1872–1906*, 7; Howell Cobb, *Analysis of the Statute Laws of Georgia* (New York: Edward O. Jenkins, 1846), 28.

40. Morris, *Elizabeth Evelyn Wright, 1872–1906*, 4.

41. Ibid., 10–11; Rhodom Greene and John Lumpkin, *The Georgia Justice* (Milledgeville, GA: P. L. & B. H. Robinson, Printers, 1835), 73.

42. Coleman, *Tuskegee to Voorhees*, 16–17.

43. Morris, *Elizabeth Evelyn Wright, 1872–1906*, 23.

44. Coleman, *Tuskegee to Voorhees*, 21–23; Morris, *Elizabeth Evelyn Wright, 1872–1906*, 14, 18.

45. Washington, "A Sunday Evening Talk," 3–4; Coleman, *Tuskegee to Voorhees*, 31. On Washington's three wives, see "The 3 Wives of Booker T. Washington," *Ebony* (September 1982): 29–30, 32, 34.

46. Coleman, *Tuskegee to Voorhees*, 38.

47. Letters from the Booker T. Washington Collection at the Library of Congress, Washington, DC, reveal his involvement with radical African American women reformers who often stayed at The Oaks, i.e., Victoria Earle Matthews, an activist reformer who worked in New York City and Boston for part of her life.

48. Margaret M. Washington, "The Negro Home," a speech delivered before the Women's Interracial Conference, Memphis, TN, October 20, 1920, Margaret Murray Washington Papers, Hollis Burke Frissell Library, Tuskegee University, Tuskegee, AL; "The Influence of Club Work in Alabama," *National Notes* (1904): 4; "Synopsis of the Lecture by Mrs. Booker T. Washington, on the Organizing of Women's Clubs," June 22, 1910, Margaret Murray Washington Papers, Hollis Burke Frissell Library, Tuskegee University, Tuskegee, AL.

49. "A Dangerous Doctrine," *State*, June 26, 1902, Voorhees Industrial School Papers, South Carolinian Library, University of South Carolina, Columbia, SC; "Negro Education Is White Insurance," *State*, July 2, 1902, Voorhees Industrial School Papers, South Carolinian Library, University of South Carolina, Columbia, SC.

50. James D. Anderson, "Black Rural Communities and the Struggle for Education During the Age of Booker T. Washington, 1877–1915," *Peabody Journal of Education* 67, no. 4 (1990): 60.

51. Morris, *Elizabeth Evelyn Wright, 1872–1906*, 54.

52. Ibid., 83–85; Coleman, *Tuskegee to Voorhees*, 61–62.

53. Morris, *Elizabeth Evelyn Wright, 1872–1906*, 61, 90–91; Superintendent of Education, *Thirty-First Annual Report of the Superintendent of Education of the State of South Carolina* (Columbia, SC: State Superintendent of Education of the State of South Carolina, 1899).

54. Morris, *Elizabeth Evelyn Wright, 1872–1906*, 78.

55. Letter from Elizabeth E. Wright to Booker T. Washington, February 20, 1900, Voorhees Industrial School Papers, South Carolinian Library, University of South Carolina, Columbia, SC.

56. Letter from Ralph Voorhees to Senator Mayfield, April 24, 1901; letter to Booker T. Washington from Elizabeth E. Wright, April 27, 1901; letter from Elizabeth Evelyn Wright to Booker T. Washington, February 18, 1904: all from Voorhees Industrial School Papers, South Carolinian Library, University of South Carolina, Columbia, SC. See also Laura Rosily Dawson, *A Vision for Victory: A Pictorial History of Voorhees College, 1897–1997* (Marceline: Walsworth Publishing Company, 16–17.

57. Voorhees, Industrial School, *The Fifth Annual Report of the Principal and Treasurer of the Voorhees Industrial School, Denmark, South Carolina, 15 May 1902* (Tuskegee: Tuskegee Institute Steam Print, 1902), n.p.

58. "The Voorhees Industrial School," 1905, n.p.; letter from Elizabeth E. Wright to Booker T. Washington, February 18, 1904: both from Voorhees Industrial School Papers, South Carolinian Library, University of South Carolina, Columbia, SC.

59. *Tuskegee Student*, November 26, 1903, Voorhees Industrial School Papers, South Carolinian Library, University of South Carolina, Columbia, SC.

60. Voorhees Industrial School, *Remarkable Career of a Remarkable Woman* (Denmark, SC: Voorhees Industrial School, 1919), 9.

61. In November 1993 the Disney Company announced plans for a third Disney theme park to be built in Virginia. The company named the theme park Disney's America and based the rides and daily shows on real historical events. Disney described the park as "a venue for [Americans] to debate the future of their nation and learn about the past by living its history . . . [as well as] a celebration of the diversity of America, the plurality of this nation and of the conflicts that have defined us as a people." For Disney's vision statement, see "Disney's America Theme Park Planned," *American History Illustrated* 29 (March/April 1994): 6. The project threatened the village of Haymarket thirty-five miles west of Washington, DC, and endangered the dozen Civil War battlefield sites within a half hour's drive of the theme park. Some sixty-four other National Register sites also exist in the proposed area—the most endangered was the Manassas National Battlefield Park. The park's playlands would include an Indigenous village, a Civil War fort, an Ellis Island replica, a factory town, a World War II airfield, and a family farm. The promotional literature also maintained that no subject was too controversial. Disney Chairman Michael Eisner said, "We will show the Civil War with all its racial conflict. We want to make you feel what it was like to be a slave or what it was like to

escape through the underground railroad." See "Learning Together: Disney and the Historians," *The Public Historian* 17, no. 4 (1995): 5–8.

62. Elizabeth Fox Genovese, *Within the Plantation Household: Black and White Women of the Old South* (Chapel Hill: University of North Carolina Press, 1988), 160–62.

63. Brenda Stevenson, *Life in Black and White: Family and Community in the Slave South* (New York: Oxford University Press, 1996), 184.

64. Deeds, Loudon County Courthouse, Leesburg, VA (DB 6F:272–73, DB 7E:133, DB 7S:285, DB 7S:482); Wills, Loudon County Courthouse, Leesburg, VA (WB 31:466–67, WB 3K:326, WB 3K:371); Probate Records, Prince William County Courthouse, Manassas, VA (WB L:355, WB Q:29–32, WB Q:244–45, WB Q: 304–5, WB T:405–6, WB T:579–80; WB X:386); Deeds, Prince William County Courthouse, Manassas, VA (DB 31:375); Prince William County, 1850 Slave Schedule, Microfilm M432, Reel #992, p. 743; Prince William County, 1860 Slave Schedule, Microfilm M653, Reel #1396, pp. 3–4; John W. Blassingame, *The Slave Community: Plantation Life in the Antebellum South* (New York: Oxford University Press, 1979), 156–61.

65. Charles L. Perdue Jr., Thomas E. Barden, and Robert K. Phillips, eds., *Weevils in the Wheat: Interviews with Virginia Ex-Slaves* (Charlottesville: University Press of Virginia, 1976), 216.

66. Stevenson, *Life in Black and White*, 187; Wilma King, "'Suffer with Them Till Death': Slave Women and Their Children in Nineteenth-Century America," in *More Than Chattel: Black Women and Slavery in the Americas*, ed. David Barry Gaspar and Darlene Clark Hine (Bloomington: Indiana University Press, 1996), 155. See also Wilma King, *Stolen Childhood: Slave Youth in Nineteenth-Century America* (Bloomington: Indiana University Press, 1998); Marie Jenkins Schwartz, *Born in Bondage: Growing Up Enslaved in the Antebellum South* (Cambridge, MA: Harvard University Press, 2000).

67. E. Franklin Frazier, "The Negro Slave Family," *The Journal of Negro History* 15, no. 2 (1930): 205–6. See also George P. Rawick, *From Sundown to Sunup: The Making of the Black Community* (Westport, CT: Greenwood Publishing Company, 1972), 90–91.

68. Tempie Cummins as quoted in Donna Wyant Howell, *I Was a Slave: Descriptions of Plantation Life* (Washington, DC: American Legacy Books, 1995), 24.

69. Charles A. Mills, *Echoes of Manassas* (Manassas, VA: Friends of the Manassas Museum, 1988), 1.

70. Matthew B. Reeves, *Views of a Changing Landscape: An Archeological and Historical Investigation of Sudley Post Office, Manassas National Battlefield Park, Manassas, Virginia* (Manassas, VA: Manassas National Battlefield Park, 1998), 2.4–2.5; Fairfax Harrison, *Landmarks of Old Prince William, a Study of Origins in Northern Virginia* (Baltimore: Gateway Press, Inc., 1987), 588–89; Martha McCartney, "Historical Background," in *Cultural Resource Survey and Inventory of a War Torn Landscape: The Stuart's Hill Tract, Manassas Battlefield Park, Virginia*, ed. Laura Galke (Washington, DC: National Park Service, 1992), 23; R. Jackson Ratcliffe, *This Was Prince William* (Leesburg, VA: Potomac Press, 1978), 2–3.

71. Reeves, *Views of a Changing Landscape*, 2.6; Ratcliffe, *This Was Prince William*, 12; McCartney, "Historical Background," 29. See also John J. Hennessy, *The First Battle of Manassas: An End to Innocence, July 18–21, 1861* (Mechanicsburg, VA: H. E.

NOTES TO PP. 79–81   145

Howard, Inc., 1989). See John J. Hennessy, *Return to Bull Run: Campaign and Battle of Second Manassas* (New York: Simon & Schuster, 1993).

72. Reeves, *Views of a Changing Landscape*, 2.6. For a firsthand account of conditions immediately after the war, see J. T. Trowbridge, *The South: A Tour of Its Battlefields and Ruined Cities: A Journey Through the Desolated States and Talks with Its People* (Hartford, CT: Stebbins, 1866), 86.

73. Stephen Johnson Lewis, *Undaunted Faith: The Story of Jennie Dean* (Manassas, VA: The Manassas Museum, 1994), 16–17. See also Laura A. Peake, "The Manassas Industrial School for Colored Youth, 1894–1916" (MA thesis, The College of William and Mary, 1995), 22–25.

74. Lucy Phinney, *Yesterday's Schools* (Manassas, VA: Lucy Phinney, 1993), 39–42; Peake, "The Manassas Industrial School for Colored Youth, 1894–1916," 25–26.

75. "Industrial School Founder Succumbs," 1.

76. Lewis, *Undaunted Faith*, 26–27.

77. "Death of the Founder of the Manassas Industrial School," *Manassas Journal*, n.d., 2; Eugene Scheel, "Several Churches Served Old Conklin," *Loudoun Times-Mirror*, August 28, 1991, D11.

78. Letter from Jane E. Thompson to Emily Howland, June 8, 1909, Emily Howland Papers, Rare and Manuscript Collections, Carl A Kroch Library, Cornell University, Ithaca, NY (reel 7). Exhaustive research on Thompson has not yielded any further information on her except for Louis Harlan's entry in Booker T. Washington's published papers. Jane E. Thompson, of Thoroughfare Gap, Virginia, was a white woman whose family had owned slaves. She helped found the Manassas Industrial School, where she served on the Board of Directors, taught, and assisted with fund-raising. She worked with Jennie Dean to help establish her many local churches. In her later years Thompson became a clerical worker in Washington, DC. Eugene M. Scheel, *Crossroads and Corners: A Tour of the Villages, Towns, and Post Offices of Prince William County, Virginia, Past and Present* (Prince William County, VA: Historic Prince William, Inc., 1996), 41–42.

79. Lewis, *Undaunted Faith*, xxiv; B. Henderson, "A Strong Pastor of a Strong Church," *The Colored American Magazine* 14, no. 1 (1906): 16.

80. Genovese, *Roll, Jordan, Roll*, 280–84.

81. Stuckey, *Slave Culture*, 30–31.

82. For a similar discussion, see Adam Fairclough, "'Being in the Field of Education and Also Being a Negro . . . Seems . . . Tragic': Black Teachers in the Jim Crow South," *The Journal of American History* 87, no. 1 (2000): 68.

83. Fuke, "Land, Lumber, and Learning," 296.

84. Rev. Alexander Kent, "Mr. Carnegie's Gospel of Wealth," *Woman's Tribune*, March 19, 1892, 84.

85. Walter Henderson Brooks, *The Pastor's Voice: A Collection of Poems* (Washington, DC: The Associated Publishers, Inc., 1945), xiv, xx. Although some discrepancies do persist in the account of these events, it seems that the work of both Dean and Brooks was believed complementary enough, as ex-slaves, to cast them together in working toward the founding of the Manassas Industrial School. Some accounts suggest that she was assisted by Rev. Phillips Brooks, which might explain some of the misunderstanding.

86. Jennie Dean, *The Beginning of the Manassas Industrial School for Colored Youth and Its Growth* (Manassas, VA: N.p., 1900), Oswald Garrison Villard Papers, Widener Library, Harvard College Library, Harvard University, Cambridge, MA, 3. Unfortunately, the first names of Dr. and Mrs. Clemens are not mentioned.

87. William I. Lee, "History of the Church," *One Hundred Anniversary of the Nineteenth Street Baptist Church, Washington, DC* (Washington, DC: N.p., 1939), 18, 26; "Industrial School Founder Succumbs," 1; Whitman, "Manassas Industrial School," 297–301. See also Lewis, *Undaunted Faith*, xxiii.

88. Mark R. Schneider, *Boston Confronts Jim Crow, 1890–1920* (Boston: Northeastern University Press, 1997), 4–5.

89. Edward Everett Hale, "Educational Status of the Colored People," *Lend a Hand: A Record of Progress* 6, no. 3 (1891): 151. For another account of a Black school, see Charlotte R. Thorn and Mabel W. Dillingham, "Calhoun Colored School," *Lend a Hand: A Record of Progress* 13, no. 1 (1894): 52–55.

90 .Hale, "Educational Status of the Colored People," 151.

91. Whitman, "Manassas Industrial School," 298; Jane E. Thompson, "Memorial to Jennie Dean," *Manassas Journal*, May 10, 1918; Edward Everett Hale Papers, Department of Rare Books and Special Collections, University of Rochester, Rochester, New York.

92. Dean becomes symbolic of women who were formerly enslaved and who furthered the progress of the race through community building.

93. See Emily Howland Papers, Rare and Manuscript Collections, Carl. A Kroch Library, Cornell University, Ithaca, NY; Emily Howland Papers, Howland Stone Store Museum, Sherwood, NY. See also Mildred D. Myers, *Miss Emily: Emily Howland, Teacher of Freed Slaves, Suffragist, and Friend of Susan B. Anthony and Harriet Tubman* (Charlotte Harbor, FL: Tabby House, 1998). Dean must have known about Washington's work at Tuskegee, although no evidence exists that she even visited the school. Howland might have introduced Dean to Washington at some point in her efforts to financially support both schools.

94. Stephanie E. Przybylek and Peter Lloyd Jones, *Images of America: Around Cayuga County* (Dover, MA: Arcadia Publishing, 1996), 60.

95. See Jeff M. O'Dell, Howland Chapel School, National Register of Historic Places Registration Form, 1990.

96. Harriet Taylor Upton, *Proceedings of the Twenty-Fifth Annual Conference of the National American Woman Suffrage Association, Held in Washington, D.C., January 16, 17, 18, 19, 1893* (Washington, DC: The Association, 1893). Suzanne Lebsock, "A Share of Honor," in *Virginia Women, 1600–1945*, ed. Suzanne Lebsock (Richmond, VA: Virginia State Library, 1987), 90; Kathleen Barry, *Susan B. Anthony: A Biography of a Singular Feminist* (New York: New York University Press, 1988), 328; Judith E. Harper, *Susan B. Anthony: A Biographical Companion* (Santa Barbara, CA: ABC-CLIO, Inc., 1998), 135–38; Lynn Sherr, *Failure Is Impossible: Susan B. Anthony in Her Own Words* (New York: Random House, 1995), 82–86. Dean could have solicited assistance from Elizabeth Cady Stanton as well, but unfortunately she was not available due to health-related matters.

97. Letter from Jane E. Thompson to Emily Howland, June 8, 1909, Emily Howland Papers, Rare and Manuscript Collections, Carl. A Kroch Library, Cornell University, Ithaca, NY.

98. Ibid.
99. Ibid.
100. Dean, *The Beginning*, 7.
101. Lewis, *Undaunted Faith*, 28.
102. The Manassas Industrial School, *The Manassas Industrial School for Colored Youth Located at Manassas, Virginia, 1902–1903 Catalog* (Manassas, VA: The Manassas Industrial School, 1902), 4.
103. The Manassas Industrial School, *The Manassas Industrial School for Colored Youth Located at Manassas, Virginia, 1908–1909 Catalog* (Manassas, VA: The Manassas Industrial School, 1908), 13.
104. Ibid.
105. Ibid.
106. Ibid., 14.
107. Letter from Jennie Dean to Emily Howland, August 18, 1909, Emily Howland Papers, Rare and Manuscript Collections, Carl. A Kroch Library, Cornell University, Ithaca, NY. It is difficult to determine if Dean actually wrote the letter herself or had someone else instead sign her name. Letter from Jane E. Thompson to Emily Howland, August 18, 1909, Emily Howland Papers, Rare and Manuscript Collections, Carl. A Kroch Library, Cornell University, Ithaca, NY.
108. The Manassas Industrial School, *1908–1909 Catalog*, 10–11.
109. Jennie Dean, *A Battleground School: A Colored Woman's Work in Uplifting Negro Boys and Girls, The Story of the Manassas Industrial School for Colored Youth* (Alexandria, VA: N.p., 1901).
110. Lewis, *Undaunted Faith*, xix. This biography is the only extant work that examines Dean's life and her efforts to build the Manassas Industrial School.
111. Ibid.
112. Literacy should be understood, among former slaves like Dean, along a spectrum of ability.
113. Whitman, "Manassas Industrial School," 297.
114. Dean, *The Beginning of the Manassas Industrial School for Colored Youth and Its Growth*.
115. Literacy must be understood as far more complex and contingent on the social, political, and economic contexts available to individuals, communities, etc. Arlette Ingram Willis, "Literacy at Calhoun Colored School, 1892–1945," *Reading Research Quarterly* 37, no. 1 (2002): 11.
116. Anderson as quoted in ibid., 14.
117. Phyllis M. Belt-Beyan, *The Emergence of African American Literacy Traditions: Family and Community Efforts in the Nineteenth-Century* (Boulder: Greenwood Publishing Group 2004), 3–5.
118. Hunter, *To 'Joy My Freedom*, vii. See also Deryck W. Holdsworth, "Landscape and Archives as Texts," in *Understanding Ordinary Landscapes*, ed. Paul Groth and Todd W. Bressi (New Haven, CT: Yale University Press, 1997), 44–55.
119. Royster, *Southern Horrors and Other Writings*, 45–46.
120. Certificate of Death, Jane Serepta Dean, Department of Health, Division of Vital Records, Commonwealth of Virginia, May 5, 1913. There is some question about Dean's actual birth date. Several secondary sources suggest that she was born in 1857 while other sources, like her death certificate, indicate that she was born in

1848. At the time of her death her sister, Ms. Ella H. Bailey, signed her death certificate and inevitably would have possibly been present at the time of Dean's birth. Some documents suggest that she was but five years old when the Civil War first broke out, still leaving open the question of her actual birth date. The year 1852 appears on her tombstone and is often cited. The almost nine-year spread between 1848 and 1857 reveals how chattel slavery had denied so many people of their basic humanity. Ella H. Dean Bailey, "The History of Miss Jennie Dean's Life," Manassas Industrial School Papers, Manassas Museum, Manassas, VA, n.d.

121. "Industrial School Founder Succumbs," 1.

122. Letter from Jane E. Thompson to Emily Howland, December 16, 1913, Emily Howland Papers, Rare and Manuscript Collections, Carl A. Kroch Library, Cornell University, Ithaca, NY.

123. Sabine Offe, "Sites of Remembrance? Jewish Museums in Contemporary Germany," *Jewish Social Studies* 5, no. 2 (1997): 84.

124. Bart Verschaffel, "The Monumental: On the Meaning of a Form," *The Journal of Architecture* 4, no. 4 (1999): 334.

125. Whitman, 301.

Chapter Five

1. Longstreth as quoted in Woods, "Charles F. McKim," 311.

2. Ibid.

3. Kimberly Alexander Shilland, "Chapter III, Ware and Van Brunt Advance the Profession" (PhD diss., Massachusetts Institute of Technology, 1999/2000), 22.

4. Arthur Rotch, "Eugène Létang," vol. 2, Eugène Létang Papers, Architectural Collections, The MIT Museum, Boston, MA.

5. Robert R. Taylor, "A Soldier's Home" (thesis, Massachusetts Institute of Technology, 1892), Architectural Collections, The MIT Museum, Boston, MA, 1. His classmates' thesis projects included a school of architecture, a clubhouse, a technical high school, an opera house, an official residence, an office building, a town hall, a villa, and an armory. See also William T. Atwood, "The Massachusetts Institute of Technology," *New England Magazine* 42 (June 1910): 405.

6. Ellen Weiss, "Robert R. Taylor of Tuskegee, An Early Professional Architect in Alabama," *Preservation Report* (March/April 1989): 3. See also Weiss, "Robert R. Taylor of Tuskegee, An Early Black American Architect," 3–19; Weiss, *Robert R. Taylor and Tuskegee*, 45–74.

7. Robert R. Taylor, "The Scientific Development of the Negro," in *Celebration of the Fiftieth Anniversary of the Granting of a Charter to the Massachusetts Institute of Technology* (New York: McGraw-Hill, 1911), 168–69.

8. Weiss, "Robert R. Taylor of Tuskegee, An Early Professional Architect in Alabama," 3.

9. Taylor, "The Scientific Development of the Negro," 169–70.

10. Ibid.

11. "Architectural Drawing at the Tuskegee Normal and Industrial Institute."

12 Scott, "Training Head and Hand," 1.

13. Ibid., 2.

14. Weiss, "Robert R. Taylor of Tuskegee, An Early Professional Architect in Alabama," 3.

15. Ibid., 4.

16. Ibid.

17. Dozier, "Tuskegee: Booker T. Washington's Contribution to the Education of Black Architects," 43; "The Negro Nevertheless a Factor in Architecture," *The Negro History Bulletin* (April 1940): 101.

18. Warren Logan, "Resources and Material Equipment," in *Tuskegee and Its People: Their Ideals and Achievements*, ed. Booker T. Washington (New York: D. Appleton and Co., 1906), 51.

19. Taylor, "The Scientific Development of the Negro," 168–69.

20. Arthur Drexler, ed., "Preface," in *The Architecture of the Ecole des Beaux-Arts* (Cambridge, MA: The MIT Press, 1977), 9; Anthony Alofsin, "Tempering the Ecole: Nathan Ricker at the University of Illinois, Langford Warren at Harvard, and Their Followers," in *The History of History in American Schools of Architecture 1865–1975*, ed. Gwendolyn Wright and Janet Parks (New York: Princeton Architectural Press, 1990), 73–75, 86, 87. See also Thomas Hastings, "The Relations of Life to Style in Architecture," *Harper's New Monthly* 88, no. 528 (1894): 959–61; Ernest Flagg, "American Architecture as Opposed to Architecture in America," *Architectural Record* 10, no. 2 (1900): 178–80.

21. Robert R. Taylor, "Tuskegee's Mechanical Department," *The Southern Workman* 50, no. 10 (1921): 463.

22. Ibid., 25.

23. Ibid., 34.

24. "Architectural Drawing at the Tuskegee Normal and Industrial Institute."

25. Scott, "Training Head and Hand," 1.

26. Ellen Weiss, "Tuskegee: Landscape in Black and White," *Winterthur Portfolio* 36, no. 1 (2001): 20.

27. Ibid., 23.

28. Ibid., 28.

29. Ibid., 23.

30. Ibid., 28.

31. Virginia McAlester and Lee McAlester, *A Field Guide to American Houses* (New York: Alfred A. Knopf, 2006), 324.

32. Ibid.

33. Ibid., 321.

34. Voorhees Industrial School, *The Fifth Annual Report; Tuskegee Student*, November 26, 1903.

35. Although Taylor has been credited with designing four of the earliest buildings at Voorhees, evidence does suggest that Pittman was involved in their actual design and construction beginning sometime in 1902 with his design for Kennerly Hall. A large part of Pittman's later private practice, both in Washington, DC, and Dallas, Texas, was engaged with the design and construction of several leading institutions for African American race leaders throughout the South. Pittman's design for the National Religious Training School and Chautauqua in Durham, North Carolina (1910), reflects his use of the Colonial Revival style with some concern for regional influences. Angel David Nieves, "Voorhees: Elizabeth Evelyn Wright's

'Small Tuskegee' and Black Education in the Post-Reconstruction South," *Arris: Journal of the Southeast Chapter of the Society of Architectural Historians* 13 (2002): 25–37; Ruth Ann Stewart, "William Sidney Pittman (1875–1958)," *African American Architects: A Biographical Dictionary, 1865–1945*, ed. Dreck Spurlock Wilson (New York: Routledge, 2004), 446–48; Weiss, *Robert R. Taylor and Tuskegee*, 49–52.

36. "William Sidney Pittman: Architect of the Race," *Washington Bee*, October 1907, 1. See also Robert W. Rydell, John E. Findling, and Kimberly D. Pelle, *Fair America: World's Fairs in the United States* (Washington, DC: Smithsonian Institution Press, 2000), 30.

37. Jessie C. D. Green, "Elizabeth E. Wright, Inspiration in Action," *Founder's Day*, April/May 1941, 11–12, Voorhees Industrial School Papers, South Carolinian Library, University of South Carolina, Columbia, SC.

38. See Voorhees College Collection, University of South Carolina.

39. J. Kenneth Morris, *Elizabeth Evelyn Wright, 1872–1906: Founder of Voorhees College* (Sewanee: University of the South, 1983), 186.

40. John E. Wells, ed., *The South Carolina Architects, 1885–1935: A Biographical Dictionary* (Richmond: New South Architectural Press, 1992), 33.

41. Claflin University, *Catalogue of Claflin University, 1897–1898* (Charleston: Walker, Evans & Cogswell, Printers, 1898), 2, University Archives, Claflin University, Orangeburg, SC. Claflin was founded in 1869 and under the general control of the Methodist Episcopal Church. A university brochure describes its intended purpose in educating African Americans: "It is the principal duty of this generation to educate the next." See also William Wilson Cooke File, University Archives, Claflin University, Orangeburg, SC. Recent work on Scandinavian Sloyd, see David J. Whittaker, *The Impact and Legacy of Educational Sloyd: Heads and Hands in Harness* (New York: Routledge, 2013), 98.

42. Betty Bird and Nancy B. Schwartz, *Thematic Study of Black Architects, Builders and Developers in Washington, D.C.* (Washington, DC: United Planning Organization, 1993), 44; "Industrial Education an Important Feature," 9; "The New Manual-Training Building, Claflin University, Orangeburg, S.C.," *Christian Educator*, August 1902, 10–11; "The Claflin Method," *Christian Educator* (May–August 1905): 2–3.

43. Claflin University, *Catalogue of Claflin University, 1897–98* (Charleston: Walker, Evans & Cogswell, Printers, 1898), University Archives, Claflin University, Orangeburg, SC, 69.

44. Claflin University, *Catalogue of Claflin University, . . . 1884–1885*. Elaborate images of the university begin to appear in the inside front cover of the catalog and continue to do so throughout the turn of the century.

45. Claflin University, *Catalogue of Claflin University, College of Agriculture, and Mechanics Institute, Orangeburg, S.C., 1890–1891* (Charleston: Walker, Evans & Cogswell, Printers, 1891), University Archives, Claflin University, Orangeburg, SC, 69.

46. R. Charles Bates, *The Elementary Principles of Architecture and Building* (Boston: Press of Geo. H. Ellis, 1892), 11, P. Charles Bates File, University Archives, Claflin University, Orangeburg, SC.

47. Ibid., 20.

48. Weiss, "Robert R. Taylor of Tuskegee, an Early Black American Architect," 11.

49. Harlan, *Booker T. Washington*, 94.

50. Morris, *Elizabeth Evelyn Wright*, 227.

51. Weiss, "Robert R. Taylor of Tuskegee, An Early Professional Architect in Alabama," 5. Weiss mentions "the rare Tuskegee fire that some thought might be arson," see *Robert R. Taylor and Tuskegee*, 224.

52. Sullivan, "Extralegal Violence," 38; Elaine Frantz Parsons, "Midnight Rangers: Costume and Performance in the Reconstruction-Era Ku Klux Klan," *Journal of American History* 92, no. 3 (2005): 811–36.

53. Weiss, "Robert R. Taylor of Tuskegee, An Early Professional Architect in Alabama," 5.

54. Cornel West, *Keeping Faith: Philosophy and Race in America* (New York: Routledge, 1993), 47.

55. Booker T. Washington, "Chapters from My Experience," *World's Work*, April 1911, 14233.

56. Taylor, "The Scientific Development of the Negro," 169.

57. Ibid., 168–69.

58. The Manassas Industrial School, *The Manassas Industrial School for Colored Youth . . . 1908–1909 Catalog*, 4, 10–11; The Manassas Industrial School, *The Manassas Industrial School for Colored Youth Located at Manassas, Virginia, 1912–1913 Catalog* (Manassas, VA: The Manassas Industrial School, 1913), 14–15.

59. Charles W. Leavitt, "Stands, Stadia, and Bowls," *Journal Proceedings* 11, no. 8 (1915): 576.

60. Heidi Hohmann, "Charles Wellford Leavitt, Jr.," in *Pioneers of American Landscape Design*, ed. Charles A. Birnbaum (New York: McGraw-Hill, 2000), 223–27; William M. Hogue, *The Jacob Tome Institute and Its Schools: The First Hundred Years* (North East, MD: Tome School, 1995); Flora Milner Harrison, *What the Berry School for Boys Is Doing* (N.p.: N.p., n.d.). Leavitt's park designs included Pennypack Park in Philadelphia; Monument Valley Park in Colorado Springs; and a parkway system along the Cooper River in Camden, New Jersey. He was chief engineer of the Palisades Interstate Park for over twelve years.

61. Mary N. Woods, "Thomas Jefferson and the University of Virginia," 266.

62. Ibid.

63. A second architect, Robert D. Kohn, a representative of V. W. Benjamin, was asked to present plans for new structures at Manassas sometime before 1910. "Lay Corner Stones for Three Buildings," *Manassas Democrat*, June 2, 1910; "Ready to Build Industrial School," *Manassas Democrat*, June 16, 1910. Kohn was a member of the Society for Ethical Culture in New York City. The Society, founded by Felix Adler in 1876, was committed to issues of social justice and moral education. The Society was made up largely of New York's leading Jewish philanthropists and businessmen committed to the ethical treatment of all people, regardless of race. It is clear that Dean must have somehow acknowledged a common bond between Blacks and Jews as African Americans often referred to themselves as a "Chosen People."

64. Ibid., 325.

65. Ibid., 324.

66. Ibid., 320.

67. Ibid.

68. "Death of the Founder of the Manassas Industrial School," 2; Manassas Industrial School for Colored Youth, *1909 Financial Report, Donors' List and Statement of Current Needs* (Manassas, VA: Manassas Industrial School for Colored Youth, 1909), 15.

69. James P. Comer, *Beyond Black and White* (New York: Quadrangle Books, 1972), 165. See also Judith Lewis Herman, *Trauma and Recovery* (New York: Basic Books, 1992), 74, 75–76, 101.

70. *Atlanta Constitution*, May 23, 1890, 1; "Confederate Soldiers' Home," *Inland Architect and News Record* 19, no. 3 (1892): 39, 52; R. B. Rosenburg, *Living Monuments: Confederate Soldiers' Homes in the New South* (Chapel Hill: University of North Carolina Press, 1993), xiii. On memory and mourning in the nineteenth century, see especially Martha Pike, "In Memory of: Artifacts Relating to Mourning in Nineteenth-Century America," in *American Material Culture: The Shape of Things Around Us*, ed. Edith P. Nieves (Bowling Green, OH: Bowling Green State University Popular Press, 1984): 48–65. For a discussion of a campus building as a memorial, see Woods, "Henry Van Brunt."

71. Fleischner, "Memory, Sickness, and Slavery," 397–98. I do not, however, agree with landscape historian Kenrick Ian Grandison, who argues that the Black college campus is a site of terror. See Kenrick Ian Grandison, "Landscapes of Terror: A Reading of Tuskegee's Historic Campus," in *The Geography of Identity*, ed. Patricia Yaeger (Ann Arbor: University of Michigan Press, 1996), 334. Instead, a much more nuanced reading suggests that the campus can be seen as a site representative of past trauma invested with new meaning for self-empowerment and as an archive of enslavement. Allan Sekula, "The Body and the Archive," *October* 39 (Winter 1986): 3–64; Cloke and Jones, *Tree Cultures*, 8, 64–66; Joshua Hagen, "Places of Memory and Memories of Places in Nazi Germany," in *Memory, Place and Identity: Commemoration and Remembrance of War and Conflict*, ed. Danielle Drozdzewski, Sarah De Nardi, and Emma Waterton (New York: Routledge, 2016), 236–54.

72. An important recent discussion of space, trauma and memory sheds important light on "the ways that victims continue to live and imagine space in the aftermath of conflict" (3). African Americans are no exception and require a more sustained and thorough analysis as I've begun to outline above. Pamela Colombo and Estela Schindel, *Space and Memories of Violence: Landscapes of Erasure, Disappearance and Exception* (New York: Palgrave Macmillan, 2014), 3.

Chapter Six

Epigraph: Curtis, "Jennie Dean's School."

1. Shirley J. Carlson, "Black Ideals of Womanhood in the Late Victorian Era," *The Journal of Negro History* 77, no. 2 (1992): 61–62; Frances Mitchell Ross, "The New Woman as Club Woman and Social Activist in Turn of the Century Arkansas," *The Arkansas Historical Quarterly* 50, no. 4 (1991): 317–18. See also Barbara Welter, "The Cult of True Womanhood: 1800–1860," in *Dimity Convictions: The American Woman in the Nineteenth Century* (Athens: Ohio University Press, 1976), 21–41; Blanche Glassman Hersh, "The True Woman and the 'New Woman' in Nineteenth Century America," in *Woman's Being, Woman's Place: Female Identity and Vocation in*

American History, ed. Mary Kelley (Boston: Hall, 1979), 271–82. For a discussion outlining the struggle of Black women during the Victorian Era, see Jennifer Devere Brody, *Impossible Purities: Blackness, Femininity and Victorian Culture* (Durham, NC: Duke University Press, 1998).

2. Susan M. Reverby and Dorothy O. Helly, "Converging on History," in *Gendered Domains: Rethinking Public and Private in Women's History*, ed. Dorothy O. Helly and Susan M. Reverby (Ithaca, NY: Cornell University Press, 1992), 6–8. Both authors even suggest "the concept of gendered and divided spheres might merely be a reflection of long-standing categories within the minds of our intellectual oppressors."

3. Troy Duster, "The Long Path to Higher Education for African Americans," *Thought and Action: The NEA Higher Education Journal* 25 (2009): 101–4; Shaun R. Harper, Lori D. Patton, and Ontario S. Wooden, "Access and Equity for African American Students in Higher Education: A Critical Race Historical Analysis of Policy Efforts," *The Journal of Higher Education* 80, no. 4 (July/August 2009): 389–414.

4. Alvin J. Schexnider, *Saving Black Colleges: Leading Change in a Complex Organization* (Basingstoke: Palgrave Macmillan, 2013), 27–44. Also consider Edward Fort, *Survival of the Historically Black Colleges and Universities: Making It Happen* (New York: Lexington Books, 2013), 42–43, 66; Stephanie K. Meeks, "Our HBCUs Are National Treasures," *HuffPost*, May 4, 2017, http://www.huffingtonpost.com/national-trust-for-historic-preservation/our-hbcus-are-national-tr_b_9828326.html.

5. Stephen Provasnik, Linda L. Shafer, and Thomas D. Snyder, *Historically Black Colleges and Universities, 1976 to 2001* (Washington, DC: National Center for Education Statistics, 2004), 2; Kevin McClain and April Perry, "Where Did They Go: Retention Rates for Students of Color at Predominantly White Institutions," *College Student Affairs Leadership*, 4, no. 1 (2017): 23–32, Article 3, https://scholarworks.gvsu.edu/csal/vol4/iss1/3/.

6. "Clyburn Statement on Passage of H.R. 1135, to Reauthorize the HBCU Historic Preservation Program," June 27, 2017, https://clyburn.house.gov/press-release/clyburn-statement-passage-hr-1135-reauthorize-hbcu-historic-preservation-program.

7. Cecil N. McKithan, "Preserving HBCUs for Future Generations," *CRM: Cultural Resource Management* 22, no. 8 (1999): 39.

8. Hannah McCann, "20 Historically Black Colleges and Universities Receive Stimulus Grants for Building Preservation," *Architect: The Journal of the American Institute of Architects*, September 18, 2009, http://www.architectmagazine.com/design/20-historically-black-colleges-and-universities-receive-stimulus-grants-for-building-preservation_o.

9. McKithan, "Preserving HBCUs for Future Generations," 40.

10. Jacqueline Conciatore, "Fighting to Preserve Black History," *Black Issues in Higher Education* 17, no. 11 (2000): 21.

11. Ibid., 22.

12 Statement from Ms. Elizabeth Nickens to Mayor Weber and Members of the Manassas City Council, March 26, 1992, Manassas Industrial School Papers, Manassas Museum, Manassas, VA.

13. James W. Loewen, "The Shrouded History of College Campuses," *Chronicle of Higher Education*, January 28, 2000, B7; Peter Halewood, "Campus Activism and Competing Racial Narratives," *Academe* 102, no. 6 (November/December 2016): 8.

14. Ibid.

15. McCann, "20 Historically Black Colleges and Universities"; The National Organization of Minority Architects, "Architecture at HBCUs: Principles, Legacy, and Preservation," Morgan State University Conference, November 5–6, 2015, http://www.noma.net/article/260/happenings/news/architecture-at-hbcus-principles-legacy-and-preservation.

16. For a discussion on contraband camps, especially in the Virginia and Washington, DC, areas, see Joseph P. Reidy, "'Coming from the Shadow of the Past': The Transition from Slavery to Freedom at Freedman's Village, 1863–1900," *Virginia Magazine of History and Biography* 95, no. 4 (1987): 403–28; Page Milburn, "The Emancipation of the Slaves in the District of Columbia," *Records of the Columbia Historical Society* (Washington, DC: Columbia Historical Society, 1913), 16:115.

17. Mrs. W. Carleton Adams, "Slave Monument Question," *Confederate Veteran* 12, no. 2 (1904): 525.

18. Scott Dyer, "Black College Beef Up Security After Receiving Hate Mail," *Black Issues in Higher Education*, February 3, 2000, 18.

19. Ibid.

20. Pierre Nora, "Between Memory and History: Les Lieux de Mémorie," in *History and Memory in African American Culture*, ed. Geneviève Fabre and Robert O'Meally (New York: Oxford University Press, 1994), 284–85; Michael Rothberg, "Between Memory and Memory: From Lieux de mémoire to Noeuds de mémoire," *Yale French Studies* 118/119 (2010): 3; Lauret Savoy, *Trace: Memory, History, Race, and the American Landscape* (Berkeley, CA: Counterpoint, 2016), 113.

21. Nora, "Between Memory and History," 285.

22. Recent works have expanded our understanding of women's reforms efforts in the Post-Reconstruction era; see Michelle Mitchell, *Righteous Propagation: African Americans and the Politics of Racial Destiny After Reconstruction* (Chapel Hill: University of North Carolina Press, 2004); Susan D. Carle, *Defining the Struggle: National Organizing for Racial Justice, 1880–1915* (New York: Oxford University Press, 2013). One of the few most recent works to include Wright in any significant way include Sharon Ferguson Beasley, "Pioneering Women of Southern Education: A Comparative Study of Northern and Southern School Founders" (PhD diss., University of South Carolina, 2014).

Bibliography

Archives

Booker T. Washington Collection. Library of Congress, Washington, DC.
Catalogue of Claflin University, College of Agriculture, and Mechanics Institute, Orangeburg, S.C., 1884–1885, 1890–1891, 1897–1898. University Archives, Claflin University, Orangeburg, SC.
Deeds. Loudon County Courthouse, Leesburg, VA.
Deeds, Prince William County Courthouse, Manassas, VA.
Division of Behavioral Science Research (reel 1). Tuskegee University Archives, Tuskegee, Alabama.
Edward Everett Hale Papers, Department of Rare Books and Special Collections, University of Rochester, Rochester, New York.
Emily Howland Papers. Howland Stone Store Museum, Sherwood, New York.
Emily Howland Papers. Rare and Manuscript Collections, Carl. A Kroch Library, Cornell University, Ithaca, NY (reel 7).
Eugène Létang Papers. Architectural Collections, The MIT Museum, Boston, MA.
Manassas Industrial School Papers. Manassas Museum, Manassas, VA.
Margaret Murray Washington Papers. Hollis Burke Frissell Library, Tuskegee University, Tuskegee, AL.
Monroe N. Work Papers, Tuskegee University Archives, Tuskegee, AL.
P. Charles Bates File. University Archives, Claflin University, Orangeburg, SC.
Probate Records. Prince William County Courthouse, Manassas, VA.
South Carolinian Library, University of South Carolina, Columbia, SC.
Tuskegee University Archives, Tuskegee, AL.
Voorhees College Collection. University of South Carolina, Columbia, SC.
Voorhees Industrial School Papers. South Carolinian Library, University of South Carolina, Columbia, SC.
William Wilson Cooke File. University Archives, Claflin University, Orangeburg, SC.
Wills. Loudon County Courthouse, Leesburg, VA.

Periodicals

Anglo-African
Appeal
Athens Banner

Atlanta Constitution
Boston Herald
Chicago Tribune
Christian Educator
Christian Index
Chronicle of Higher Education
Cleveland Daily Leader
Confederate Veteran
Daily Missouri Democrat
Freedman's Journal
Independent
Indianapolis Freeman
Kansas City American Citizen
Loudoun Times-Mirror
Manassas Democrat
Manassas Journal
Metropolitan Post
National Freedman
New National Era
New York Age
New York Times
Norfolk Journal
Philadelphia Inquirer
Savannah Tribune
State
St. Paul Dispatch
Tallahassee Democrat
Tuskegee Student
Washington Bee
Washington Post
Washington Tribune
Woman's Tribune
World's Work

Other Sources

Adams, Alice Dana. *The Neglected Period of Anti-Slavery in America.* Boston: Radcliffe College Monographs No. 14, 1908.

Adams, John Coleman. "What a Great City Might Be—A Lesson from the White City." *The New England Magazine* 14, no. 1 (1896): 3–13.

Adams, Mrs. W. Carleton. "Slave Monument Question." *Confederate Veteran* 12, no. 2 (1904): 525.

Ahmed, Sara. *Living a Feminist Life.* Durham, NC: Duke University Press, 2017.

Alderson, William T. "The Freedmen's Bureau in Virginia." MA thesis, Vanderbilt University, 1949.

Allen, James. *Without Sanctuary: Lynching Photography in America.* Santa Fe, NM: Twin Palms Publishers, 2000.
Alofsin, Anthony. "Tempering the Ecole: Nathan Ricker at the University of Illinois, Langford Warren at Harvard, and Their Followers." In *The History of History in American Schools of Architecture 1865–1975*, edited by Gwendolyn Wright and Janet Parks, 73–87. New York: Princeton Architectural Press, 1990.
Ammons, Elizabeth. *Conflicting Stories: American Women Writers at the Turn into the Twentieth Century.* New York: Oxford University Press, 1992.
Anderson, Benedict. *Imagined Communities: Reflections on the Origin and Spread of Nationalism.* New York: Verso, 1991.
Anderson, Eric, and Alfred A. Moss Jr. *Dangerous Donations: Northern Philanthropy and Southern Black Education, 1902–1930.* Columbia: University of Missouri Press, 1999.
Anderson, James D. "Black Rural Communities and the Struggle for Education During the Age of Booker T. Washington, 1877–1915." *Peabody Journal of Education* 67, no. 4 (1990): 46–62.
———. *The Education of Blacks in the South, 1860–1935.* Chapel Hill: University of North Carolina Press, 1988.
Anderson, Kay J. "The Idea of Chinatown: The Power of Place and Institutional Practice in the Making of a Racial Category." *Annals of the Association of American Geographers* 77, no. 4 (1987): 580–98.
Appelbaum, Stanley. *The Chicago World's Fair of 1893: A Photographic Record.* New York: Dover Publications, Inc., 1980.
"Architectural Drawing at the Tuskegee Normal and Industrial Institute." *Architects' and Builders' Magazine* 5, no. 8 (1904): 377–78.
"Architecture Among Negroes in America." *The Negro History Bulletin* (April 1940): 99–100.
Armstrong, Catherine. "Slavery and Landscape." *Slavery and Abolition* 38, no. 1 (2017): 1–5.
Armstrong, Samuel C. "General Armstrong's Memoranda." *The Southern Workman and Hampton School Record* 20, no. 12 (December 1893): 178.
Armstrong, Warren B. "Union Chaplains and the Education of the Freedmen." In *The Price of Freedom, Slavery and the Civil War*, edited by Martin H. Greenberg and Charles G. Waugh, 104–15. Nashville: Cumberland House, 2000.
Atchinson, Ray M. "The Land We Love: A Southern Post-Bellum Magazine of Agriculture, Literature, and Military History." *The North Carolina Historical Review* 37, no. 4 (1960): 506–15.
Atwood, William T. "The Massachusetts Institute of Technology." *New England Magazine* 42 (June 1910): 396–405.
Auslander, Mark. "The Other Side of Paradise: Glimpsing Slavery in the University's Utopian Landscapes." *Southern Spaces*, May 13, 2010. https://southernspaces.org/2010/other-side-paradise-glimpsing-slavery-universitys-utopian-landscapes.
Ayers, Edward L. *The Promise of the New South: Life After Reconstruction.* New York: Oxford University Press, 1992.

Bachin, Robin. "Cultural Boundaries: Constructing Urban Space and Civic Culture on Chicago's South Side, 1890–1919." PhD diss., University of Michigan, 1996.

Bachin, Robin F. *Building the South Side: Urban Space and Civic Culture in Chicago, 1890–1919.* Chicago: University of Chicago Press, 2004.

Bacon, Mardges. "Toward a National Style of Architecture: The Beaux-Arts Interpretation of the Colonial Revival." In *The Colonial Revival in America*, edited by Alan Axelrod, 92–95. New York: W. W. Norton & Company, 1985.

Baer, Hans A. "The Role of the Bible and Other Sacred Texts in African American Denominations and Sects." In *African Americans and the Bible: Sacred Texts and Social Textures*, edited by Vincent L. Wimbush, 92–102. Eugene, OR: Wipf and Stock Publishers, 2012.

Bailey, Fred. "The Textbooks of the 'Lost Cause': Censorship and the Creation of Southern State Histories." *Georgia Historical Quarterly* (Summer 1991): 507–33.

Baker, Lee D. *From Savage to Negro: Anthropology and the Construction of Race, 1896–1954.* Berkeley: University of California Press, 1998.

Baker, Ray Stannard. "What Is a Lynching? A Study of Mob Justice, South and North." *McClure's Magazine* 24 (January 1905): 299–314.

Bank, Rosemarie K. "Representing History: Performing the Columbian Exposition." *Theatre Journal* 54, no. 4 (December 2002): 589–606.

Barry, Kathleen. *Susan B. Anthony: A Biography of a Singular Feminist.* New York: New York University Press, 1988.

Barton, Craig. *Sites of Memory: Perspectives on Architecture and Race.* Princeton, NJ: Princeton Architectural Press, 2001.

Bates, Gerri. "The Hallowed Halls: African American Women College and University Presidents." *The Journal of Negro Education* 76, no. 3 (2007): 373–90.

Bates, R. Charles. *The Elementary Principles of Architecture and Building.* Boston: Press of Geo. H. Ellis, 1892. P. Charles Bates File, University Archives, Claflin University, Orangeburg, SC.

Bay, Mia. "The Battle for Womanhood Is the Battle for Race: Black Women and Nineteenth-Century Racial Thought." In *Toward an Intellectual History of Black Women*, edited by Mia Bay and Farah J. Griffin, 79–80. Baltimore: Johns Hopkins University Press, 2015.

———. *To Tell the Truth Freely: The Life of Ida B. Wells.* New York: Hill and Wang, 2010.

Beasley, Sharon Ferguson. "Pioneering Women of Southern Education: A Comparative Study of Northern and Southern School Founders." PhD diss., University of South Carolina, 2014.

Bederman, Gail. "'Civilization,' the Decline of Middle-Class Manliness, and Ida B. Wells's Antilynching Campaign (1892–94)." *Radical History Review* no. 52 (1992): 5–30.

Bell, Thomas J. "The Chicago Fair." *Bulletin of Atlanta University,* July 1893, 3.

Belt-Beyan, Phyllis M. *The Emergence of African American Literacy Traditions: Family and Community Efforts in the Nineteenth-Century.* Boulder: Greenwood Publishing Group, 2004.

Bender, Thomas. *New York Intellect: A History of Intellectual Life in New York City, from 1750 to the Beginnings of Our Own Time.* Baltimore: The Johns Hopkins University Press, 1987.
Bennett, Michael Anthony. "What Are the Buildings Saying: A Study of First Year Undergraduate Students Attributions About College Campus Architecture." PhD diss., Kansas State University, 1995.
Berg, Manfred. *Popular Justice: A History of Lynching in America.* New York: Rowman & Littlefield Publishers, 2015.
Bethel, Elizabeth Rauh. *Promiseland: A Century of Life in a Negro Community.* Philadelphia: Temple University Press, 1981.
Biemiller, Lawrence. "Planning the College Campus: The Evolution of a 'Distinctively American Form.'" *Chronicle of Higher Education,* May 30, 1984, 5–7.
Billings, Dwight B. *Planters and the Making of a "New South": Class, Politics, and Development in North Carolina, 1865–1900.* Chapel Hill: University of North Carolina Press, 1979.
Bird, Betty, and Nancy B. Schwartz. *Thematic Study of Black Architects, Builders and Developers in Washington, D.C.* Washington, DC: United Planning Organization, 1993.
Blassingame, John W. *The Slave Community: Plantation Life in the Antebellum South.* New York: Oxford University Press, 1979.
———. "The Union Army as an Educational Institution for Negroes, 1862–1865." *Journal of Negro Education* 34, no. 2 (1965): 152–59.
Blassingame, Tia Marie. "Breaking Through a 'Thounderous Silence': The African American in the Evolution of American Architecture." Senior thesis, Princeton University, n.d., American Institute of Architects (AIA) Archives, Washington, DC.
Blight, David W. "'For Something Beyond the Battlefield': Frederick Douglass and the Struggle for the Memory of the Civil War." *The Journal of American History* 75, no. 4 (1989): 229–1158.
———. *Race and Reunion: The Civil War in American Memory.* Cambridge, MA: Harvard University Press, 2001.
Bogart, Michele H. *Public Sculpture and the Civic Ideal in New York City, 1890–1930.* Chicago: University of Chicago Press, 1989.
Bolotin, Norman. *Chicago's Grand Midway: A Walk around the World at the Columbian Exposition.* Urbana–Champaign: University of Illinois Press, 2017.
Boyer, M. Christine. *The City of Collective Memory: Its Historical Imagery and Architectural Entertainments.* Cambridge, MA: The MIT Press, 1994.
Bracey, John H., Jr., August Meier, and Elliott Rudwick, eds. *Black Nationalism in America.* New York: The Bobbs-Merrill Company, Inc., 1970.
Bragdon, Claude Fayette. *The Beautiful Necessity: Seven Essays on Theosophy and Architecture.* Rochester, NY: Mansas Press, 1910.
Breisch, Kenneth A. *Henry Hobson Richardson and the Small Public Library in America: A Study in Typology.* Cambridge, MA: The MIT Press, 2003.
Bridges, Tony. "Halls Evacuated After FAMU Explosion." *Tallahassee Democrat,* September 1, 1999.
Brockliss, Laurence. "Gown and Town: The University and the City in Europe, 1200–2000, *Minerva* 38, no. 2 (2000): 147–70.

Brody, Jennifer Devere. *Impossible Purities: Blackness, Femininity and Victorian Culture.* Durham, NC: Duke University Press, 1998.

Brooks, Walter Henderson. *The Pastor's Voice: A Collection of Poems.* Washington, DC: The Associated Publishers, Inc., 1945.

Brosnan, AnnMarie. "Representations of Race and Racism in the Books Used in Southern Black Schools During the American Civil War and Reconstruction Era, 1861–1876." *Paedagogica Historica: International Journal of the History of Education* 52, no. 6 (2016): 718–33.

Brown, Elsa Barkley. "Negotiating and Transforming the Public Sphere: African American Political Life in the Transition from Slavery to Freedom." *Public Culture* 7, no. 1 (1994): 107–46.

Brown, Thomas J. *Civil War Canon: Sites of Confederate Memory in South Carolina.* Chapel Hill: University of North Carolina Press, 2015.

Brundage, W. Fitzhugh. *Booker T. Washington and Black Progress: Up from Slavery 100 Years Later.* Gainesville: University Press of Florida, 2003.

———, ed. "Introduction." In Brundage, *Under Sentence of Death*, 1–20.

———, ed. *Under Sentence of Death: Lynching in the South.* Chapel Hill: University of North Carolina Press, 1997.

———. "White Women and the Politics of Historical Memory in the New South, 1880–1920," 1–2. Unpublished paper, University of Florida, 2000.

Bullock, Henry Allen. *A History of Negro Education in the South, from 1619 to the Present.* New York: Praeger, 1970.

Bunting, Bainbridge. *Harvard: An Architectural History.* Cambridge, MA: Harvard University Press, 1998.

Burg, David F. *Chicago's White City of 1893.* Lexington: University Press of Kentucky, 1976.

Burnett, Frances Hodgson. *Two Little Pilgrims' Progress: A Story of the City Beautiful.* New York: Charles Scribner's Sons, 1895.

Bush-Brown, Albert. "Image of a University: A Study of Architecture as an Expression of Education at Colleges and Universities in the United States between 1800–1900." PhD diss., Princeton University, 1959.

Butchart, Ronald E. "Remapping Racial Boundaries Teachers as Border Police and Boundary Transgressors in Post-Emancipation Black Education, USA, 1861–1876." *Paedagogica Historica: International Journal of the History of Education* 43, no. 1 (2007): 61–78.

Carby, Hazel. *Reconstructing Womanhood: The Emergence of the Afro-American Woman Novelist.* New York: Oxford University Press, 1987.

Carle, Susan D. *Defining the Struggle: National Organizing for Racial Justice, 1880–1915.* New York: Oxford University Press, 2013.

Carlson, Shirley J. "Black Ideals of Womanhood in the Late Victorian Era." *The Journal of Negro History* 77, no. 2 (1992): 61–62.

Carroll, Rebecca. *Uncle Tom or New Negro? African Americans Reflect on Booker T. Washington and Up from Slavery One Hundred Years Later.* New York: Broadway Books, 2006.

Certificate of Death, Jane Serepta Dean. Department of Health, Division of Vital Records, Commonwealth of Virginia, May 5, 1913.

Chase, Lisa. "Imagining Utopia: Landscape Design at Smith College, 1871–1910." *New England Quarterly* 65, no. 4 (1992): 560–86.
Cho, Sumi, Kimberlé Williams Crenshaw, and Leslie McCall. "Toward a Field of Intersectionality Studies: Theory, Applications, and Praxis." *Signs: Journal of Women and Culture in Society* 38, no. 4 (2013): 785–810.
Christen, Barbara Snowden. "Cass Gilbert and the Ideal of the City Beautiful: City and Campus Plans, 1900–1916." PhD diss., The City University of New York, 1997.
Clark, Kathleen. *Defining Moments: African American Commemoration and Political Culture in the South, 1863–1913*. Chapel Hill: University of North Carolina Press, 2006.
Clark-Lewis, Elizabeth, ed. *First Freed: Washington, D.C. in the Emancipation Era*. Washington, DC: A. P. Foundation Press, 1998.
Cloke, Paul, and Owain Jones. *Tree Cultures: The Place of Trees and Trees in Their Place*. New York: Bloomsbury Academic, 2002.
"Clyburn Statement on Passage of H.R. 1135, to Reauthorize the HBCU Historic Preservation Program," June 27, 2017. https://clyburn.house.gov/press-release/clyburn-statement-passage-hr-1135-reauthorize-hbcu-historic-preservation-program.
Cobb, Howell. *Analysis of the Statute Laws of Georgia*. New York: Edward O. Jenkins, 1846.
Coleman, Dr. J. F. B. *Tuskegee to Voorhees: The Booker T. Washington Idea Projected by Elizabeth Evelyn Wright*. Columbia, SC: The R. L. Bryan Company, 1922.
Collins, Patricia Hill, and Sirma Bilge. *Intersectionality*. Cambridge, MA: Polity Press, 2016.
Colombo, Pamela, and Estela Schindel. *Space and Memories of Violence: Landscapes of Erasure, Disappearance and Exception*. New York: Palgrave Macmillan, 2014.
Comer, James P. *Beyond Black and White*. New York: Quadrangle Books, 1972.
Conciatore, Jacqueline. "Fighting to Preserve Black History." *Black Issues in Higher Education* 17, no. 11 (2000): 20–22.
Cone, James H. *The Cross and the Lynching Tree*. Ossining, NY: Orbis Books, 2013.
"Confederate Soldiers' Home." *Inland Architect and News Record* 19, no. 3 (1892): 39, 52.
Confederated Southern Memorial Association. *A History of the Confederated Memorial Associations of the South*. New Orleans: The Graham Press, 1904.
The Confederate Home and School, Charlestown, S.C. Charleston, SC: The News and Courier Book Presses, 1886.
Conn, Steven. *Museums and American Intellectual Life, 1876–1926*. Chicago: University of Chicago Press, 1998.
Cooks, Bridget R. "Fixing Race: Visual Representations of African Americans at the World's Columbian Exposition, Chicago, 1893." *Patterns of Prejudice* 41, no. 5 (2007): 435–65.
Cooper, Anna Julia. *A Voice from the South*. Xenia, OH: The Aldine Printing House, 1892.
Cooper, Brittney C. *Beyond Respectability: The Intellectual Thought of Race Women*. Urbana: University of Illinois Press, 2017.

Cooper, Frederick. "Elevating the Race: The Social Thought of Black Leaders 1827–1850." *American Quarterly* 24 (December 1972): 604–26.

Cox, Karen L. "Women, the Lost Cause, and the New South: The United Daughters of the Confederacy and the Transmission of Confederate Culture." PhD diss., University of Southern Mississippi, 1997.

Crenshaw, Kimberlé. "Mapping the Margins: Intersectionality, Identity Politics, and Violence against Women of Color." *Stanford Law Review* 43, no. 6 (1991): 1241–99.

Cruea, Susan M. "Changing Ideals of Womanhood During the Nineteenth-Century Woman Movement." *American Transcendental Quarterly* 19, no. 3 (2005): 187–204.

Curtis, William E. "Jennie Dean's School." *Washington Star*, February 5, 1907, n.p.

Dailey, Jane. "Deference and Violence in the Postbellum South: Manners and Massacres in Danville, Virginia." *The Journal of Southern History* 63, no. 3 (1997): 557–58.

Dagbovie, Pero Gaglo. "Black Women Historians from the Late Nineteenth Century to the Dawning of the Civil Rights Movement." *Journal of African American History* 89, no. 3 (Summer 2004): 241–61.

———. "Exploring a Century of Historical Scholarship on Booker T. Washington." *The Journal of African American History* 92, no. 2 (2007): 239–64.

Dahms, Harry F. "Retheorizing Global Space in Sociology: Towards a New Kind of Discipline." In *The Spatial Turn: Interdisciplinary Perspectives*, edited by Barney Warf and Santa Arias, 88–101. New York: Routledge, 2008.

Daugherty, Ellen. "Negotiating the Veil: Tuskegee's Booker T. Washington Monument." *American Art* 24, no. 3 (Fall 2010): 52–77.

Davidson, James West. *"They Say": Ida B. Wells and the Reconstruction of Race*. New York: Oxford University Press, 2008.

Davis, Patricia. "Memories in Transition: Black History Museums, New South Narratives, and Urban Regeneration." *Southern Communication Journal* 78, no. 2 (2013): 107–27.

Dawson, Laura Rosily. *A Vision for Victory: A Pictorial History of Voorhees College, 1897–1997*. Marceline: Walsworth Publishing Company, 1997.

Dean, Andrea Oppenheimer. "Revisiting the White City." *Historical Preservation* 45, no. 2 (1993): 42–49, 97–98.

Dean, Jennie. *A Battleground School: A Colored Woman's Work in Uplifting Negro Boys and Girls, The Story of the Manassas Industrial School for Colored Youth*. Alexandria, VA: N.p., 1901.

———. *The Beginning of the Manassas Industrial School for Colored Youth and Its Growth*. Manassas, VA: N.p., 1900. Oswald Garrison Villard Papers, Widener Library, Harvard College Library, Harvard University, Cambridge, MA.

Dennis, Michael. "Reforming the 'Academical Village': Edwin A. Alderman and the University of Virginia, 1904–1915." *The Virginia Magazine of History and Biography* 105, no. 1 (1997): 53–86.

———. "Schooling Along the Color Line: Progressives and the Education of Blacks in the New South." *Journal of Negro Education* 67 (Spring 1998): 142–56.

Denton, Virginia Lantz. *Booker T. Washington and the Adult Education Movement*. Gainesville: University Press of Florida, 1993.

Deutsch, Sarah. "Reconceiving the City: Women, Space, and Power in Boston, 1870–1910." *Gender and History* 6, no. 2 (1994): 202–23.

———. *Women and the City: Gender, Space and Power in Boston, 1870–1940*. New York: Oxford University Press, 2002.

di Leonardo, Micaela. *Exotics at Home: Anthropologies, Others, American Modernity*. Chicago: University of Chicago Press, 1998.

Dill, Bonnie Thornton, Amy McLaughlin, and Angel David Nieves. "Future Directions of Feminist Research: Intersectionality." In *Handbook of Feminist Research: Theory and Praxis*, edited by Sharlene Nagy Hesse-Biber, 629–37. New York: Sage Publications, 2007.

Dill, Bonnie Thornton, and Ruth Enid Zambrana. "Critical Thinking About Inequality: An Emerging Lens." In Dill and Zambrana, *Emerging Intersections*, 1–21.

———, eds. *Emerging Intersections: Race, Class, and Gender in Theory, Policy, and Practice*. New Brunswick, NJ: Rutgers University Press, 2009.

"Disney's America Theme Park Planned." *American History Illustrated* 29 (March/April 1994): 6.

Dossett, Kate. *Bridging Race Divides: Black Nationalism, Feminism, and Integration in the United States, 1896–1935*. Gainesville: University Press of Florida, 2008.

Douglass, Frederick. "Introduction." In *The Reason Why the Colored American Is Not in the World's Columbian Exposition*, 12. Chicago: Miss Ida B. Wells, 1892.

Douglass, Frederick, and Ida B. Wells. *The Reason Why the Colored American Is Not in the World's Columbia Exposition, The Afro-American's Contribution to Columbian Literature*. Chicago: Ida B. Wells, 1893.

Dozier, Richard K. "A Historical Survey: Black Architects and Craftsmen." *Black World* (May 1974): 5–7.

———. "Tuskegee: Booker T. Washington's Contribution to the Education of Black Architects." PhD diss., University of Michigan, 1990.

———. "Tuskegee Institute: From Humble Beginnings to National Shrine." *Historic Preservation* 33, no. 1 (1981): 42–137.

Drexler, Arthur, ed. "Preface." *The Architecture of the Ecole des Beaux-Arts*, 3–4. Cambridge, MA: The MIT Press, 1977.

Drinkwater, Lawrence Ray. "Scholarship, Honor, and the Lost Cause: A History of McCabe's University School, 1865–1901." PhD diss., Virginia Commonwealth University, 1994.

Drummond, Tammerlin. "Black Schools Go White." *Time*, March 20, 2000, 57.

Du Bois, W. E. B. *Black Reconstruction in America*. New York: A Touchstone Book, 1992.

———. *Black Reconstruction in America 1860–1880: An Essay Toward a History of the Part Which Black Folk Played in the Attempt to Reconstruct Democracy in America*. Atlanta: Classic Textbooks, 1935.

———. "The Late Booker T. Washington," *The Crisis* 11, no. 2 (December 1915): 82–89.

———. *The Souls of Black Folk*. New York: Random House, 1993.

Dubrow, Gail Lee. "Preserving Her Heritage: American Landmarks of Women's History." PhD diss., University of California–Los Angeles, 1991.

———. "Restoring a Female Presence." In *Architecture: A Place for Women*, edited by Ellen Perry Berkeley and Matilda McQuaid, 159–70. Washington, DC: Smithsonian Institution Press, 1989.

Dubrow, Gail Lee, and Jennifer B. Goodman. *Restoring Women's History Through Historic Preservation*. Baltimore: Johns Hopkins University Press, 2002.

Durant, Susan Speare. "The Gently Furled Banner: The Development of the Myth of the Lost Cause, 1865–1900." PhD diss., University of North Carolina at Chapel Hill, 1972.

Duster, Troy. "The Long Path to Higher Education for African Americans." *Thought and Action: The NEA Higher Education Journal* 25 (2009): 99–110.

Dyer, Scott. "Black College Beef Up Security After Receiving Hate Mail." *Black Issues in Higher Education*, February 3, 2000, 18.

"Editor's Easy Chair." *Harper's New Monthly Magazine* 34, no. 201 (1867): 389–90.

"Editor's Easy Chair." *Harper's New Monthly Magazine* 34, no. 204 (1890): 804.

Ernest, John. *Resistance and Reformation in Nineteenth-Century African-American Literature*. Jackson: University Press of Mississippi, 1995.

Evans, Sara M., and Harry C. Boyte. *Free Spaces: The Sources of Democratic Change in America*. New York: Harper & Row Publishers, Inc., 1986.

Fabre, Geneviève. "African-American Commemorative Celebrations in the Nineteenth Century." In *History and Memory in African-American Culture*, 72–91. New York: Oxford University Press, 1994.

Fabre, Geneviève, and Robert O'Meally, eds. *History and Memory in African-American Culture*. New York: Oxford University Press, 1994.

Fairclough, Adam. "'Being in the Field of Education and Also Being a Negro . . . Seems . . . Tragic': Black Teachers in the Jim Crow South." *The Journal of American History* 87, no. 1 (2000): 65–91.

Faulkner, Carol. *Women's Radical Reconstruction: The Freedmen's Aid Movement*. Philadelphia: University of Pennsylvania Press, 2007.

Faulkner, Carol, and Alison M. Parker, eds. *Interconnections: Gender and Race in American History*. Rochester, NY: University of Rochester Press, 2012.

Faust, Drew Gilpin. *Mothers of Invention: Women of the Slaveholding South in the American Civil War*. New York: Vintage Books, 1996.

Feimster, Crystal N. *Southern Horrors: Women and the Politics of Rape and Lynching*. Cambridge, MA: Harvard University Press, 2011.

Fernandez, James W. "Architectonic Inquiry." *Semiotica* 89, no. 1/3 (1992): 215–26.

Fielding, Fanny. "Southern Homestead." *The Land We Love* 4, no. 6 (1868): 504.

The Fifth Annual Report of the Principal and Treasurer of the Voorhees Industrial School. Tuskegee, AL: Tuskegee Institute Steam Print, 1902.

Fitzpatrick, Sandra, and Maria R. Goodwin. *The Guide to Black Washington*. New York: Hippocrene Books, 1990.

Flagg, Ernest. "American Architecture as Opposed to Architecture in America." *Architectural Record* 10, no. 2 (1900): 178–80.

Fleischner, Jennifer. "Memory, Sickness, and Slavery." In *Mastering Slavery: Memory, Family, and Identity in Women's Slave Narratives*, 397–99. New York: New York University Press, 1996.

Flexner, Abraham. *Universities: American, English, German*. New York: Oxford University Press, 1930.

Flinn, John J. *The Best Things to Be Seen at the World's Fair.* Chicago: Columbian Guide Co., 1893.

Foner, Eric. *Reconstruction: America's Unfinished Revolution, 1863–1877.* New York: Harper & Row, Publishers, 1988.

Foner, Philip S. "Oration in Memory of Abraham Lincoln, Delivered at the Unveiling of the Freedmen's Monument in Memory of Abraham Lincoln." In *The Life and Writings of Frederick Douglass,* edited by Philip S. Foner, 26–312. New York: International Publishers, 1955.

Foreman, P. Gabrielle. *Activist Sentiments: Reading Black Women in the Nineteenth Century.* Urbana: University of Illinois Press, 2009.

Fort, Edward. *Survival of the Historically Black Colleges and Universities: Making It Happen.* New York: Lexington Books, 2013.

Foster, Gaines M. *Ghosts of the Confederacy: Defeat, the Lost Cause, and the Emergence of the New South 1865–1913.* New York: Oxford University Press, 1987.

Franklin, John Hope. *Schools for All: The Blacks and Public Education in the South, 1865–1877.* Lexington: University Press of Kentucky, 1974.

Franklin, Vincent P., and James D. Anderson, eds. *New Perspectives on Black Educational History.* Boston: G. K. Hall & Co., 1978.

Franklin, V. P., and Bettye Collier-Thomas. "Biography, Race Vindication, and African-American Intellectuals: Introductory Essay." *Journal of Negro History* 81, no. 1–4 (1996): 1.

Frazier, E. Franklin. "The Negro Slave Family." *The Journal of Negro History* 15, no. 2 (1930): 198–259.

Freeman, Dale H. "The Crispus Attucks Monument Dedication." *Historical Journal of Massachusetts* 25, no. 2 (Summer 1997): 125–40.

Frey, Sylvia R. *Water from the Rock: Black Resistance in a Revolutionary Age.* Princeton, NJ: Princeton University Press, 1991.

Fuke, Richard Paul. "Land, Lumber, and Learning: The Freedmen's Bureau, Education, and the Black Community in Post-Emancipation Maryland." In *The Freedmen's Bureau and Reconstruction: Reconstructions,* edited by Paul A. Cimbala and Randall M. Miller, 292–96. New York: Fordham University Press, 1999.

Gaines, Kevin. *Uplifting the Race: Black Leadership, Politics, and Culture in the Twentieth Century.* Chapel Hill: University of North Carolina Press, 1996.

Gaston, Paul M. *The New South Creed: A Study in Southern Mythmaking.* New York: Vintage Books, 1973.

Geiger, Roger L. "The Era of Multipurpose Colleges in American Higher Education, 1850–1890." In *The American College in the Nineteenth Century,* edited by Roger L. Geiger, 127–52 Nashville: Vanderbilt University Press, 2000.

Genovese, Elizabeth Fox. *Within the Plantation Household: Black and White Women of the Old South.* Chapel Hill: University of North Carolina Press, 1988.

Genovese, Eugene. *Roll, Jordan, Roll: The World the Slaves Made.* New York: Vintage, 1976.

Giddings, Paula. *When and Where I Enter: The Impact of Black Women on Race and Sex in America.* New York: Bantam Books, 1984.

Gilbert, James. *Perfect Cities: Chicago Utopias of 1893.* Chicago: University of Chicago Press, 1991.

Gill, Valerie. "Catharine Beecher and Charlotte Perkins Gilman: Architects of Female Power." *Journal of American Culture* 21, no. 2 (1998): 17–24.

Gillette, Howard F., Jr. "White City, Capital City." *Chicago History: The Magazine of the Chicago Historical Society* 18, no. 4 (1989–90): 26–45.

Gillis, John, ed. *Commemorations: The Politics of National Identity*. Princeton, NJ: Princeton University Press, 1994.

Gilmore, Glenda Elizabeth. *Defying Dixie: The Radical Roots of Civil Rights, 1919–1950*. New York: W. W. Norton & Company, 2009.

———. *Gender and Jim Crow: Women and the Politics of White Supremacy in North Carolina, 1896–1920*. Chapel Hill: University of North Carolina Press, 1996.

Ginsburg, Rebecca, and Clifton Ellis, eds. *Cabin, Quarter, Plantation: Architecture and Landscapes of North American Slavery*. New Haven, CT: Yale University Press, 2010.

———. *Slavery in the City: Architecture and Landscapes of Urban Slavery in North America*. Charlottesville: University of Virginia Press, 2017.

Girouard, Mark. *Sweetness and Light: The "Queen Anne" Movement, 1860–1900*. New York: Oxford University Press, 1977.

Githens, Alfred Morton. "The Group Plan I: A Theory of Composition; The Carnegie Technical Schools." *The Brickbuilder* 15, no. 7 (1906): 134–38.

———. "The Group Plan II: The Elemental Types of Composition." *The Brickbuilder* 15, no. 9 (1906): 179–82.

Glassberg, David. "Monuments and Memories." *American Quarterly* 43, no. 1 (1991): 143–56.

Glaude, Eddie S., Jr. *Exodus! Religion, Race, and Nation in Early Nineteenth-Century Black America*. Chicago: University of Chicago Press, 2000.

Gore, Blinzy L. *"On a Hilltop High": The Origin and History of Claflin College to 1984*. Spartanburg, SC: The Reprint Company, 1994.

Grandison, Kenrick Ian. "From Plantation to Campus: Progress, Community, and the Lay of the Land in Shaping the Early Tuskegee Campus." *Landscape Journal* 15, no. 1 (1996): 6–22.

———. "Landscapes of Terror: A Reading of Tuskegee's Historic Campus." In *The Geography of Identity*, edited by Patricia Yaeger, 334–67. Ann Arbor: University of Michigan Press, 1996.

Green, Constance McLaughlin. *The Secret City: A History of Race Relations in the Nation's Capital*. Princeton, NJ: Princeton University Press, 1967.

Greene, Vivian. "Utopia/Dystopia." *American Art* 25, no. 2 (2011): 2–7.

Grier, Katherine. *Culture and Comfort: Parlor Making and Middle Class Identity, 1850–1930*. Washington, DC: Smithsonian Institution Press, 2013.

Gulley, H. E. "Women and the Lost Cause: Preserving a Confederate Identity in the American Deep South." *Journal of Historical Geography* 19, no. 2 (1993): 125–41.

Hage, Ghassan. *White Nation: Fantasies of White Supremacy in a Multicultural Society*. Annandale: Pluto Press Australia, 1998.

Hagen, Joshua. "Places of Memory and Memories of Places in Nazi Germany." In *Memory, Place and Identity: Commemoration and Remembrance of War and Conflict*, edited by Danielle Drozdzewski, Sarah De Nardi, and Emma Waterton, 236–54. New York: Routledge, 2016.

Hahn, Steven. *A Nation under Our Feet: Black Political Struggles in the Rural South from Slavery to the Great Migration.* Cambridge, MA: The Belknap Press of Harvard University Press, 2003.

Hale, Edward Everett. "Educational Status of the Colored People." *Lend a Hand: A Record of Progress* 6, no. 3 (1891): 149–52.

Halewood, Peter. "Campus Activism and Competing Racial Narratives." *Academe* 102, no. 6 (November/December 2016): 8–12.

Hall, Jacquelyn Dowd. "'You Must Remember This': Autobiography as Social Critique." *The Journal of American History* 85, no. 2 (September 1998): 439–65.

Hamilton, Kenneth M. *Booker T. Washington in American Memory.* Urbana-Champaign: University of Illinois Press, 2017.

Hamlin, A. D. F. *A Text-Book of the History of Architecture.* New York: Longmans & Green, 1896.

Hanson, Joyce Ann. *Mary McLeod Bethune and Black Women's Political Activism.* Columbia: University of Missouri Press, 2003.

Harlan, Louis R. *Booker T. Washington: The Wizard of Tuskegee, 1901–1915.* New York: Oxford University Press, 1983.

———. *Separate and Unequal.* New York: Praeger, 1970.

Harper, Frances E. W. *Iola Leroy or Shadows Uplifted.* Philadelphia: Carrigues Brothers, 1893.

Harper, Frances Ellen Watkins. "Woman's Political Future." In *World's Congress of Representative Women,* edited by May Wright Sewal, 433–37. Chicago: Rand McNally, 1894.

Harper, Judith E. *Susan B. Anthony: A Biographical Companion.* Santa Barbara, CA: ABC-CLIO, Inc., 1998.

Harper, Shaun R., Lori D. Patton, and Ontario S. Wooden. "Access and Equity for African American Students in Higher Education: A Critical Race Historical Analysis of Policy Efforts." *The Journal of Higher Education* 80, no. 4 (July/August 2009): 389–414.

Harris, Dianne. "Social History: Identity, Performance, Politics, and Architectural History." *Journal of the Society of Architectural Historians* 64, no. 4 (December 2005): 421–23.

Harris, Neil. *Building Lives: Constructing Rites and Passages.* New Haven, CT: Yale University Press, 1999.

Harris, Neil, Wim de Wit, James Gilbert, and Robert W. Rydell, eds. *Grand Illusions: Chicago's World's Fair of 1893.* Chicago: Chicago Historical Society, 1993.

Harris, William C. *With Charity for All: Lincoln and the Restoration of the Union.* Lexington: University Press of Kentucky, 1997.

Harrison, Fairfax. *Landmarks of Old Prince William, A Study of Origins in Northern Virginia.* Baltimore: Gateway Press, Inc., 1987.

Harrison, Flora Milner. *What the Berry School for Boys Is Doing.* N.p.: N.p., n.d.

Harvey, Bruce G. *World's Fairs in a Southern Accent: Atlanta, Nashville, and Charleston, 1895–1902.* Knoxville: University of Tennessee Press, 2014.

Harvey, David. "Between Space and Time: Reflections on the Geographical Imagination." *Annals of the Association of American Geographers* 80, no. 3 (1990): 418–34.

———. *Spaces of Hope.* Berkeley: University of California Press, 2000.

Hastings, Thomas. "The Relations of Life to Style in Architecture." *Harper's New Monthly* 88, no. 528 (1894): 959–61.
Heathcott, Joseph, "Review, Buildings, Landscapes, and Memory: Case Studies in Historic Preservation by Daniel Bluestone." *Winterthur Portfolio* 46, no. 4 (Winter 2012): 309–10.
Henderson, B. "A Strong Pastor of a Strong Church." *The Colored American Magazine* 14, no. 1 (1906): 16–20.
Hennessy, John J. *The First Battle of Manassas: An End to Innocence, July 18–21, 1861.* Mechanicsburg, VA: H. E. Howard, Inc., 1989.
Hennessy, John J. *Return to Bull Run: Campaign and Battle of Second Manassas.* New York: Simon & Schuster, 1993.
Heningburg, Alphonse. "The Relation of Tuskegee Institute to Education in the Lower South." *The Journal of Educational Sociology* 7, no. 3 (November 1933): 157–62.
Herman, Judith Lewis. *Trauma and Recovery.* New York: Basic Books, 1992.
Hersh, Blanche Glassman. "The True Woman and the 'New Woman' in Nineteenth Century America." In *Woman's Being, Woman's Place: Female Identity and Vocation in American History*, edited by Mary Kelley, 271–82. Boston: Hall, 1979.
Higginbotham, Evelyn Brooks. "African American Women's History and the Metalanguage of Race." In *We Specialize in the Wholly Impossible*, edited by Darlene Clark Hine, Wilma King, and Linda Reed, 251–74. New York: Carlson Publishing, 1995.
Hobson, J. A. "'Lynching' in the Southern States." *Speaker* 8 (August 29, 1903): 498–99.
Hoelscher, Steven, and Derek H. Alderman. "Memory and Place: Geographies of a Critical Relationship." *Social and Cultural Geography* 5, no. 3 (September 2004): 347–55.
Hogan, Pendleton. *The Lawn: A Guide to Jefferson's University.* Charlottesville: University of Virginia Press, 1987.
Hogue, William M. *The Jacob Tome Institute and Its Schools: The First Hundred Years.* North East, MD: Tome School, 1995.
Hohmann, Heidi. "Charles Wellford Leavitt, Jr." In *Pioneers of American Landscape Design*, edited by Charles A. Birnbaum, 223–27. New York: McGraw-Hill, 2000.
Holdsworth, Deryck W. "Landscape and Archives as Texts." In *Understanding Ordinary Landscapes*, edited by Paul Groth and Todd W. Bressi, 45–55. New Haven, CT: Yale University Press, 1997.
Horowitz, Helen Lefkowitz. "Designing for the Genders: Curricula and Architecture at Scripps College and the California Institute of Technology." *Pacific Historical Review* 54, no. 4 (1985): 439–61.
Hood, Aurelius P. *The Negro at Mound Bayou: Being an Authentic Story of the Founding, Growth and Development of the "Most Celebrated Town in the South."* Mound Bayou: A. P. Hood, 1909.
Hooff, Ruth Round. *Glimpses of George Carr Round.* Manassas, VA: George C. Round Elementary School, 1986.
hooks, bell. "Choosing the Margin as a Space of Radical Openness." In *Yearnings: Race, Gender and Cultural Politics*, 145–54. London: Turnaround Press, 1989.

———. *Feminist Theory from Margin to Center.* Cambridge, MA: South End Press, 2000.
Horton, James Oliver. *Landmarks of African American History.* New York: Oxford University Press, 2005.
Hoskins, Janet. *Biographical Objects: How Things Tell the Stories of People's Lives.* New York: Routledge, 1998.
Howell, Donna Wyant. *I Was a Slave: Descriptions of Plantation Life.* Washington, DC: American Legacy Books, 1995.
Howell, Troy Dean. "William Gordon McCabe, Headmaster: The 'Old Boy' Academy in Transition." MA thesis, University of Virginia, 1989.
Hunter, Arthur Lloyd. "The Sacred South: Postwar Confederates and the Sacrilization of Southern Culture." PhD diss., Saint Louis University, 1978.
Hunter, Tera. *To 'Joy My Freedom: Southern Black Women's Lives and Labors After the Civil War.* Cambridge, MA: Harvard University Press, 1997.
Inaugural Ceremonies of the Freedmen's Memorial Monument to Abraham Lincoln. Saint Louis: Levison & Blythe, 1876.
"The Influence of Club Work in Alabama." *National Notes* (1904): 4.
The Inter Ocean. *Centennial History of the City of Chicago. Its Men and Institutions. Biographical Sketches of Leading Citizens.* Chicago: Inter Ocean, 1905.
Jackson, John Brinckerhoff. *Discovering the Vernacular Landscape.* New Haven, CT: Yale University Press, 1984.
Jackson, Luther P. "The Educational Efforts of the Freedmen's Bureau and Freedmen's Aid Societies in South Carolina, 1862–1872." *The Journal of Negro History* 8, no. 1 (January 1923): 1–40.
Jacob, Kathryn Allamong. *Testament to Union: Civil War Monuments in Washington, D.C.* Baltimore: The Johns Hopkins University Press, 1998.
Janney, Caroline E. *Burying the Dead But Not the Past: Ladies' Memorial Associations and the Lost Cause.* Chapel Hill: University of North Carolina Press, 2008.
Johnson, Joan Marie. "'Ye Gave Them a Stone': African American Women's Clubs, the Frederick Douglass Home, and the Black Mammy Monument." *Journal of Women's History* 17, no. 1 (2005): 62–86.
Johnson, Karen A., Abdul Pitre, and Kenneth L. Johnson, eds. *African American Women Educators: A Critical Examination of Their Pedagogies, Educational Ideas, and Activism from the Nineteenth to the Mid-Twentieth Century.* New York: R&L Education, 2014.
Johnson, Rossiter. *A History of the World's Columbian Exposition Held in Chicago in 1893.* Vol. II. New York: D. Appleton and Co., 1898.
Jones, Allen W. "The Role of Tuskegee Institute in the Education of Black Farmers." *The Journal of Negro History* 60, no. 2 (April 1975): 252–67.
Jones, Jacqueline. *Soldiers of Light and Love: Northern Teachers and Georgia Blacks, 1865–1873.* Athens: University of Georgia Press, 1992.
Kearney, Amanda. *Violence in Place, Cultural and Environmental Wounding.* New York: Routledge, 2016.
Kent, Rev. Alexander. "Mr. Carnegie's Gospel of Wealth." *The Woman's Tribune*, March 19, 1892, 84.
King, Wilma. *Stolen Childhood: Slave Youth in Nineteenth-Century America.* Bloomington: Indiana University Press, 1998.

———. "'Suffer with Them Till Death': Slave Women and Their Children in Nineteenth-Century America." In *More Than Chattel: Black Women and Slavery in the Americas*, edited by David Barry Gaspar and Darlene Clark Hine, 147–68. Bloomington: Indiana University Press, 1996.

Krieger, Alex. "Civic Lessons of an Ephemeral Monument, Monumentality and the City." *Monumentality and the City, The Harvard Architecture Review* 4 (Spring 1984): 149–55.

Lane, Elizabeth E. "Tuskegee School: A Practical Solution of the Negro Problem." *Lend a Hand: A Record of Progress* 13, no. 1 (1894): 17–21.

Lane, Linda Rochelle. *A Documentary of Mrs. Booker T. Washington*. New York: Edwin Mellen Press, 2001.

Lanning, Michael Lee. *Defenders of Liberty: African Americans in the Revolutionary War*. New York: Birch Lane, 1999.

Lasch-Quinn, Elisabeth. *Black Neighbors: Race and the Limits of Reform in the American Settlement House Movement, 1890–1945*. Chapel Hill: University of North Carolina Press, 1993.

"Learning Together: Disney and the Historians." *The Public Historian* 17, no. 4 (1995): 5–8.

Lears, T. J. Jackson. *No Place for Grace: Antimodernism and the Transformation of American Culture, 1880–1920*. Chicago: University of Chicago Press, 1991.

Leavitt, Charles W. "Stands, Stadia, and Bowls." *Journal Proceedings* 11, no. 8 (1915): 16.

Lebsock, Suzanne. "A Share of Honor" In *Virginia Women, 1600–1945*, edited by Suzanne Lebsock, 89–91. Richmond: Virginia State Library, 1987.

Lee, William I. "History of the Church." One Hundred Anniversary of the Nineteenth Street Baptist Church, Washington, DC. Washington, DC: N.p., 1939.

LeLoudis, James L. *Schooling the New South: Pedagogy, Self, and Society in North Carolina, 1880–1920*. Chapel Hill: University of North Carolina Press, 1996.

Levy, James. "Forging African American Minds: Black Pragmatism, 'Intelligent Labor,' and a New Look at Industrial Education, 1879–1900." *American Nineteenth Century History* 17, no. 1 (2016): 44–45.

Lewis, Mary L. "The White Rose Industrial Association, the Friend of the Strange Girl in New York." *The Messenger: World's Greatest Negro Monthly* 7, no. 4 (1925): 158.

Lewis, Stephen Johnson. *Undaunted Faith: The Story of Jennie Dean*. Manassas, VA: The Manassas Museum, 1994.

Litwack, Leon. *Trouble in Mind: Black Southerners in the Age of Jim Crow*. New York: Alfred A. Knopf, 1998.

Loewen, James W., and Edward H. Sebesta, eds. *The Confederate and Neo-Confederate Reader: The "Great Truth" about the "Lost Cause."* Jackson: University Press of Mississippi, 2011.

Logan, Warren. "Resources and Material Equipment." In *Tuskegee and Its People: Their Ideals and Achievements*, edited by Booker T. Washington, 35–55. New York: D. Appleton and Co., 1906.

Lorini, Alessandra. *Rituals of Race: American Public Culture and the Search for Racial Democracy*. Charlottesville: University of Virginia Press, 1999.

Lovett, Bobby L. *America's Historically Black Colleges and Universities: A Narrative History, 1837–2009.* Macon, GA: Mercer University Press, 2015.
Mabee, Carleton. "Sojourner Truth, Bold Prophet: Why Did She Never Learn to Read." *New York History* 69 (January 1988): 55–77.
The Manassas Industrial School. *The Manassas Industrial School for Colored Youth Located at Manassas, Virginia, 1902–1903 Catalog.* Manassas, VA: The Manassas Industrial School, 1902.
———. *The Manassas Industrial School for Colored Youth Located at Manassas, Virginia, 1908–1909 Catalog.* Manassas, VA: The Manassas Industrial School, 1908.
———. *The Manassas Industrial School for Colored Youth Located at Manassas, Virginia, 1912–1913 Catalog.* Manassas, VA: The Manassas Industrial School, 1913.
Manassas Industrial School for Colored Youth. *1909 Financial Report, Donors' List and Statement of Current Needs.* Manassas, VA: Manassas Industrial School for Colored Youth, 1909.
Manring, M. M. *Slave in a Box: The Strange Career of Aunt Jemima.* Charlottesville: University of Virginia Press, 1998.
Marable, Manning. "Introduction." *Souls* 2, no. 4 (Fall 2000): 6–7.
———. "Tuskegee and the Politics of Illusion in the New South." *Journal of Black Studies and Research* 8, no. 7 (1977): 13–24.
Marling, Karal Ann. *George Washington Slept Here: Colonial Revivals and American Culture.* Cambridge, MA: Harvard University Press, 1988.
Mason, Randy. *The Once and Future New York: Historic Preservation and the Modern City.* Minneapolis: University of Minnesota Press, 2009.
Massa, Ann. "Black Women in the 'White City.'" *Journal of American Studies* 8, no. 3 (1974): 319–37.
Matthews, Virginia. "The Redemption of Our City." *Federation* 2 (July 1902): 57–58.
Matthews-Gardner, A. Lanethea. "The Postwar Black Women's Club Movement: The Intersection of Gender, Race, and American Political Development, 1940–1960." *Journal of Women, Politics and Policy* 31, no. 3 (2010): 260–85.
McAlester, Virginia, and Lee McAlester. *A Field Guide to American Houses.* New York: Alfred A. Knopf, 2006.
McCann, Hannah. "20 Historically Black Colleges and Universities Receive Stimulus Grants for Building Preservation." *Architect: The Journal of the American Institute of Architects*, September 18, 2009. http://www.architectmagazine.com/design/20-historically-black-colleges-and-universities-receive-stimulus-grants-for-building-preservation_o.
McCartney, Martha. "Historical Background." In *Cultural Resource Survey and Inventory of a War Torn Landscape: The Stuart's Hill Tract, Manassas Battlefield Park, Virginia*, edited by Laura Galke, 23–29. Washington, DC: National Park Service, 1992.
McClain, Kevin, and April Perry. "Where Did They Go: Retention Rates for Students of Color at Predominantly White Institutions." *College Student Affairs Leadership*, 4, no. 1 (2017): 23–32. Article 3, https://scholarworks.gvsu.edu/csal/vol4/iss1/3/.
McCluskey, Audrey Thomas. *A Forgotten Sisterhood: Pioneering Black Women Educators and Activists in the Jim Crow South.* New York: Rowman & Littlefield Publishers, 2014.

McElya, Micki. *Clinging to Mammy: The Faithful Slave in Twentieth-Century America.* Cambridge, MA: Harvard University Press, 2007.
McKithan, Cecil N. "Preserving HBCUs for Future Generations." *CRM: Cultural Resource Management* 22, no. 8 (1999): 39–40.
McMillen, Neil R. *Dark Journey: Black Mississippians in the Age of Jim Crow.* Urbana: University of Illinois Press, 1990.
McMurry, Linda O. *To Keep the Waters Troubled: The Life of Ida B. Wells.* New York: Oxford University Press, 1998.
McPherson, James M. *The Struggle for Equality: Abolitionists and the Negro in the Civil War and Reconstruction.* Princeton, NJ: Princeton University Press, 1964.
Meeks, Stephanie K. "Our HBCUs Are National Treasures." *HuffPost,* May 4, 2017. http://www.huffingtonpost.com/national-trust-for-historic-preservation/our-hbcus-are-national-tr_b_9828326.html.
"Memorial to Stonewall Jackson's Army." *Confederate Veteran* 25, no. 6 (1917): 246.
Milburn, Page. "The Emancipation of the Slaves in the District of Columbia." *Records of the Columbia Historical Society* 16:115. Washington, DC: Columbia Historical Society, 1913.
Miller, Carroll L. L., and Anne S. Pruitt-Logan. *Faithful to the Task at Hand: The Life of Lucy Diggs Slowe.* Albany, NY: SUNY Press, 2012.
Miller, Donald L. *City of the Century: The Epic of Chicago and the Making of America.* New York: Touchstone Books, 1997.
Mills, Charles A. *Echoes of Manassas.* Manassas, VA: Friends of the Manassas Museum, 1988.
Mitchell, John L. "Shall the Wheels of Race Agitation Be Stopped." *The Colored American Magazine* 5 (September 1902): 386–91.
Mitchell, Michelle. *Righteous Propagation: African Americans and the Politics of Racial Destiny After Reconstruction.* Chapel Hill: University of North Carolina Press, 2004.
Mitchell, Tia. "Bomb Rocks FAMU—Again." *The FAMUAN,* September 23, 1999.
Mohawk, John C. *Utopian Legacies: A History of Conquest and Oppression in the Western World.* Santa Fe, NM: Clear Light Publishing, 2000.
Monroe, Harriet, and John Wellborn Root. *A Study of His Life and Work.* Boston: Houghton Mifflin & Co., 1896.
"The Monumental Spirit of the South." *Confederate Veteran* 22, no. 8 (1914): 344.
Moody, Wesley. *Demon of the Lost Cause: Sherman and Civil War History.* Columbia: University of Missouri, 2011.
Moore, Jacqueline M. *Booker T. Washington, W. E. B. DuBois, and the Struggle for Racial Uplift.* New York: Rowman & Littlefield Publishers, 2003.
Morales-Velazquez, Rubil. "Imagining Washington: Monuments and Nation Building in the Early Capital." *Washington History* 12, no. 1 (2000): 12–29.
Morris, J. Kenneth. *Elizabeth Evelyn Wright, 1872–1906: Founder of Voorhees College.* Sewanee, TN: University of the South, 1983.
Morris, Robert C. *Reading, 'Riting, and Reconstruction: The Education of Freedmen in the South, 1861–1870.* Chicago: University of Chicago Press, 1981.
Moses, William J. "National Destiny and the Black Bourgeois Ministry." *The Wings of Ethiopia: Studies in African American Life and Letters.* Ames: Iowa State University Press, 1990.

Moses, Wilson Jeremiah, ed. *Classical Black Nationalism: From the American Revolution to Marcus Garvey.* New York: New York University Press, 1996.

"Mound Bayou—Past and Present." *The Negro History Bulletin* (April 1940): 105–6, 109–11.

Muccigrosso, Robert. *Celebrating the New World: Chicago's Columbian Exposition of 1893.* Chicago: Ivan R. Dee, 1993.

Mugleston, William F., ed. "The Freedmen's Bureau and Reconstruction in Virginia: The Diary of Marcus Sterling Hopkins, a Union Officer." *The Virginia Magazine of History and Biography* 86, no. 1 (1978): 45–102.

Mumford, Lewis. *The Brown Decades: A Study of the Arts in America, 1865–1895.* New York: Dover Publications, Inc., 1931.

Myers, Mildred D. *Miss Emily: Emily Howland, Teacher of Freed Slaves, Suffragist, and Friend of Susan B. Anthony and Harriet Tubman.* Charlotte Harbor, FL: Tabby House, 1998.

Naples, Nancy A. *Feminism and Method: Ethnography, Discourse Analysis, and Activist Research.* New York: Routledge, 2003.

Nash, Jennifer C. "Re-thinking Intersectionality." *Feminist Review* 89, no. 1 (2008): 1–15.

Nasaw, David. "The City as Playground: The World's Fair Midways." In *Going Out: The Rise and Fall of Public Amusements*, edited by David Nasaw, 62–79. Cambridge, MA: Harvard University Press, 1993.

Nast, Thomas. "'The Nigger Must Go,' 'The Chinese Must Go,' and 'The Poor Barbarians Can't Understand Our Civilized Republication Form of Government.'" *Harper's Weekly: Journal of Civilization* 23, no. 1185 (September 13, 1879): 1.

National Lincoln Monument Association. *Constitution of the Educational Monument Association to the Memory of Abraham Lincoln.* Washington, DC: McGill & Witherow, 1865.

The National Organization of Minority Architects. "Architecture at HBCUs: Principles, Legacy, and Preservation." Morgan State University Conference, November 5–6, 2015. http://www.noma.net/article/260/happenings/news/architecture-at-hbcus-principles-legacy-and-preservation.

"The Negro Nevertheless a Factor in Architecture." *The Negro History Bulletin* (April 1940): 101–2.

Nelson, Dana D. *National Manhood: Capitalist Citizenship and the Imagined Fraternity of White Men.* Durham, NC: Duke University Press, 1998.

Newton, James E., and Ronald L. Lewis, eds. *The Other Slaves: Mechanics, Artisans, and Craftsmen.* Boston: G. K. Hall & Co., 1978.

Nieves, Angel David. "Voorhees: Elizabeth Evelyn Wright's 'Small Tuskegee' and Black Education in the Post-Reconstruction South." *Arris: Journal of the Southeast Chapter of the Society of Architectural Historians* 13 (2002): 25–37.

Nora, Pierre. "Between Memory and History: Les Lieux de Mémorie." In *History and Memory in African American Culture*, edited by Geneviève Fabre and Robert O'Meally, 284–300. New York: Oxford University Press, 1994.

Norrell, Robert J. *Up from History: The Life of Booker T. Washington.* Cambridge, MA: Harvard University Press, 2009.

O'Connor, Mrs. T. P. *My Beloved South.* New York: G. P. Putnam's Sons, 1914.

O'Dell, Jeff M. Howland Chapel School, National Register of Historic Places Registration Form, 1990.
Offe, Sabine. "Sites of Remembrance? Jewish Museums in Contemporary Germany." *Jewish Social Studies* 5, no. 2 (1997): 78–84.
O'Gorman, James. "Marshall Field Wholesale Store." *Journal of the Society of Architectural Historians* 36 (October 1978): 180–88.
Paddon, Anna R., and Sally Turner. "African Americans and the World's Columbian Exposition." *Illinois Historical Journal* 88 (Spring 1995): 22–28.
Page, Max. *The Creative Destruction of Manhattan, 1900–1940*. Chicago: University of Chicago Press, 2001.
Page, Thomas Nelson. "Pen Picture of Yourselves, Your Mothers, and Grandmothers." *Confederate Veteran* 25, no. 7 (1917): 340.
Painter, Nell Irvine. *Exodusters: Black Migration to Kansas after Reconstruction*. New York: Knopf, 1977.
———. "Representing Truth: Sojourner Truth's Knowing and Becoming Known." *The Journal of American History* 81, no. 2 (September 1994): 461–92.
———. "Sojourner Truth in Life and Memory: Writing the Biography of an American Exotic." *Gender and History* 2, no. 1 (1990): 3–16.
Parks, Janet, and Barry Bergdoll. *Mastering McKim's Plan: Columbia's First Century on Morningside Heights*. New York: Miriam and Ira D. Wallach Art Gallery, Columbia University, 1997.
Parsons, Elaine Frantz. "Midnight Rangers: Costume and Performance in the Reconstruction-Era Ku Klux Klan." *Journal of American History* 92, no. 3 (2005): 811–36.
Patton, June O. "Moonlight and Magnolias in Southern Education: The Black Mammy Memorial Institute." *The Journal of Negro History* 65, no. 2 (1980): 149–55.
Payne, E. George. *Principles of Educational Sociology: An Outline*. New York: New York University Press, 1928.
Peake, Laura A. "The Manassas Industrial School for Colored Youth, 1894–1916." MA thesis, The College of William and Mary, 1995.
Pearson, Noel. "White Guilt, Victimhood and the Quest for a Radical Centre." *Griffith Review* 16 (May 2007). https://griffithreview.com/articles/white-guilt-victimhood-and-the-quest-for-a-radical-center/.
Pease, William, and Jane Pease. *Black Utopia: Negro Communal Experiments in America*. Madison: State Historical Society of Wisconsin, 1972.
Perdue, Charles L., Jr., Thomas E. Barden, and Robert K. Phillips, eds. *Weevils in the Wheat: Interviews with Virginia Ex-Slaves*. Charlottesville: University Press of Virginia, 1976.
Perlman, Merrill. "Black and White: Why Capitalization Matters." *Columbia Journalism Review*. http://www.cjr.org/analysis/language_corner_1.php.
Peterson, Jon A. "The City Beautiful Movement: Forgotten Origins and Lost Meanings." *Journal of Urban History* 2, no. 4. (1976): 415–34.
Pethel, Mary Ellen, and Sarah Wilkerson Freeman. "Lifting Every Female Voice: Education and Activism in Nashville's African American Community, 1870–1940." In *Tennessee Women: Their Lives and Times*, vol. 1, edited by Beverly

Greene Bond and Sarah Wilkerson Freeman, 239–69. Athens: University of Georgia Press, 2009.
Pfeifer, Michael J. *Lynching Beyond Dixie: American Mob Violence Outside the South.* Urbana-Champaign: University of Illinois Press, 2013.
Phinney, Lucy. *Yesterday's Schools.* Manassas, VA: Lucy Phinney, 1993.
Pike, Martha. "In Memory of: Artifacts Relating to Mourning in Nineteenth-Century America." In *American Material Culture: The Shape of Things Around Us,* edited by Edith P. Mayo, 48–65. Bowling Green, OH: Bowling Green State University Popular Press, 1984.
Prince William County. 1850 Slave Schedule, Microfilm M432, Reel #992, p. 743.
———. 1860 Slave Schedule, Microfilm M653, Reel #1396, p. 3–4.
Prosser, Charles A. "Facilities for Industrial Education." In *Proceedings of the National Education Association,* edited by National Education Association, 189–203. Ann Arbor: National Education Association, 1912.
Provasnik, Stephen, Linda L. Shafer, and Thomas D. Snyder. *Historically Black Colleges and Universities, 1976 to 2001.* Washington, DC: National Center for Education Statistics, 2004.
Przybylek, Stephanie E., and Peter Lloyd Jones. *Images of America: Around Cayuga County.* Dover, MA: Arcadia Publishing, 1996.
Quarles, Benjamin. *Black Abolitionists.* New York: Oxford University Press, 1969.
———. *Lincoln and the Negro.* New York: Oxford University Press, 1962.
———. *The Negro in the American Revolution.* New York: Collier Books, 1961.
———. *The Negro in the Civil War.* 1953; repr., Boston: Little, Brown and Company, 1969.
Raboteu, Albert J. *Slave Religion: The "Invisible Institution" in the Antebellum South.* New York: Oxford University Press, 1978.
Ratcliffe, R. Jackson. *This Was Prince William.* Leesburg: Potomac Press, 1978.
Rawick, George P. *From Sundown to Sunup: The Making of the Black Community.* Westport, CT: Greenwood Publishing Company, 1972.
"Recollections of the 'Lost Cause' by a Southern Cavalry Officer." *The Land We Love* 4, no. 1 (1867): 38–49.
Redcay, Edward E. *County Training Schools and Public Secondary Education for Negroes in the South.* Washington, DC: The John F. Slater Fund, 1935.
Reed, Christopher Robert. "All the World Is Here." In *The Black Presence at White City,* 143–92. Bloomington: Indiana University Press, 2000.
Reeves, Matthew B. *Views of a Changing Landscape: An Archeological and Historical Investigation of Sudley Post Office, Manassas National Battlefield Park, Manassas, Virginia.* Manassas, VA: Manassas National Battlefield Park, 1998.
Reidy, Joseph P. "'Coming from the Shadow of the Past': The Transition from Slavery to Freedom at Freedman's Village, 1863–1900." *Virginia Magazine of History and Biography* 95, no. 4 (1987): 403–28.
Report of the Board of General Managers of the Exhibit of the State of New York at the World's Columbian Exposition. Albany, NY: James B. Lyon, State Printer, 1894.
Reps, John W. *The Making of Urban America: A History of City Planning in the U.S.* Princeton, NJ: Princeton University Press, 1965.

Reverby, Susan M., and Dorothy O. Helly. "Converging on History." In *Gendered Domains: Rethinking Public and Private in Women's History*, edited by Dorothy O. Helly and Susan M. Reverby, 1–27. Ithaca, NY: Cornell University Press, 1992.

Rhoads, William B. "The Colonial Revival and the Americanization of Immigrants." In *The Colonial Revival in America*, edited by Alan Axelrod, 239–342. New York: W. W. Norton & Company, 1985.

Rhodes, Jane. *Mary Ann Shadd Cary: The Black Press and Protest in the Nineteenth Century*. Bloomington: Indiana University Press, 1998.

Robertson, Ashley N. *Mary McLeod Bethune in Florida: Bringing Social Justice to the Sunshine State*. Mount Pleasant, SC: Arcadia Publishing, 2015.

Robinson, Cedric J. *Black Movements in America*. New York: Routledge, 1997.

Robnett, Belinda. "External Political Change, Collective Identities, and Participation in Social Movement Organizations." In *Social Movements: Identity, Culture, and the State*, edited by David S. Meyer, Nancy Whittier, and Belinda Robnett, 266–85. New York: Oxford University Press, 2002.

Rosenburg, R. B. *Living Monuments: Confederate Soldiers' Homes in the New South*. Chapel Hill: University of North Carolina Press, 1993.

Ross, Frances Mitchell. "The New Woman as Club Woman and Social Activist in Turn of the Century Arkansas." *The Arkansas Historical Quarterly* 50, no. 4 (1991): 317–18.

Roth, Leland M. *McKim, Mead & White, Architects*. New York: Harper & Row Publishers, 1983.

Rothberg, Michael. "Between Memory and Memory: From Lieux de mémoire to Noeuds de mémoire." *Yale French Studies* 118/119 (2010): 3–12.

Rothblatt, Sheldon. "The Writing of University History at the End of Another Century." *Oxford Review of Education* 23, no. 2 (1997): 151–67.

Round, George C. "History of Manassas." Manassas, VA: N.p., 1897.

Royster, Jacqueline Jones, ed. *Southern Horrors and Other Writings: The Anti-Lynching Campaign of Ida B. Wells, 1892–1900*. New York: Bedford Books, 1997.

Rubin, Anne Sarah. "Redefining the South: Confederates, Southerners, and Americans, 1863–1868." PhD diss., University of Virginia, 1999.

Rudolph, Frederick. *The American College and University: A History*. Athens: University of Georgia Press, 1990.

Rudolph, Marva L. "Emma J. Wilson." In *Notable Black American Women, Book II*, edited by Jessie Carney Smith, 721–23. New York: Gale Research, 1992.

Rudwick, Elliott M., and August Meier. "Black Man in the 'White City': Negroes and the Columbian Exposition, 1893." *Phylon* 26, no. 4. (1965): 27–28, 354.

Ryan, Dennis P. "The Crispus Attucks Monument Controversy of 1887." *Negro History Bulletin* 40, no. 1 (1977): 656–57.

Ryan, Mary P. *Civic Wars: Democracy and Public Life in the American City During the Nineteenth Century*. Berkeley: University of California Press, 1997.

Rydell, Robert. *All the World's a Fair: Visions of Empire at American International Expositions, 1876–1916*. Chicago: University of Chicago Press, 1987.

———. "A Cultural Frankenstein? The Chicago World's Columbian Exposition." In *Grand Illusions: Chicago's World's Fair of 1893*, edited by Neil Harris et al., 141–70. Chicago: Chicago Historical Society, 1993.

———. "Editor's Introduction." *The Reason Why the Colored American Is Not in the World's Columbian Exposition: The Afro-American's Contribution to Columbian Literature*, xiii. Chicago: University of Illinois Press, 1999.

Rydell, Robert W. "The City as Playground: The World's Fair Midways." In *Going Out: The Rise and Fall of Public Amusements*, edited by David Nasaw, 62–79. Cambridge, MA: Harvard University Press, 1993.

Rydell, Robert W., John E. Findling, and Kimberly D. Pelle. *Fair America: World's Fairs in the United States*. Washington, DC: Smithsonian Institution Press, 2000.

Sandercock, Leonie. "Feminist and Multicultural Perspectives on Preservation Planning." In *Making the Invisible Visible: A Multicultural Planning History*, edited by Leonie Sandercock, 57–77. Berkeley: University of California Press, 1998.

Savage, Kirk. "Race, Memory, and Identity: The National Monuments of the Union and the Confederacy." PhD diss., University of California–Berkeley, 1990.

———. *Standing Soldiers, Kneeling Slaves: Race, War, and Monument in Nineteenth-Century America*. Princeton, NJ: Princeton University Press, 1997.

Savoy, Lauret. *Trace: Memory, History, Race, and the American Landscape*. Berkeley, CA: Counterpoint, 2016.

Schechter, Patricia. *Ida B. Wells-Barnett and American Reform, 1880–1930*. Chapel Hill: University of North Carolina Press, 2001.

Scheel, Eugene M. *Crossroads and Corners: A Tour of the Villages, Towns, and Post Offices of Prince William County, Virginia, Past and Present*. Prince William County, VA: Historic Prince William, Inc., 1996.

Schein, Richard. "Race and Landscape in the United States." In *Landscape and Race in the United States*, edited by Richard Schein, 1–22. New York: Routledge, 2006.

Schexnider, Alvin J. *Saving Black Colleges: Leading Change in a Complex Organization*. Basingstoke, UK: Palgrave Macmillan, 2013.

Schiller, Ben. "Learning Their Letters: Critical Literacy, Epistolary Culture, and Slavery in the Antebellum South." *Southern Quarterly* 45, no. 3 (2008): 11–29.

Schneider, Mark R. *Boston Confronts Jim Crow, 1890–1920*. Boston: Northeastern University Press, 1997.

Schoelwer, Susan Prendergast. "Curious Relics and Quaint Scenes: The Colonial Revival at Chicago's Great Fair." In *The Colonial Revival in America*, edited by Alan Axelrod, 184–85. New York: W. W. Norton & Company, 1985.

Schuyler, David. "Frederick Law Olmsted and the Origins of Modern Campus Design." *Planning for Higher Education* 25, no. 2 (1996–97): 2–10.

———. "Frederick Law Olmsted and the World's Columbian Exposition." *Journal of Planning History* 15, no. 1 (2016): 3–28.

Schuyler, David, Gregory Kaliss, and Jeffrey Schlossberg, eds. *The Papers of Frederick Law Olmsted: The Last Great Projects, 1890–1895*. Baltimore: The Johns Hopkins University Press, 2015.

Schuyler, Montgomery. "Architecture of American Colleges." *The Architectural Record* 27, no. 6 (1910): 145–66.

Schwartz, Marie Jenkins. *Born in Bondage: Growing Up Enslaved in the Antebellum South*. Cambridge, MA: Harvard University Press, 2000.

Scipio, L. Albert. *Pre-War Days at Tuskegee: Historical Essay on Tuskegee Institute, 1881–1943*. Silver Spring, MD: Roman Publications, 1987.

Scott, Emmett J. "Training Head and Hand: Architectural and Mechanical Drawing at Tuskegee." *The Tuskegee Student*, April 20, 1901, 1–2.

Scott, James C. *Domination and the Arts of Resistance: Hidden Transcripts*. New Haven, CT: Yale University Press, 1990.

Scott, Kenneth. "The Slave Insurrection in New York in 1712." *The New York Historical Society Quarterly* 45, no. 1 (1961): 43–74.

Sekula, Allan. "The Body and the Archive." *October* 39 (Winter 1986): 3–64.

Sewall, May Wright, ed. *The World's Congress of Representative Women*. Chicago: Rand, McNally, 1894.

Sharp, Joanne P. "'Gendering Nationhood': A Feminist Engagement with National Identity." In *BodySpace*, edited by Nancy Duncan, 97–108. New York: Routledge, 1996.

Shaw, Mariann. *World's Fair Notes, a Woman Journalist Views Chicago's 1893 Columbian Exposition*. Chicago: Pogo Press, 1992.

Sherer, Robert G. *Subordination or Liberation? The Development and Conflicting Theories of Black Education in Nineteenth Century Alabama*. Tuscaloosa: University of Alabama Press, 1977.

Sherr, Lynn. *Failure Is Impossible: Susan B. Anthony in Her Own Words*. New York: Random House, 1995.

Sherwood, Patricia C., and Joseph Michael Lasala. "Education and Architecture: The Evolution of the University of Virginia's Academical Village." In *Thomas Jefferson's Academical Village: The Creation of an Architectural Masterpiece*, edited by Richard Guy Wilson, 1–9. Charlottesville: University of Virginia Press, 1993.

Shilland, Kimberly Alexander. "Chapter III, Ware and Van Brunt Advance the Profession." PhD diss., Massachusetts Institute of Technology, 1999/2000.

Sibley, David. "Survey 13: Purification of Space." *Environment and Planning D: Society and Space* 6, no. 4 (1988): 409–10.

Silber, Nina. *The Romance of Reunion: Northerners and the South, 1865–1900*. Chapel Hill: University of North Carolina Press, 1993.

Silkey, Sarah L. *Black Woman Reformer: Ida B. Wells, Lynching, and Transatlantic Activism*. Athens: University of Georgia Press, 2015.

Simpson, John A. "The Cult of the 'Lost Cause.'" *Tennessee Historical Quarterly* 34, no. 4 (1975): 350–51.

Smangs, Mattias. "The Lynching of African Americans in the U.S. South: A Review of Sociological and Historical Perspectives." *Sociology Compass* 11, no. 8 (2017): 1–13.

Smith, Shawn Michelle. *American Archives: Gender, Race, and Class in Visual Culture*. Princeton, NJ: Princeton University Press, 1999.

———. "Photographing the 'American Negro': Nation, Race, and Photography at the Paris Exposition of 1900." In *With Other Eyes: Looking at Race and Gender in Visual Culture*, edited by Lisa Bloom, 72–85. Minneapolis: University of Minnesota Press, 1999.

Snyder, Tom. *120 Years of American Education: A Statistical Portrait*. Washington, DC: National Center for Education Statistics, 1993.

Soja, Edward W. *Postmodern Geographies: The Reassertion of Space in Critical Social Theory*. New York: Verso, 1997.

Spivey, Donald. *Schooling for the New Slavery: Black Industrial Education, 1868–1915.* New York: Greenwood Press, 1978.
Starnes, Richard D. "Forever Faithful: The Southern Historical Society and Confederate Historical Memory." *Southern Cultures* 2, no. 2 (1996): 177–94.
Starr, Frederick. "Anthropology at the World's Fair." *Popular Science Monthly* 43, no. 5 (1893): 610–21.
"State Pride." *Our Living and Our Dead* 1, no. 1 (1874): 46–47.
Stevenson, Brenda, ed. *The Journals of Charlotte Forten Grimké.* New York: Oxford University Press, 1988.
———. *Life in Black and White: Family and Community in the Slave South.* New York: Oxford University Press, 1996.
Stevenson, Bryan. *Lynching in America: Confronting the Legacy of Racial Terror.* Montgomery, AL: Equal Justice Initiative, 2015.
Stewart, O. A. "Greenwood: A Dream Come True." *Tuskegee Messenger* 10 (July 1934): 1–4.
Stewart, Ruth Ann, "William Sidney Pittman (1875–1958)." In *African American Architects: A Biographical Dictionary, 1865–1945*, edited by Dreck Spurlock Wilson, 446–48. New York: Routledge, 2004.
Stuckey, Sterling. *Slave Culture: Nationalist Theory and the Foundations of Black America.* New York: Oxford University Press, 1987.
Suggs, Vickie L. "Mary McLeod Bethune: The Significance of Rhetorical Action in the Development of Black College Leader." In *Historically Black College Leadership and Social Transformation: How Past Practices Inform the Present and Future*, edited by Vickie L. Suggs, 23–42. Charlotte: Information Age Publishing, Inc., 2014.
Sullivan, Sarah. "Extralegal Violence: The Ku Klux Klan in the Reconstruction Era." *Elements* 12, no. 2 (2016): 35–46.
Superintendent of Education. *Thirty First Annual Report of the Superintendent of Education of the State of South Carolina.* Columbia, SC: State Superintendent of Education of the State of South Carolina, 1899.
Swain, Martha H. "Clubs and Voluntary Organizations." *The New Encyclopedia of Southern Culture* 13 (2009): 74–77.
Swint, Henry L. *Dear Ones at Home: Letters from Contraband Camps.* Nashville: Vanderbilt University Press, 1966.
Tate, Claudia. *Domestic Allegories of Political Desire: The Black Heroine's Text at the Turn of the Century.* New York: Oxford University Press, 1992.
Taylor, Robert R. "The Scientific Development of the Negro." In *Celebration of the Fiftieth Anniversary of the Granting of a Charter to the Massachusetts Institute of Technology*, 168–70. New York: McGraw-Hill, 1911.
———. "A Soldier's Home." Thesis, Massachusetts Institute of Technology, 1892. Architectural Collections, The MIT Museum, Boston, MA.
———. "Tuskegee's Mechanical Department." *The Southern Workman* 50, no. 10 (1921): 457–68.
Taylor, Ula. *The Veiled Garvey: The Life and Times of Amy Jacques Garvey.* Chapel Hill: University of North Carolina Press, 2002.

Tenth Annual Report of the Principals of the Calhoun Colored School, of Calhoun, Lowndes County, Alabama, with the Reports of the Heads of Departments. Boston: Geo. H. Ellis Co., Printers, 1902.

Testimony Taken by the Joint Select Committee to Inquire into the Condition of Affairs in the Late Insurrectionary States, Alabama. Washington, DC: Government Printing Office, 1872.

Thelin, John R., and James Yankovich. "Bricks and Mortar: Architecture and the Study of Higher Education." In *Higher Education: Handbook of Theory and Research*, edited by John C. Smart, 3:57–83. New York: Agathon Press, Inc., 1987.

Thorn, Charlotte R., and Mabel W. Dillingham. "Calhoun Colored School." *Lend a Hand: A Record of Progress* 13, no. 1 (1894): 52–55.

Thornbrough, Emma Lou. "Booker T. Washington as Seen by His White Contemporaries." *Journal of Negro History* 53 (April 1968): 161–82.

"The 3 Wives of Booker T. Washington." *Ebony*, September 1982, 29–30, 32, 34.

Thurston, Robert W. *Lynching: American Mob Murder in Global Perspective.* New York: Routledge, 2016.

Tolles, Bryant F. *Architecture and Academe: College Buildings in New England Before 1860.* Lebanon: University Press of New England, 2011.

"To the Patrons of the Land We Love." In *The Land We Love*. N.p.: N.p., n.d.

Towns, W. Stuart. *Enduring Legacy: Rhetoric and Ritual of the Lost Cause.* Tuscaloosa: University of Alabama Press, 2012.

———. "Honoring the Confederacy in Northwest Florida: The Confederate Monument Ritual." *The Florida Historical Quarterly* 57, no. 2 (1978): 205–12.

Trachtenberg, Alan. *Brooklyn Bridge: Fact and Symbol.* Chicago: University of Chicago Press, 1979.

———. *The Incorporation of America: Culture and Society in the Gilded Age.* New York: Hill and Wang, 1982.

Trachtenberg, Marvin. *The Statue of Liberty.* New York: Viking, 1976.

Trowbridge, J. T. *The South: A Tour of Its Battlefields and Ruined Cities: A Journey Through the Desolated States and Talks with Its People.* Hartford, CT: Stebbins, 1866.

Tselos, Dimitri. "The Chicago Fair and the Myth of the 'Lost Cause.'" *Journal of the Society of Architectural Historians* 46, no. 4 (1967): 259–68.

Tucker, David M. "Miss Ida B. Wells and Memphis Lynching." *Phylon* 32, no. 2 (1971): 117.

Turner, Paul Venable. *Campus: An American Planning Tradition.* Cambridge, MA: The MIT Press, 1984.

Upton, Dell. *Architecture in the United States.* New York: Oxford University Press, 1999.

Upton, Harriet Taylor. *Proceedings of the Twenty-Fifth Annual Conference of the National American Woman Suffrage Association, Held in Washington, D.C., January 16, 17, 18, 19, 1893.* Washington, DC: The Association, 1893.

Van Brunt, Henry. "The Columbian Exposition and American Civilization." *Atlantic Monthly*, May 1893, 577–88.

Vance, Mary. *Campus Planning: A Bibliography.* Monticello: Vance Bibliographies, 1986.

Vaughn, William Preston. *Schools for All: The Blacks and Public Education in the South, 1865–1877.* Lexington: University Press of Kentucky, 1974.
Verney, Kevern. *The Art of the Possible: Booker T. Washington and Black Leadership in the United States, 1881–1925.* New York: Routledge, 2014.
Verschaffel, Bart. "The Monumental: On the Meaning of a Form." *The Journal of Architecture* 4, no. 4 (1999): 334.
Veysey, Laurence. *The Emergence of the American University.* Chicago: University of Chicago Press, 1965.
Voorhees Industrial School. *The Fifth Annual Report of the Principal and Treasurer of the Voorhees Industrial School, Denmark, South Carolina, 15 May 1902.* Tuskegee, AL: Tuskegee Institute Steam Print, 1902.
———. *Remarkable Career of a Remarkable Woman.* Denmark, SC: Voorhees Industrial School, 1919,
———. *Voorhees Industrial School, Denmark, South Carolina.* Bamberg: A. W. Knight, 1907.
Wadelington, Charles W., and Richard F. Knapp. *Charlotte Hawkins Brown and Palmer Memorial Institute: What One Young African American Woman Could Do.* Chapel Hill: University of North Carolina Press, 1999.
Wallace-Sanders, Kimberly. *Mammy: A Century of Race, Gender, and Southern Memory.* Ann Arbor: University of Michigan Press, 2009.
Waller, Rev. C. D. "A Living Monument." *Confederate Veteran* 8, no. 7 (1900): 334.
Washington, Booker T. "Address." *Exercises at the Dedication of the Monument to Colonel Robert Gould Shaw and the Fifty-Fourth Regiment of Massachusetts Infantry,* 59–61. Boston: Municipal Printing Office, 1897.
———. *My Larger Education: Being Chapters from My Experience.* New York: Doubleday, 1911.
———. *The Negro Problem.* New York: James Pott & Company, 1903.
———. *Tuskegee and Its People: Their Ideals and Achievements.* Freeport, ME: Books for Libraries Press, 1971.
———. *Up from Slavery: An Autobiography.* New York: A. L. Burt Company, Publishers, 1900.
———. *Working with the Hands: Being a Sequel to "Up from Slavery" Covering the Author's Experiences in Industrial Training at Tuskegee.* New York: Doubleday, Page & Company, 1904.
Washington, Mary Helen. "Introduction." In *A Voice from the South,* xxxiii–xxxix. New York: Oxford University Press, 1988.
Watkins, William H. "Teaching and Learning in the Black Colleges: A 130-Year Retrospective." *Journal of Teaching Education* 3, no. 1 (1990): 10–25.
Weimann, Jeanne Madeline. *The Fair Women.* Chicago: Academy, 1981.
Weisenfeld, Judith. *African American Women and Christian Activism: New York's Black YMCA, 1905–1945.* Cambridge, MA: Harvard University Press, 1997.
Weiss, Ellen. "Booker T. Washington's Architectural Strategies." In *Space Unveiled: Invisible Cultures in the Design Studio,* edited by Carla Jackson Bell, 14–25. New York: Routledge, 2015.
———. *Robert R. Taylor and Tuskegee: An African American Architect Designs for Booker T. Washington.* Montgomery, AL: New South Books, 2012.

———. "Robert R. Taylor of Tuskegee, An Early Black American Architect." *ARRIS: Journal of the Southeast Chapter of the Society of Architectural Historians* 2 (1991): 3–19.
———. "Robert R. Taylor of Tuskegee, An Early Professional Architect in Alabama." *Preservation Report* (March/April 1989): 3–6.
———. "Tuskegee: Landscape in Black and White." *Winterthur Portfolio* 36, no. 1 (2001): 20–34.
Wells, Ida B. "Lynch Laws in All Its Phases." *Our Day* 11 (May 1893): 333–37. ———. *Mob Rule in New Orleans.* Chicago: Miss Ida B. Wells, 1900.
———. *A Red Record.* Chicago: Miss Ida B. Wells, 1895.
———. *Southern Horrors. Lynch Law in All Its Phases.* New York: The New York Age Print, 1892.
———. *United State Atrocities: Lynch Law.* London: Lux, 1893.
Wells-Barnett, Ida B. *The Reason Why the Colored American Is Not in the World's Columbian Exposition: The Afro-American's Contribution to Columbian Literature.* Edited by Robert W. Rydell. Urbana-Champaign: University of Illinois Press, 1999.
Wells, John E., ed. *The South Carolina Architects, 1885–1935: A Biographical Dictionary.* Richmond, VA: New South Architectural Press, 1992.
Welter, Barbara. "The Cult of True Womanhood: 1800–1860." *Dimity Convictions: The American Woman in the Nineteenth Century,* 21–41. Athens: Ohio University Press, 1976.
West, Cornel. *Keeping Faith: Philosophy and Race in America.* New York: Routledge, 1993.
West, Michael R. *The Education of Booker T. Washington: American Democracy and the Idea of Race Relations.* New York: Columbia University Press, 2006.
West, Patricia. "'The Bricks of Compromise Settle into Place': Booker T. Washington's Birthplace and the Civil Rights Movement." In *Domesticating History: The Political Origins of America's House Museums,* edited by Patricia West, 128–57. Washington, DC: Smithsonian Institution Press, 1999.
Wheeler, Candace. "A Dream City." *Harper's New Monthly Magazine* 86, no. 516 (1893): 836–49.
Whipps, Judy. "Local Community: Place-Based Pragmatist and Feminist Education." *The Pluralist* 9, no. 2 (Summer 2014): 29–41.
Whitman, Mrs. Bernard. "Manassas Industrial School." *Lend a Hand: A Record of Progress* 14, no. 4 (1895): 297–301.
Whittaker, David J. *The Impact and Legacy of Educational Sloyd: Heads and Hands in Harness.* New York: Routledge, 2013.
Wiener, Jonathan M. *Social Origins of the New South: Alabama, 1860–1885.* Baton Rouge: Louisiana State University Press, 1978.
Wilcox, David R. "Going National: American Anthropology Successfully Redefines Itself as an Accepted Academic Discipline." In *Coming of Age in Chicago: The 1893 World's Fair and the Coalescence of American Anthropology,* edited by Curtis M. Hinsley and David R. Wilcox, 413–54. Lincoln: University of Nebraska Press, 2016.
Willard, Ashton R. "The Development of College Architecture in America." *The New England Magazine* 16, no. 5 (1897): 513–14.

Williams, Clarence. *Technology and the Dream: Reflections on the Black Experience at MIT, 1941–1999.* Cambridge, MA: The MIT Press, 2001.

Williams, Heather Andrea. *Self-Taught: African American Education in Slavery and Freedom.* Chapel Hill: University of North Carolina Press, 2007.

Williams-Forson, Psyche A. *Building Houses Out of Chicken Legs: Black Women, Food and Power.* Durham, NC: University of North Carolina Press, 2006.

Willis, Arlette Ingram. "Literacy at Calhoun Colored School, 1892–1945." *Reading Research Quarterly* 37, no. 1 (2002): 8–44.

Wills, Gary. *Mr. Jefferson's University.* Washington, DC: National Geographic Society, 2002.

Wilson, Dreck Spurlock, ed. *African American Architects: A Biographical Dictionary, 1865–1945.* New York: Routledge, 2004.

Wilson, Richard Guy, ed. *Thomas Jefferson's Academical Village: The Creation of an Architectural Masterpiece.* Charlottesville: Bayly Art Museum of the University of Virginia, 1993.

Wilson, Richard Guy, and Sara A. Butler. *University of Virginia: Campus Guides.* Princeton, NJ: Princeton Architectural Press, 1999.

Winchester, Hilary. "The Construction and Deconstruction of Women's Roles in the Urban Landscape." In *Inventing Places: Studies in Cultural Geography*, edited by Kay Anderson and Fay Gale, 140–41. Melbourne: Longman Cheshire, 1992.

Wolcott, Victoria. *Remaking Respectability: African American Women in Interwar Detroit.* Chapel Hill: University of North Carolina Press, 2001.

Wood, Amy Louise. *Lynching and Spectacle: Witnessing Racial Violence in America, 1890–1940.* Durham: University of North Carolina Press, 2011.

Woods, Mary N. "Charles F. McKim and the Foundation of the American Academy in Rome." In *Light on the Eternal City: Observations and Discoveries in the Art and Architecture of Rome*, edited by Hellmut Hager and Susan Scott Munshower, 307–11. University Park: The Pennsylvania State University, 1987.

———. *From Craft to Profession: The Practice of Architecture in Nineteenth-Century America.* Berkeley: University of California Press, 1999.

———. "Henry Van Brunt: The Historic Styles, Modern Architecture." In *American Public Architecture: European Roots and Native Expressions*, edited by Craig Zabel and Susan Munshower, 82–113. College Park: The Pennsylvania State University, 1989.

———. "Thomas Jefferson and the University of Virginia: Planning the Academic Village." *Journal of the Society of Architectural Historians* 44 (October 1985): 266–83.

Woodson, Carter G. *The Education of the Negro Prior to 1861.* Washington, DC: The New Era Printing Company, 1919.

"The World's Fair of 1892." *Scientific American*, January 4, 1890, 2.

Wright, Gavin. *Old South, New South: Revolutions in the Southern Economy Since the Civil War.* New York: Basic Books, 1986.

Yeatman, James E. "The Freedmen's Monument to Lincoln." *The National Freedman*, October 15, 1865.

Yetter, George Humphrey. "Stanford White at the University of Virginia: The New Building on the South Lawn and the Reconstruction of the Rotunda in 1896." MA thesis, University of Virginia, 1980.

Young, James E. *The Texture of Memory: Holocaust Memorials and Meanings.* New Haven, CT: Yale University Press, 1993.

Zerubavel, Yael. *Recovered Roots: Collective Memory and the Making of the Israeli National Tradition.* Chicago: University of Chicago Press, 1995.

Index

An italicized page locator signifies a graphic.

Adams, Lewis, 54–55
Adeleke, Tunde, 4
agency, 13, 15, 27, 51, 105; Dean and Wright seizure of, 2, 6, 9, 111
Alabama State University, 111
A&M University, 111
Americanization, 38, 41–42
amnesia: collective, 14, 40; historical, 109
Anderson, Benedict, 51
Anderson, James D., 59, 85–86
Anthony, Susan B., 83
Archie-Hudson, Marguerite, 108
architectural education, 64; at Tuskegee, 55–56, 91–92, 99
architectural symbolism, 98–99
architecture: American college, 53–54; Beaux Arts style of, 35, 42, 52, 53, 89–90, 93, 94, 95, 103–4; of bourgeois mansions, 35–36; Colonial Revival style of, 36, 44, 94, 98, 100, 103, 104, 131n82; of Columbian Exposition, 35, 36–37, 45, 53; Gothic style of, 89; of Manassas, 10, 28, 100–105, *fig. 8*; and nation making, 42, 60–61; and nationalism, 97–98; professionalization of American, 89–90; and race uplift, 60–61, 93, 98; Southern Colonial style of, 98–99; of Taylor, 89, 90–94, 98, 99; of Tuskegee, 60, 93, 98–99; vernacular, 62, 63, 91, 93–94, 100; of Voorhees, 28, 94–99, 100
Armstrong, Samuel, 4
Atlanta University, 32, 142n33

Atwood, Charles B., 36

Bailey, Lewis H., 81
Banner of the South, 17
Barnett, Ferdinand Lee, 30
Bates, R. Charles: *The Elementary Principles of Architecture and Building*, 97–98
Beaux Arts style, 35, 42, 52, 89–90, 93; and campus design, 53, 103; at Manassas, 103–4; at Voorhees, 94, 95
Beginning of the Manassas Industrial School for Colored Youth and Its Growth, The, 85
Bell, Thomas J., 32
Bender, Thomas, 22
Bethune, Mary McLeod, 69
Black artisans, 48–49, 55
Black consciousness, 67; pragmatic, 68, 140n16
Black education: Booker T. Washington view of, 58–59; contested historiography on, 3–4; Douglass on, 22–23; early postbellum African American, 22, 27, 68–71, 80; under slavery, 69, 88, 141n21; vocational and industrial, 3–4, 29, 58–59, 67–68, 71; whites' view of, 81, 86. *See also* historically black colleges and universities; industrial schools
"Black Mammy," 18, 21, 22, 110
Black nationalism, 47, 63; and Black women, 31–32, 66, 139–40n6; as concept and term, 4, 5, 139–40n6; and Dean, 45, 81; expressed through built environment, 5, 6, 43, 51, 52;

Black nationalism—*(cont'd)*
  gendered definitions of, 31–32; and nation making, 5, 50–51, 120n13; and women reformers, 4–6, 19–20, 66; and Wright, 45, 139n6. *See also* nation making
Black towns, 61–64
Black women: agency seized by, 2, 6, 9, 15, 27, 111; and Black nationalism, 31–32, 66, 139–40n6; church role of, 50; and civilization redefinition, 47–48; clubs organized by, 66–67; and Columbian Exposition, 31, 32, 33, 43, 44; and community feminism, 67; creation of educational institutions by, 27–28, 42–43; idealized, 106; at industrial schools, 70–71; and lynching, 33; patriarchal paradigms challenged by, 4, 66, 67, 106–7; and race uplift, 4, 5, 20, 66, 88; and race woman concept, 27, 65–66; during Reconstruction, 3, 65, 69; as social reformers, 2–3, 7, 11, 26–27, 31–32, 44, 45, 51, 66–67; and storytelling, 86; as writers, 19–20. *See also* Dean, Jennie; Wright, Elizabeth Evelyn
Boston, MA, 25
Bowen, Cornelia, 69
Boyer, M. Christine: *The City of Collective Memory*, 63
Boyte, Harry C., 130n62
Bragdon, Claude, 52
Brickbuilder, The, 54
Brooks, Walter H., 80, 81, 82, 145n85
Brown, Charlotte Hawkins, 4
Brown, John, 24
Brundage, W. Fitzhugh, 18
built environment, 3, 68, 91, 102–3; Black nationalist agenda expressed through, 5, 6, 43, 51, 52; of Columbian Exposition, 7, 38, 43–44; narratives created through, 25, 26; and nation building, 120n13; and race uplift, 1–2, 4, 62, 65, 66; transformative power of, 40; and women's social reform work, 11, 25, 45, 118n51. *See also* architecture
Burnham, Daniel, 36

Calhoun, John C., 109
Calhoun Colored School, 4
campus planning and design, 8, 10, 52–54, 60–61; Booker T. Washington view of, 10, 61, 93, 99; and Beaux Arts style, 53, 94, 95, 103–4; and Colonial Revival style, 84, 94, 98, 100, 103, 104; at Manassas, 101–3, *fig. 5*, *fig. 38*; at Tuskegee, 10, 60, 61, 93, 96, 99; at Voorhees, 10, 96, *fig. 4*; for women's colleges, 134n35
Carby, Hazel, 40
Carr-Burdette College for Women, 21
Castells, Manuel, 11
Centennial Exposition of 1876, 36
Charleston, SC, 21, 48–49
Cherokees, 72
Chesnut, Mary, 19
churches, 49, 50, 68
City Beautiful movement, 43–44, 52, 54, 131n79
Civil War, 2–3, 19, 79, 90; commemoration of, 13–15; and Lost Cause mythology, 16–17
civilization: Columbian Exposition discourse of, 34, 38, 44–45; redefining, 45, 47–48; Victorian view of, 37–38
Claflin University, 60–61, 97, 150n41
classicism, 36–37; and neoclasicism, 89
Clemens, Dr., 83
club movement, 66–67
Clyburn, James, 108
Coleman, J. F. B., 74
collective amnesia, 14, 40
collective memory, 16–17, 28, 50, 63–64
colleges and universities: growth of in US, 20–21, 22, 52; historically black, 71, 107–11, 142n33; women's, 134n35. *See also* industrial schools
Collier's, 37
Colonial Revival style, 36, 44, 131n82; at Manassas, 94, 100, 103, 104; at Tuskegee, 98; at Voorhees, 94
Colored American, 20

INDEX 187

Colored People's Educational Monument Association, 22–23
Colored People's National Lincoln Monument, 24
Columbia University, 53, 56
Columbian Exposition, 7–8, 33–35; African American exclusion from, 30–31, 32–33; architecture of, 35, 36–37, 45, 53; Auditorium Building at, 35; and Black women, 31, 32, 33, 43, 44; and City Beautiful movement, 43–44; and "civilization" discourse, 34, 38, 44–45; Court of Honor at, 34, 36, 37, 40, 42, *fig. 16*; exposition grounds, 34–35, *fig. 6, fig. 15, fig. 18*; mechanical arts palace at, *fig. 23*; Midway Plaisance at, 7–8, 34, 38–39, 42, *fig. 17, fig. 19, fig. 20*; and social control, 41; and Wells, 20, 32–33, 43, 44–45, 125n1; Woman's building at, *fig. 14*; women's participation in, 31. *See also* Midway Plaisance; White City
community building, 10, 52, 61, 80, 99
community feminism, 67
Compensated Emancipation Act, 13
Confederate Home and School, 21
Confederate monuments, 40, 123n54; building of, 10–11, 16–17, 18, 21–22
Confederate Veteran, 17
Confederated Southern Memorial Association, 18–19
Cooke, William Wilson, 97
Cooper, Anna Julia, 46, 139n6; *A Voice from the South*, 9, 26–27, 47–48
Cooper, Brittney C.: *Beyond Respectability*, 66
Cornell University, 89
Country Gentlemen, The, 37
Crane, Stephen: *The Red Badge of Courage*, 19
Crenshaw, Kimberlé, 2
Crummell, Alexander, 31–32
Cummins, Tempie, 78–79

Danville, SC, 41
Davidson, Olivia, 3

Daytona Educational and Industrial Institute, 69
Dean, Charles, 78, 79
Dean, Jennie, 2, 10, 77–88, 108, *fig. 3*; birth and death of, 87, 147–48n120; and Black nationalism, 45, 81; and campus buildings, 104, 105; childhood of, 77–78; as domestic servant, 12, 79–80; Douglass honoring of, 86–87; educational vision of, 3, 9–10, 65, 86; as former slave, 13, 78, 146n92; fund-raising work by, 71, 83, 84, 85, 100; legacy of, 104; and Manassas founding, 1, 81–83; race uplift project of, 68, 81, 85; schooling and literacy of, 80, 85–86, 105; social agenda of, 11, 45, 68
Delany, Martin, 31–32
Denmark, SC, 75–76
Deutsch, Sarah, 118n51
DeVos, Betsy, 109
Dillingham, Mabel, 4
Disney's America, 143–44n61
Douglass, Frederick, 126–27n17; and Columbian Exposition, 30, 31; on Lincoln, 15, 22, 23, 110; at Lincoln statue dedication, 14–15, 22; at Manassas, 86–87, 88; on monuments, 23, 24
Dowell, W. Fred, 100; photos by, *figs. 3, 36, 37, 39, 40*
Drexler, Arthur, 93
Du Bois, W. E. B., 15, 45; and Booker T. Washington, 115n15, 137n74; *The Talented Tenth*, 24
Dubrow, Gail Lee, 118n51
Dunbar, U. S. J., *fig. 11*

Eastman, George, 56
Eaton, John, 141n21
Eisner, Michael, 143–44n61
Ellerbe, J. E., 75–76
Emancipation Monument, 12, 13–14, 110, *fig. 10*
Evans, Sara M., 130n62
Evers, Medgar, 109
Exodus, 9, 49

families, slave, 27
Faulkner, Carol, 2
Faust, Drew Gilpin, 18
Felton, Rebecca, 31
Fisk University, 107–8, 110–11, 142n33
Foreman, P. Gabrielle, 133n22
Forten, Charlotte, 69
Fortune, T. Thomas, 58
Foucault, Michel, 11
Fowlkes, Stephen, 72
Franklin, John Hope, 1
Frazier, E. Franklin, 78
Freedmen's Bureau, 3, 13, 24–25, 68–69, 70

Garnet, Henry Highland, 23–24
Garvey, Amy Jacques, 67
gender: and educational conceptions, 68, 71; and intersectionality, 2–3; and nation building, 43; and patriarchal paradigms, 4, 66, 67, 106–7; and womanhood ideals, 66, 67, 140n8. *See also* Black women
General Federation of Women's Clubs (CFWC), 66
Genovese, Eugene D., 50
Giddens, Anthony, 11
Gilmore, Glenda, 71
Girouard, Mark, 26
Githens, Alfred Morton, 54
Goodman, Jennifer B., 118n51
Gothic style, 89
Grandison, Kenrick Ian, 152n71
Grant, Ulysses S., 141n21
Greene, Beverly, 89
Greenwood Village, 62–63, 93–94, 96, *fig. 28*
Guess, S. M., 76

Hage, Ghassan, 41
Hahn, Steven, 116n29
Haines Normal Institute, 69
Hale, Edward Everett, 82
Hamer, Fannie Lou, 109
Hamlin, A. D. F., 52

Hampton Normal and Agricultural Institute, 4, 32, 80; Booker T. Washington at, 54, 55, 136n56
Harlan, Louis R., 58–59, 62, 137n74
Harper, Frances Ellen Watkins, 20, 32, 49, 139n6; *Iola Leroy or Shadows Uplifted*, 47
Harper's Bazaar, 37
Harper's New Monthly Magazine, 43–44
Harper's Weekly, 37
Harrell College, 98
Harvey, David, 40
Hayden, Sophia, 31, 89
Hicks, Margaret, 89
hidden transcripts, 28–29
Hill, Walter Barnard, 101
historic preservation, 5, 6, 45, 86, 87, 107; contemporary efforts for, 108–10; and race literature, 11, 20
Historic Preservation Initiative, 108
historical amnesia, 109
historically black colleges and universities (HBCUs), 107–8; growth of, 71, 142n33; as memory sites, 108–10; racial harassment at, 110–11
Holtzclaw, Mary Paterson, 115n18
Hopkins, Pauline E., 20, 46
Hopper, Grace Murray, 109
Howard, Joan Imogene, 32
Howe, Frank Maynard, 36
Howe, Julia Ward, 19
Howland, Emily, 82–83
Hughes, Louis, 48
Hunt, Richard Morris, 36, 90
Hunter, Tera, 120–21n17

industrial and vocational training: and black consciousness, 67–68, 140n16; Booker T. Washington view of, 29, 58–59; contested historiography on, 3–4; and gender, 71
industrial schools: as community laboratories, 59–60; curriculum at, 9–10, 77, 83–84, 97; defined, 113n1; growth of after Civil War, 70–71. *See also* Manassas Industrial

School; Tuskegee Institute; Voorhees College
intersectionality, 4, 71; about, 2–3, 114n7
Ionic porticos, 91, 98, 99

Jackson, J. B., 63
Jackson, Stonewall, 21, 69, 123n54
Jamestown Tercentenary Exposition, 95
Jefferson, Thomas, 8, 10, 36–37, 41–42, 101
Jim Crow, 29, 31, 40, 57–58; imposition of, 8–9; intimidation and terror under, 59, 74–75, 98; lynching under, 33, 39–40, *fig. 21, fig. 22*; resistance to, 81, 82, 105; segregationist laws under, 4, 7, 38, 88, 91
Johnson, Andrew, 12
Johnson, James Weldon, 48
Johnson, Jonas Edward, 115n18
Johnston, Frances Benjamin, 71, 100; *Hampton (Institute) Album*, 56; photos by, *figs. 15, 23, 24, 25, 26, 27, 31, 41*
Jones, Graces Morris Allen, 115n18
Jones, Jacqueline, 65–66; *Soldiers of Light and Love*, 27
Journal of Negro History, The, 78
Jubilee Hall (Fisk University), 107–8

Kearney, Amanda, 118n51
Kohn, Robert D., 151n63
Krieger, Alex, 37
Ku Klux Klan, 75, 98

La Branche, Bertha, 115n18
Lainey, Lucy, 69
Land We Love, The, 17, 20
landscaping, 94, 101
Langston University, 61
Leavitt, Charles Wellford, 101–2, 104, 151n60, *fig. 38*
Lee, Robert E., 21, 79, 123n54
Lefebvre, Henri, 11
Lend a Hand Society, 82
Létang, Eugène, 90
Levy, James, 67–68

Lewis, Ronald L., 48
Lewis, Stephen Johnson: *Undaunted Faith: The Story of Jennie Dean*, 85
Lincoln, Abraham, 12, 13; Douglass view of, 15, 22, 23, 110
Lincoln Park/Square, 12, 13–14, 110, *fig. 10*
literacy (African American), 69, 76, 80, 147n115; and Dean, 85–86, 105; Jim Crow tests for, 57–58; whites' view of, 86, 88
Litwack, Leon, 40
Loewen, James W., 109–10
Logan, Warren, 92–93
Longstreth, Richard, 89–90
Lost Cause, 10–11, 15, 16–22, *fig. 9*
Low, Seth, 56
lynching, 33, 39–40, *fig. 21, fig. 22*

Macon County, AL, 56–58
Manassas battles, 79
Manassas Industrial School: architecture of, 10, 28, 100–105, *fig. 8*; campus design of, 101–3, *fig. 5, fig. 38*; closing of, 86, 87; curriculum at, 9–10, 83–84; Dean founding of, 1, 81–83; Douglass at, 86–87, 88; educational vision of, 3, 9–10, 65, 86; financial support for, 82–83, 84, 100, 101; quadrangle at, 102
Manassas Industrial School buildings: Bailey Hall, 102, *fig. 36*; Berwind Hospital, 102, 104; Carnegie Library, 100–101, 102, 103–4, *fig. 37*; Charter Cottage, 102, 104; Hackley Hall, 100–101, 102, 103, *fig. 40*; Howland Hall, 100, 102, 103, *fig. 39*; Orchard Cottage, 102, 104; Roof Tree, 102, 104
Manassas Society for the Preservation of Black Heritage, 108–9
Massachusetts Infantry, 54th Regiment, 25
Massachusetts Institute of Technology (MIT), 31, 55, 89, 91
Matthews, Victoria Earle, 58

190　INDEX

Matthews-Gardner, A. Lanethea, 114n7
Mayesville Institute, 69
Mayfield, Stanwix, 75
McCabe, William Gordon, 21
McKim, Charles F., 36, 53, 90
McKim, Mead, and White, 53
Meeks, Stephanie, 110
Meharry Medical College, 110–11, 142n33
Meier, August, 4
memory sites, 63–64, 108–10
Memphis Free Speech, 39
Midway Plaisance, *fig. 17*; Cairo section at, *fig. 19*; racialized display at, 7–8, 34, 38–39, 42; West African village at, 38–39, *fig. 20*. See also Columbian Exposition
mission schools, 68
Mississippi Valley State University, 109
monuments: and ceremonial places, 50, 63; Confederate, 10–11, 16–17, 18, 21–22, 40, 123n54; Douglas-Garnet debate over, 23–24; as hidden transcripts, 28–29; in Lincoln Park, 12, 13–14, 110, *fig. 10*
Mooney, Barbara, 60
Morgan State University, 110
Moses, Wilson J., 4, 116n25
Mound Bayou, MS, 61–62
Mount Holyoke College, 134n35
Mount Meigs Institute, 69
Mount Olive Baptist Church, 62
Murray, Margaret, 3, 74

nation making: architecture's role in, 42, 60–61; and Black nationalism, 5, 50–51, 120n13; impact of literary culture on, 97; institutions as central to, 3–4, 25, 29, 45, 49–50; and national identity, 42, 49, 50; and women reformers, 4, 5, 25, 43. See also Black nationalism
National Association of Colored Women/Women's Clubs (NACW), 67, 114n7
National Trust for Historic Preservation, 110

nationalism: American, 14, 43, 120n13; and architectural design, 97–98; as imagined community, 51. See also Black nationalism
Negro Society for Historical Research, 46
neoclassicism, 89
New Echota, 72
New South, 15, 17–18, 42, 120–21n17
Newton, James E., 48
Nora, Pierre: "Between Memory and History," 111

Oakwood College, 111
O'Connor, T. P.: *My Beloved South*, 26
Offe, Sabine, 87–88
Old South, 10, 17–18, 21, 22
Olmsted, Frederick Law, 36; *A Few Things to Be Thought of before Proceeding to Plan Buildings for the National Agricultural College*, 54
Omnibus Parks Bill of 1996, 108
Our Living and Our Dead, 17

Page, Mary Louisa, 89
Page, Thomas Nelson, 18, 26
Palmer, Bertha, 31
Palmer Memorial Institute, 4
Parker, Alison M., 2
Peabody, George Foster, 101
Peabody and Stearns, 36
Peake, Mary, 69
Penn, Irvine Garland, 30
Piney Woods School, 4, 115n18
Pittman, William Sidney, 95, 96, 149n35
place, 28–29; ceremonial places, 50, 63; and monument sites, 110; and trauma, 11, 118n51
Plessy v. Ferguson, 8, 38, 129n49
Pope, John, 79
Post, George B., 36
Prentiss Normal and Industrial School, 115n18
Progressive era, 3, 67, 69–70, 106; architecture during, 52–53, 89, 98–99; Jim Crow system during, 7, 15, 110

quadrangles, campus, 61, 102

race literature, 11, 19–20
race uplift, 10, 13; and Black women, 4, 5, 20, 66, 88; Booker T. Washington view of, 58–59; and built environment, 1–2, 4, 62, 65, 66; Dean and Wright promotion of, 68, 81, 85; religious undertones to, 116n25; role of architecture in, 60–61, 93, 98; as term, 113n2; as tradition, 1
race woman concept, 27, 65–66. *See also* Black women
racial terror and intimidation, 74–75, 98, 110–11. *See also* lynching
Reconstruction: Black education during, 3, 24–25; failures of, 40, 47, 58, 107; and race woman concept, 27, 65
religion, 49–50
Rhoads, William B., 42
Richardson, Henry Hobson, 35
Ricker, Nathan, 55, 56
Rolfe, Lydia, 73
Rolfe, Virginia, 72
Ruskin, John, 89

Schuyler, Montgomery, 35–36
Scott, Charlotte, 22
Scott, Emmett J., 62–63, 92, 93
segregation, 7, 29, 59, 88; and *Plessy v. Ferguson*, 8, 38, 129n49
self-determination, 3–4, 19, 47, 50; collective, 5, 27, 51, 99
settlement house movement, 45, 132n87
Shadd, Mary Ann, 4
Shaw, Robert Gould, 25
Sillers, Walter, Jr., 109
slavery, 78, 104; Black literacy under, 69, 88; buildings as counternarrative to, 104–5; Dean under, 13, 78, 146n92; and family, 27; slaves as builders under, 48; trauma of, 1, 27, 88, 104–5, 107
Smith, Ezekiel B., 73
Smith College, 134n35

social Darwinism, 38
Southern Association of Colored Women's Clubs, 67
Southern Colonial style, 98–99
Southern Historical Society, 16–17
Southern University, 110
space, 28–29; and Black nationalism, 63; and democratic movements, 130n62; public, 40–41, 61; scholars of, 11, 118n50
State Normal School (Montgomery, AL), 60
Stewart, Annie, 78
Stewart, Maria, 4
Stillman College, 111
Stonewall Jackson Institute, 21
storytelling, 86
Stowe, Harriet Beecher, 19
Sullivan, Louis, 35
Sunny South, The, 20

Talbotton, GA, 72–73
Taylor, Robert R., 89, 99; background of, 90–91; at Tuskegee, 91–94, 98
Taylor, Ula, 67
teachers: Black, 57, 69, 73, 76; at Manassas, 9–10, 83; at Tuskegee, 55, 59; at Voorhees, 77; white, 3, 68–69
Thomas, Jeff, 83
Thompson, Jane E., 83, 87, 145n78
Thorn, Charlotte, 4
Tolge, Jus W., 73
Trachentenberg, Alan, 42
trauma: black colleges as sites of, 107, 152n71; and place, 11, 118n51; of slavery, 1, 27, 88, 104–5
Truth, Sojourner, 86
Turner, Paul Venable, 54
Tuskegee Institute, 82, *fig. 29, fig. 41*; architectural education at, 55–56, 91–92, 99; architectural styles at, 60, 93, 98–99; and Booker T. Washington, 8, 9, 29, 54–55, 59, 137–38n79; campus design of, 10, 60, 61, 93, 96, 99; construction of, 61, *fig. 26, fig. 27*; educational project of, 3, 54–56, 93; founding of, 8, 54; and

Tuskegee Institute—*(cont'd)*
  Greenwood Village, 62–63; as model Black City, 59, 137–38n79; and Taylor, 91–94, 98; Wright at, 3, 9, 72, 73–74
Tuskegee Institute buildings: Alabama Hall, 60; Armstrong Hall, 60; Emery dormitories, 92; Pavilion, 60; Porter Hall, 60; Rockefeller Hall, 92; Threasher Hall, 92
Tuskegee Veterans Hospital, 98
Tuskegee Women's Club, 66–67

Uncle Tom, 21
United Confederate Veterans, 16–17
United Daughters of the Confederacy, 16–17
University of Georgia, 101, 103
University of Illinois, 55, 56, 89
University of the South, 21
University of Virginia, 53, 101, *fig. 7*
University School for Boys, 21
Upton, Dell, 131n82
urbanism, 36–37, 93. *See also* City Beautiful movement
Utica Normal and Industrial Institute, 4, 115n18

Van Brunt, Henry, 36, 53
vernacular architecture, 62, 63, 91, 93–94, 100
Vernon, M. E., 83
Vesey, Denmark, 48–49
Voorhees, Ralph, 9, 76
Voorhees College: architecture of, 28, 94–99, 100; Booker T. Washington view of, 66; campus design of, 10, 96, *fig. 4*; curriculum at, 77, 96; educational vision of, 3–4, 9, 65; financial support for, 9, 76; site of, 94, *fig. 32*; trades taught at, 9, *fig. 31*; Wright founding of, 1, 72, 75–77, 94
Voorhees College buildings: Bedford Hall, 94; Blanton Hall, 94–95, *fig. 35*; Kennerly Hall, 76, 94, 95–96, *fig. 30*; Menafee Trades Building, 95, 96, *fig. 34*; Voorhees Hall, 94, 95–96; Washington Hall, 94, 95, *fig. 33*; Washington Hospital, 97; Wright Hall, 94, 95–96, 109; Wright Library, 95

Waller, C. D., 21
Ware, William Robert, 55
Washington, Booker T., 4, 25, 57, *fig. 24*; and Black women, 1, 66; and campus planning and design, 10, 61, 93, 99; contested legacy of, 58–59, 137n74; and Du Bois, 115n15, 137n74; educational perspective of, 58–59; and Greenwood Village, 62–63; at Hampton Institute, 54, 55, 136n56; and Tuskegee Institute, 8, 9, 29, 54–55, 59, 137–38n79; whites' view of, 75; and Wright, 3, 66, 74, 76
Washington, DC, 22–23; Lincoln Park in, 12, 13–14, 110, *fig. 10*
Washington, Margaret Murray, 66–67
Washington College, 21
Weir, William I., 79
Weiss, Ellen, 8, 92
Wells, Ida B., 7, 31, 39, 45, *fig. 13*; and Columbian Exposition, 20, 32–33, 43, 44–45, 125n1; *The Reason Why the Colored American Is Not in the World's Columbian Exposition*, 20, 125n1
West, Cornel, 99
White City, 42, 43, 45, *fig. 23*; architecture of, 36–37; Auditorium Building at, 35; as celebration of "civilization," 34, 38, 44; Court of Honor at, 34, 36, 37, 40, 42, *fig. 16*; Woman's building at, *fig. 14*. *See also* Columbian Exposition
white women, 2–3, 18, 21–22, 39, 66, 106; and Lost Cause mythology, 10–11, 18
Wilberforce University, 32, 61, 81
Willard, Ashton, 52
Williams, Marshall D., 81
Wilson, Emma J., 69
Winchester, Hilary, 28
Wolcott, Victoria, 113n2

This volume focuses broadly on the history of the social welfare reform work of nineteenth-century African American women who founded industrial and normal schools in the American South. Through their work in architecture and education, these women helped to memorialize the trauma and struggle of black Americans. Author Angel David Nieves tells the story of women such as Elizabeth Evelyn Wright (1872–1906), founder of the Voorhees Industrial School (now Voorhees College) in Denmark, South Carolina, in 1897, who not only promoted a program of race uplift through industrial education but also engaged with many of the pioneering African American architects of the period to design a school and surrounding community. Similarly, Jane (Jennie) Serepta Dean (1848–1913), a former slave, networked with elite Northern white designers to found the Manassas Industrial School in Manassas, Virginia, in 1892.

An Architecture of Education examines the work of these women educators and reformers as a form of nascent nation building, noting the ways in which the social and political ideology of race uplift and gendered agency that they embodied was inscribed on the built environment through the design and construction of these model schools. In uncovering these women's role in the shaping of African American public spheres in the post-Reconstruction South, the book makes an important contribution to the history of African Americans' long struggle for equality and civil rights in the United States.

www.ingramcontent.com/pod-product-compliance
Lightning Source LLC
Chambersburg PA
CBHW060948230426
43665CB00015B/2110